TEACHER'S MANUAL
AND ACHIEVEMENT TESTS

NorthStar 4
READING AND WRITING
THIRD EDITION

AUTHORS
Andrew K. English
Laura Monahon English

SERIES EDITORS
Frances Boyd
Carol Numrich

PEARSON
Longman

NorthStar: Reading and Writing Level 4, Third Edition
Teacher's Manual and Achievement Tests

Pearson Education, 10 Bank Street, White Plains, NY 10606

Teacher's Manual by Deborah B. Gordon. Activities for secondary schools by Ann Hilborn.

Achievement Tests developed by Dr. Joan Jamison and Dr. Carol Chapelle.

Achievement Tests by Lynn Stafford-Yilmaz.

Staff credits: The people who made up the *NorthStar: Reading and Writing Level 4, Third Edition Teacher's Manual* team, representing editorial, production, design, and manufacturing, are Dave Dickey, Christine Edmonds, Ann France, Margot Gramer, Gosia Jaros-White, Dana Klinek, Melissa Leyva, Sherry Preiss, Robert Ruvo, Debbie Sistino, Kathleen Smith, Paula Van Ells, and Adina Zoltan.

Text credits: **Page T-3** "Peeping Tom Journalism" from *Sensational TV—Trash or Journalism?* By Nancy Day. Copyright © 1996 by Nancy Day. Published by Enslow Publishers, Inc., Berkeley Heights, NJ. All rights reserved. **Page T-10** "The Miracle: She altered our perception of the disabled and remapped the boundaries of sights and sense" by Diane Schuur from *Time*, June 14, 1999. Copyright © 1999 by Time Inc. Reprinted by permission; **Page T-23** Excerpt from HOW SMART ARE ANIMALS?, copyright © 1990 by Dorothy Hinshaw Patent, reprinted by permission of Harcourt, Inc.; **Page T-30** "Toward Immortality: The Social Burden of Longer Lives" by Ker Than. LiveScience.com, May 22, 2006. Reprinted with permission from Imaginova/Starry Night; **Page T-36** "Justin Lebo" from *It's Our World, Too! Stories of Young People Who are Making a Difference* by Phillip Hoose. Copyright © 1993, 2002 by Phillip Hoose. Published by Farrar, Straus and Giroux. Reprinted by permission of the Gersh Agency and Farrar, Straus and Giroux, LLC. All rights reserved; **Page T-44** "The Satisfied Learner: How Families Homeschool Their Teens" from March–April 2000 *Mothering Magazine* by Cafi Cohen. Reprinted by permission of Cafi Cohen; **Page T-50** "Taking time to savor joys of Slow Food" by Cathy Heiner from *USA Today*, August 31, 1998. Reprinted with permission; **Page T-57** "Nostalgia" by Virgilio Dávila from *Obras Completas*, Institute de Cultura Puertorriquena, San Juan, Puerto Rico, 1964; **Page T-63** "Plugged in at Home" from "Inside the House" (Newsweek 11/27/95) from *The Road Ahead* by Bill Gates. Copyright © 1995, 1996 by William H. Gates III. Used with permission of Viking Penguin, a division of Penguin Group (USA) Inc.

Cover Art: Silvia Rojas/Getty Images
Text composition: ElectraGraphics, Inc.
Text font: 11.5/13 Minion

ISBN-10: 0-13-613319-3
ISBN-13: 978-0-13-613319-3

PEARSON LONGMAN ON THE WEB

Pearsonlongman.com offers online resources for teachers and students. Access our Companion Websites, our online catalog, and our local offices around the world.

Visit us at **www.pearsonlongman.com**.

Printed in the United States of America
1 2 3 4 5 6 7 8 9 10—BRR—13 12 11 10 09 08

CONTENTS

UNIT-BY-UNIT TEACHING SUGGESTIONS

ACHIEVEMENT TESTS

WELCOME TO **NORTHSTAR**
THIRD EDITION

NorthStar, now in its third edition, motivates students to succeed in their **academic** as well as **personal** language goals.

For each of the five levels, the two strands—*Reading and Writing* and *Listening and Speaking*—provide a fully integrated approach for students and teachers.

WHAT IS SPECIAL ABOUT THE THIRD EDITION?

NEW THEMES

New themes and **updated content**—presented in a **variety of genres**, including literature and lectures, and in **authentic reading and listening selections**—challenge students intellectually.

ACADEMIC SKILLS

More purposeful **integration of critical thinking** and an enhanced focus on **academic skills** such as inferencing, synthesizing, note taking, and test taking help students develop strategies for **success** in the **classroom** and on **standardized tests.** A **culminating productive task** galvanizes content, language, and **critical thinking skills**.

➤ In the *Reading and Writing* strand, a new, **fully integrated writing section** leads students through the **writing process** with engaging writing assignments focusing on various rhetorical modes.

➤ In the *Listening and Speaking* strand, a **structured approach** gives students opportunities for **more extended and creative oral practice**, for example, presentations, simulations, debates, case studies, and public service announcements.

NEW DESIGN

Full **color pages** with more **photos**, **illustrations**, **and graphic organizers** foster student engagement and make the content and activities come alive.

MyNorthStarLab

MyNorthStarLab, an easy-to-use **online learning and assessment program**, offers:

➤ Unlimited access to reading and listening selections and DVD segments.

➤ Focused test preparation to help students succeed on international exams such as TOEFL® and IELTS®. Pre- and post-unit assessments improve results by providing individualized instruction, instant feedback, and personalized study plans.

➤ Original activities that support and extend the *NorthStar* program. These include pronunciation practice using voice recording tools, and activities to build note taking skills and academic vocabulary.

➤ Tools that save time. These include a flexible gradebook and authoring features that give teachers control of content and help them track student progress.

THE NORTHSTAR APPROACH

The *NorthStar* series is based on **current research in language acquisition** and on the **experiences of teachers and curriculum designers**. Five principles guide the *NorthStar* approach.

PRINCIPLES

1 The more profoundly students are stimulated intellectually and emotionally, the more language they will use and retain.

The thematic organization of *NorthStar* promotes intellectual and emotional stimulation. The 50 sophisticated themes in *NorthStar* present intriguing topics such as recycled fashion, restorative justice, personal carbon footprints, and microfinance. The authentic content engages students, links them to language use outside of the classroom, and encourages personal expression and critical thinking.

2 Students can learn both the form and content of the language.

Grammar, vocabulary, and culture are inextricably woven into the units, providing students with systematic and multiple exposures to language forms in a variety of contexts. As the theme is developed, students can express complex thoughts using a higher level of language.

3 Successful students are active learners.

Tasks are designed to be creative, active, and varied. Topics are interesting and up-to-date. Together these tasks and topics (1) allow teachers to bring the outside world into the classroom and (2) motivate students to apply their classroom learning in the outside world.

4 Students need feedback.

This feedback comes naturally when students work together practicing language and participating in open-ended opinion and inference tasks. Whole class activities invite teachers' feedback on the spot or via audio/video recordings or notes. The innovative new MyNorthStarLab gives students immediate feedback as they complete computer-graded language activities online; it also gives students the opportunity to submit writing or speaking assignments electronically to their instructor for feedback later.

5 The quality of relationships in the language classroom is important because students are asked to express themselves on issues and ideas.

The information and activities in *NorthStar* promote genuine interaction, acceptance of differences, and authentic communication. By building skills and exploring ideas, the exercises help students participate in discussions and write essays of an increasingly complex and sophisticated nature.

THE NorthStar UNIT

① FOCUS ON THE TOPIC

This section introduces students to the unifying theme of the reading selections.

> **PREDICT** and **SHARE INFORMATION** foster interest in the unit topic and help students develop a personal connection to it.
>
> **BACKGROUND** AND **VOCABULARY** activities provide students with tools for understanding the first reading selection. Later in the unit, students review this vocabulary and learn related idioms, collocations, and word forms. This helps them explore content and expand their written and spoken language.

UNIT 9
The Grass Is Always Greener...

Jamaica Kincaid
Born: Antigua,[1] 1949
Occupation: Writer
Immigrated to the U.S. in 1966

Arnold Schwarzenegger
Born: Graz, Austria, 1947
Occupation: Actor/
Governor of California
Immigrated to the U.S. in 1968

Gloria Estefan
Born: Havana, Cuba, 1957
Occupation: Singer
Immigrated to the U.S. in 1959

① FOCUS ON THE TOPIC

A PREDICT

Look at the photographs and the unit title. Then discuss the questions with a partner.

1. What do the people have in common?
2. How do you think their life would have been different if they had not immigrated?
3. The unit title is part of a famous saying, "The grass is always greener on the other side of the fence.[2]" Do you think the saying is about other things besides grass and fences? What do you think the unit will be about?

[1] **Antigua:** an island in the Caribbean
[2] **fence:** a structure made of wood, metal, etc. that surrounds a piece of land

201

B SHARE INFORMATION

Throughout history, people have sought immortality. People today are living longer than at any time in history; however, we are still a long way from reaching immortality.

Work with a partner or in a small group and discuss the questions.

1. If scientists could create a pill that would allow you to live twice as long while staying healthy, would you take it?
2. How would life be different if you lived longer? How would it be better? How would it be worse? Think about how such issues as relationships, marriage, family structure, and career might be affected.

C BACKGROUND AND VOCABULARY

Reading One is a story about Marilisa and her husband, Leo. Read the letter Marilisa wrote to a friend about Leo. Choose the definition that best defines the boldfaced word.

1. a. mean
   b. energetic
   c. lazy
2. a. on time
   b. well dressed
   c. considerately
3. a. understandably
   b. incredibly
   c. to some extent
4. a. difficult
   b. fascinating
   c. different
5. a. slightly
   b. always
   c. completely
6. a. complicated
   b. impressive
   c. terrible
7. a. doing things slowly after thinking about them
   b. doing things because somebody told you to
   c. doing things quickly without thinking
8. a. annoying
   b. friendly
   c. interesting

Dear Susannah,

I know you are worried about my marrying Leo, but please realize he has many good qualities. For example, he is quite **(1) vigorous.** Despite his age, he still exercises for hours and then works in the garden. In addition, he is very thoughtful. Unlike some of my friends, he always arrives **(2) punctually.** If he says he will meet me at 10 o'clock, he will be there exactly at 10.

He is also **(3) immeasurably** wise. He has so much knowledge and experience and is interested in so many **(4) disparate** subjects such as Greek history, diamond mining, dinosaurs, and alternative medicine. Even though they are not related, he enjoys them all. I find this quality **(5) utterly** fascinating. I am totally amazed by his vast knowledge. Leo really has had an **(6) awesome** life when you think about everything he has done. It is so exciting living with someone who has had so many incredible experiences.

However, I'm not claiming Leo is perfect. For one thing, he can be very **(7) impetuous.** Just last week, he bought a new car. He didn't even think about the fact that we needed that money to pay our credit card bills!

Furthermore, at times, he can be **(8) insufferable.** I was trying to watch television last night and he was constantly interrupting me to ask questions. Couldn't he understand that I was trying to concentrate on the show? His family is another problem. Take his ex-wife, Katrin, for example. I don't understand why he ever married her. Leo, of course, is very nice and friendly to everyone.

92 UNIT 5

---

② FOCUS ON READING

This section focuses on understanding two contrasting reading selections.

READING ONE is a literary selection, academic article, news piece, blog, or other genre that addresses the unit topic. In levels 1 to 3, readings are based on authentic materials. In levels 4 and 5, all the readings are authentic.

READ FOR MAIN IDEAS and **READ FOR DETAILS** are comprehension activities that lead students to an understanding and appreciation of the first selection.

---

② FOCUS ON READING

A READING ONE: The Education of Frank McCourt

Read the first two paragraphs of The Education of Frank McCourt. Work with a partner to answer the questions. Then read the rest of the article.

1. Where is Frank McCourt now?
2. What do you think he means by "They gave me so much more than I gave them?"
3. What do you think happened to Frank between 1949 and 1997?

THE EDUCATION OF FRANK McCOURT

By Barbara Sande Dimmitt
(from Reader's Digest)

1 Frank McCourt sat on a stage in New York City's Lincoln Center, his white hair glistening under the lights overhead. He was still boyish of expression at 66, and smile lines radiated from hazel eyes bright with inquisitiveness. Soon he would be addressing the 1997 graduating class of Stuyvesant High School, where he had taught English for 18 years.

2 He let his mind wander as he gazed out at the great hall. *I've learned so much from kids like these,* he thought. *They gave me much more than I gave them.*

3 "Yo, Teach!" a voice boomed. Frank McCourt scanned the adolescents in his classroom. It was the fall of 1970 and his first week of teaching at Seward Park High School, which sat in the midst of **dilapidated** tenement buildings on Manhattan's Lower East Side. McCourt located the speaker and nodded. "You talk funny," the student said, "Where ya from?"

4 "Ireland," McCourt replied. With more than ten years of teaching experience under his

belt, this kind of interrogation[1] no longer surprised him. But one question in particular still made him squirm[2] "Where'd you go to high school?" someone else asked.

5 If I tell them the truth, they'll feel superior to me, McCourt thought. They'll throw it in my face. Most of all, he feared an accusation he'd heard before—from himself: You come from nothing, so you are nothing.

6 But McCourt's heart whispered another possibility: Maybe these kids are **yearning for** a way of figuring out this new teacher. Am I willing to risk being humiliated in the classroom to find out?

[1] **interrogation:** intense questioning
[2] **squirm:** feel embarrassed or ashamed

◀ READ FOR MAIN IDEAS

Reading One has four main ideas. What does the reading say about each idea? Circle the sentence that best summarizes the idea.

1. Reporting of facts
   a. Journalists sometimes use their own judgment and leave out certain facts when reporting a story.
   b. Journalists usually report all the facts that they know about a story.

2. Reporting about famous people
   a. In the old days, certain facts about famous people were held back from the public. This is not always true today.
   b. In the old days, certain facts about famous people were held back from the public. This is still the case today.

3. Choosing to report all stories
   a. The decision to report or not report a story is based only on the reporter's judgment.
   b. The decision to report or not report a story is influenced by many factors. The reporter's judgment is just one of these factors.

4. Respecting the right to privacy
   a. All people agree that the public has a right to know about a famous person's life.
   b. Some people believe that you lose the right to privacy when you are famous. Others disagree.

◀ READ FOR DETAILS

Complete the chart with examples or details the author uses to support each main idea.

MAIN IDEA	EXAMPLE OR DETAIL THAT SUPPORTS THE MAIN IDEA
1. Reporting of facts	*retired minister*
2. Reporting about famous people	
3. Choosing to report all stories	
4. Respecting the right to privacy	

Following this comprehension section, the **MAKE INFERENCES** activity prompts students to "read between the lines," move beyond the literal meaning, exercise critical thinking skills, and understand the text on a more academic level. Students follow up with pair or group work to discuss topics in the **EXPRESS OPINIONS** section.

READING TWO offers another perspective on the topic and usually belongs to another genre. Again, in levels 1 to 3, the readings are based on authentic materials, and in levels 4 and 5, they are authentic. This second reading is followed by an activity that challenges students to question ideas they formed about the first reading, and to use appropriate language skills to analyze and explain their ideas.

INTEGRATE READINGS ONE AND TWO presents culminating activities. Students are challenged to take what they have learned, organize the information, and synthesize it in a meaningful way. Students practice skills that are essential for success in authentic academic settings and on standardized tests.

B READING TWO: The Miracle

Diane Schuur is an accomplished jazz musician who is blind. She compares her struggles and triumphs with those of Helen Keller, the famous writer and political activist who was not only blind, but deaf as well.

1 *Discuss the questions with a partner. Then read the article by Diane Schuur.*

1. What do you think the title, "She [Helen Keller] altered our perception of the disabled and remapped the boundaries of sight and sense" means?

2. How do you think Diane Schuur "remapped" her boundaries?

THE MIRACLE:
She altered our perception of the disabled and remapped the boundaries of sight and sense.

By Diane Schuur (from *Time*)

1 Helen Keller was less than two years old when she came down with a fever. It struck dramatically and left her unconscious. The fever went just as suddenly. But she was blinded and, very soon after, deaf. As she grew up, she managed to learn to do tiny errands, but she also realized that she was missing something. "Sometimes," she later wrote, "I stood between two persons who were conversing and touched their lips. I could not understand, and was vexed. I moved my lips and gesticulated[1] frantically without result. This made me so angry at times that I kicked and screamed until I was exhausted." She was a wild child.

Diane Schuur

2 I can understand her rage. I was born two months prematurely and was placed in an incubator. The practice at the time was to pump a large amount of oxygen into the incubator,

something doctors have since learned to be extremely cautious about. But as a result, I lost my sight. I was sent to a state school for the blind, but I flunked first grade because Braille[2] just didn't make any sense to me. Words were a weird concept. I remember being hit and slapped. And you act all that in. All rage is anger that is acted in, bottled in for so long that it just pops out. Helen had it harder. She was both blind and deaf. But, oh, the transformation that came over her when she discovered that words were related to things! It's like the lyrics of that song: "On a clear day, rise and look around you, and you'll see who you are."

3 I can say the word see. I can speak the language of the sighted. That's part of the first great achievement of Helen Keller. She proved how language could liberate the blind and the

¹ **gesticulated:** motioned
² **Braille:** a form of printing with raised round marks that blind people can read by touching

34 UNIT 2

• "You must understand that even more than sighted people, we need to be touched. When you look at a person, eye to eye, I imagine it's like touching them. We don't have that convenience. But when I perform, I get that experience from a crowd."

_____

_____

_____

C INTEGRATE READINGS ONE AND TWO

◀ **STEP 1: Organize**

Both Frank McCourt and Diane Schuur faced many obstacles and challenges in their lives. These same challenges also helped them to discover and develop their talent and become successful. Complete the chart comparing Frank McCourt and Diane Schuur.

	READING ONE Frank McCourt	READING TWO Diane Schuur
1. Obstacles they faced		
2. Person or people who influenced and inspired them		
3. Personal values, traits, or characteristics that helped them face their obstacles		
4. Talent or gift that resulted from the challenges they faced		

◀ **STEP 2: Synthesize**

On a separate piece of paper, write a short paragraph comparing the lives of Frank McCourt and Diane Schuur using the information from Step 1. Describe their obstacles and triumphs.

36 UNIT 2

③ FOCUS ON WRITING

This section emphasizes development of productive skills for writing. It includes sections on vocabulary, grammar, and the writing process.

The **VOCABULARY** section leads students from reviewing the unit vocabulary, to practicing and expanding their use of it, and then working with it—using it creatively in both this section and in the final writing task.

Students learn useful structures for writing in the **GRAMMAR** section, which offers a concise presentation and targeted practice. Vocabulary items are recycled here, providing multiple exposures leading to mastery. For additional practice with the grammar presented, students and teachers can consult the GRAMMAR BOOK REFERENCES at the end of the book for corresponding material in the *Focus on Grammar* and Azar series.

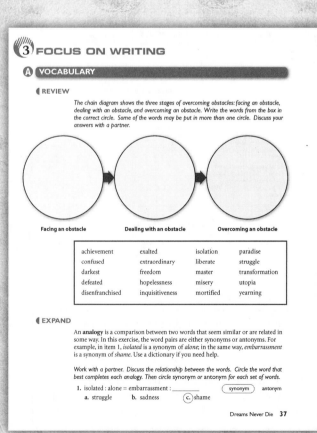

③ FOCUS ON WRITING

Ⓐ VOCABULARY

◀ REVIEW

The chain diagram shows the three stages of overcoming obstacles: facing an obstacle, dealing with an obstacle, and overcoming an obstacle. Write the words from the box in the correct circle. Some of the words may be put in more than one circle. Discuss your answers with a partner.

Facing an obstacle   **Dealing with an obstacle**   **Overcoming an obstacle**

achievement	exalted	isolation	paradise
confused	extraordinary	liberate	struggle
darkest	freedom	master	transformation
defeated	hopelessness	misery	utopia
disenfranchised	inquisitiveness	mortified	yearning

◀ EXPAND

An **analogy** is a comparison between two words that seem similar or are related in some way. In this exercise, the word pairs are either synonyms or antonyms. For example, in item 1, *isolated* is a synonym of *alone*; in the same way, *embarrassment* is a synonym of *shame*. Use a dictionary if you need help.

Work with a partner. Discuss the relationship between the words. Circle the word that best completes each analogy. Then circle synonym or antonym for each set of words.

1. isolated : alone = embarrassment : _____   (synonym) antonym
   a. struggle   b. sadness   c. shame

Dreams Never Die **37**

Ⓑ GRAMMAR: Contrasting the Simple Past, Present Perfect, and Present Perfect Continuous

1 *Examine the sentences and answer the questions with a partner.*

a. Marilisa and Leo **went** to Nairobi and Venice on their honeymoon three years ago.

b. Leo **has been** an architect, an archeologist, a space-habitats developer, a professional gambler, an astronomer, and a number of other disparate and dazzling things.

c. People **have been searching** for the "fountain of youth" since the beginning of recorded history.

1. In sentence *a*, is Leo and Marilisa's honeymoon over? How do you know?
2. In sentence *b*, is Leo still an architect, an archeologist . . . ? How do you know?
3. In sentence *c*, are people still searching for the fountain of youth? How do you know? When did people start searching?
4. What verb tenses are used in sentences *a*, *b*, and *c*?

CONTRASTING THE SIMPLE PAST, PRESENT PERFECT, AND PRESENT PERFECT CONTINUOUS	
The Simple Past 1. Use the simple past for things that happened in the past and were completed.	Leo **watched** the movie. *(Leo is no longer watching the movie. He finished watching the movie.)*
2. Use past time expressions such as: *last, ago, in, on, at, yesterday, when* . . . to indicate that an action or event was completed at a definite time in the past.	Leo **watched** the movie **yesterday**. *(Leo is no longer watching the movie. He finished watching the movie yesterday.)*
The Present Perfect 3. Use the present perfect for completed actions that happened at an indefinite time in the past.	Marilisa **has eaten** breakfast. *(She has finished her breakfast, but we don't know exactly when she ate it, or it is not important.)*
4. You can also use the present perfect for repeated actions that were completed in the past, but that may happen again in the future.	Leo **has visited** Paris six times. *(Those six visits are finished. However, he may visit Paris again in the future.)*

(continued on next page)

Longevity: Too Much of a Good Thing? **107**

The **WRITING** section of each unit leads students through the writing process and presents a challenging and imaginative writing task that directs students to integrate the content, vocabulary, and grammar from the unit.

- Students practice a short **pre-writing strategy**, such as freewriting, clustering, brainstorming, interviewing, listing, making a chart or diagram, categorizing, or classifying.

- Then students organize their ideas and write, using a **specific structural or rhetorical pattern** that fits the subject at hand.

- Students then learn **revising techniques** within a sentence-level or paragraph-level activity to help them move towards **coherence and unity** in their writing.

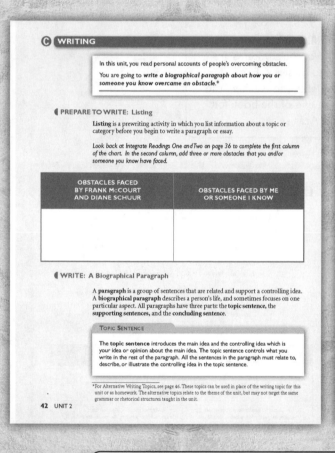

© WRITING

In this unit, you read personal accounts of people's overcoming obstacles.

You are going to *write a biographical paragraph about how you or someone you know overcame an obstacle.**

◄ PREPARE TO WRITE: Listing

Listing is a prewriting activity in which you list information about a topic or category before you begin to write a paragraph or essay.

Look back at Integrate Readings One and Two on page 36 to complete the first column of the chart. In the second column, add three or more obstacles that you and/or someone you know have faced.

OBSTACLES FACED BY FRANK McCOURT AND DIANE SCHUUR	OBSTACLES FACED BY ME OR SOMEONE I KNOW

◄ WRITE: A Biographical Paragraph

A **paragraph** is a group of sentences that are related and support a controlling idea. A **biographical paragraph** describes a person's life, and sometimes focuses on one particular aspect. All paragraphs have three parts: the **topic sentence**, the **supporting sentences**, and the **concluding sentence**.

TOPIC SENTENCE

The **topic sentence** introduces the main idea and the controlling idea which is your idea or opinion about the main idea. The topic sentence controls what you write in the rest of the paragraph. All the sentences in the paragraph must relate to, describe, or illustrate the controlling idea in the topic sentence.

*For Alternative Writing Topics, see page 46. These topics can be used in place of the writing topic for this unit or as homework. The alternative topics relate to the theme of the unit, but may not target the same grammar or rhetorical structures taught in the unit.

42   UNIT 2

5. Read paragraph 8. Write a one-sentence summary of the main idea.

6. Read paragraphs 9 and 10. Write a one-sentence summary of the main idea.

3 Now write your first draft of your summary of Reading Two. Use the information from Prepare to Write and Write to plan your summary. Make sure you state the thesis and eliminate any unimportant details. Be sure to use grammar and vocabulary from the unit.

◄ REVISE: Paraphrasing

Summary writing often requires the writer to restate an author's ideas. It is very important to restate the author's ideas in your own words while keeping true to the author's ideas. This is called **paraphrasing**. (*Note:* When you choose to use author's direct words, you must use quotation marks.)

AUTHOR'S OWN WORDS	PARAPHRASED TEXT
"The things that are important to animals can be different than those that matter to humans. When studying animals, we must test them in situations that have meaning for their lives, not ours, and not just look to see how much they **resemble** us."	Hinshaw concludes that testing an animal's intelligence is very difficult and we should not apply our own human beliefs about what intelligence is to them. Specifically, animals must be tested against measures that are important and useful to them, not to the human world.
When using a direct quote, use these punctuation rules:	When paraphrasing or quoting, use a variety of reporting verbs to introduce an author's ideas:
1. Lift the quote directly as is from the text. Do not change the capitalization or punctuation.	says notes tells mentions acknowledges thinks concedes writes states believes explains concludes
2. Place a comma before the quote: Hinshaw does however acknowledge that, "Animals that are easy to train may also be highly intelligent."	
3. Place the final punctuation mark at the end of the sentence before the final quotation mark: Hinshaw does however acknowledge that, "Animals that are easy to train may also be highly intelligent,"	

When paraphrasing, first think of the main idea or what the author is trying to tell you. Think of ways to say the same thing using your own words. Do not just replace words in a sentence with synonyms.

Original   Paraphrase

Many animals have extreme perception.   ~~Many animals have excellent awareness.~~

88   UNIT 4

In the final phase of the writing process, students **edit** their work with the help of a **checklist** that focuses on mechanics, completeness, enhancing style, and incorporating the vocabulary and grammar from the unit.

ALTERNATIVE WRITING TOPICS are provided at the end of the unit. They can be used as *alternatives* to the final writing task, or as *additional* assignments. RESEARCH TOPICS tied to the theme of the unit are organized in a special section at the back of the book.

MyNorthStarLab

MyNorthStarLab supports students with **individualized instruction, feedback**, and **extra help**. A wide array of resources, including a flexible **gradebook**, helps teachers manage student progress.

The MyNorthStarLab **WELCOME** page **organizes assignments and grades**, and **facilitates communication** between students and teachers.

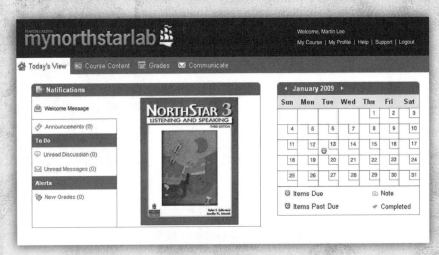

For each unit, MyNorthStarLab provides a **READINESS CHECK**.

➤ Activities **assess** student knowledge **before** beginning the unit and **follow up** with individualized instruction.

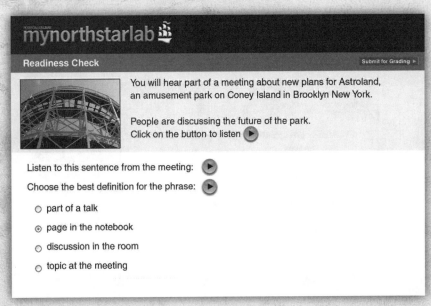

Student book material and **new** practice activities are available to students online.

➤ Students benefit from virtually unlimited **practice anywhere, anytime**.

Interaction with **Internet** and **video** materials will:

➤ Expand students' knowledge of the topic.

➤ Help students practice new vocabulary and grammar.

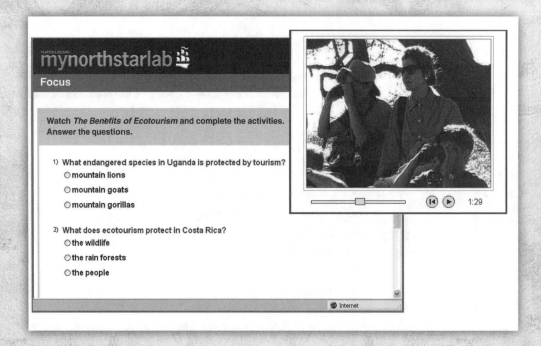

INTEGRATED SKILL ACTIVITIES in MyNorthStarLab challenge students to bring together the **language skills** and **critical thinking skills** that they have practiced throughout the unit.

The MyNorthStarLab **ASSESSMENT** tools allow instructors to customize and deliver achievement tests online.

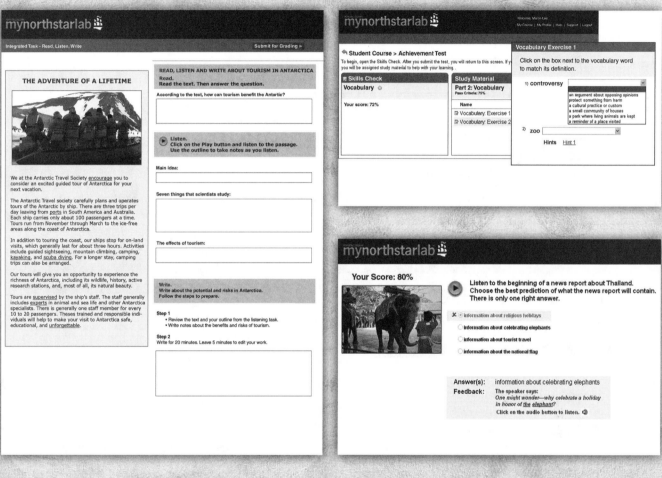

OVERVIEW OF THE TEACHER'S MANUAL AND ACHIEVEMENT TESTS

The *NorthStar Teacher's Manual* includes:

➤ Specific suggestions for teaching each unit

➤ Student Book Answer Key

➤ An alphabetized-by-unit word list of the key vocabulary items practiced in each unit

➤ Reproducible Achievement Tests with Answer Keys

UNIT-BY-UNIT TEACHING SUGGESTIONS

Unit-by-unit overview (scope and sequence), list of skills practiced in each section of the student book, suggested teaching times, teaching suggestions, suggestions on how to use *NorthStar* in secondary classes, Expansion/Homework activities, cross-references to the companion strand, techniques and instructions for using MyNorthStarLab

---

UNIT 2 — Dreams Never Die

OVERVIEW

Theme: Overcoming obstacles
This unit focuses on people who have faced and overcome obstacles and suffering in their lives and how those obstacles have shaped them. Students reflect on their own personal stories and describe their own thoughts on personal suffering and overcoming challenges.

Reading One: *The Education of Frank McCourt* by Frank McCourt describes how the author overcame extreme poverty to become a loved and respected teacher, and a successful writer.

Reading Two: *The Miracle*, from *Time*, tells the story of Diane Schuur, a woman who overcame blindness to become a jazz musician.

Critical Thinking

Infer word meaning from context	Interpret quotations
Interpret meaning of a text	Differentiate between main ideas and details
Evaluate the role of obstacles and character in personal success	Support answers with information from a text

Reading

Scan for information	Organize and synthesize information in different texts
Identify chronology in a text by using a timeline	
Find correlations between two texts	Form and express opinions based on a text

Writing

Write a compare and contrast paragraph	Write concluding sentences
Use a list as a pre-writing device	Recognize sentences that do not support main ideas
Write supporting sentences using transitional expressions	Summarize research in a report

Vocabulary	Grammar
Find and use synonyms	Gerunds and infinitives
Categorize vocabulary words	
Use context clues to find meaning	
Use idiomatic expressions	

MyNorthStarLab	NorthStar: Listening and Speaking 4
Readiness Check, Background and Vocabulary, Readings One and Two, Notetaking and Academic Skills Practice, Vocabulary and Grammar, Writing the Final Draft, Achievement Test	Unit 2 focuses on disabled people who have overcome obstacles in order to meet challenges.

12

A — READING ONE: The Education of Frank McCourt

Go to www.mynorthstarlab.com to read and listen to *The Education of Frank McCourt*.

Suggested Time: 25 minutes

In Reading One, students read about Frank McCourt and how becoming a teacher "educated" him in many ways. The article should get students thinking more about the different ways in which people look at their specific obstacles and the different ways they strive to overcome them.

1. Have students work individually to read the first two paragraphs, and as students finish reading, put them in pairs to discuss the three questions. Go over the questions as a class. Ask students to predict what the rest of the article is going to be about.

2. Have students read the rest of the article independently. The reading can be assigned as homework or lab work using MyNorthStarLab. You can also choose to play the recording of the reading and have students listen as they read.

Expansion/Homework
Have students research Frank McCourt online and find out if he has written any other books since *Angela's Ashes*.

READING STRATEGY: Flashback

1. Tell students that writers sometimes use a technique called a flashback to provide information from the past. Often this is given as a memory or a dream.

2. To help students see this clearly, have them read paragraphs 1, 2, 34, 35, 36, and 37. Then have them work in small groups to retell that story to each other (setting, character, and events) until they have a clear sense of the present time in the narrative. Then have students find the sentence that sets up the flashback in this article (He let his mind wander . . .). Once they have this piece, they can approach the rest of the article and the stories within this frame as coming from Frank McCourt's memory.

READ FOR MAIN IDEAS   Suggested Time: 15 minutes

Have students work individually to scan the reading to fill in the timeline with the events of Frank McCourt's life. Then go over the answers as a class.

Expansion/Homework
This is a good opportunity to work with students on highlighting strategies. Ask students to highlight the main events in Frank McCourt's life. Also, have students put the ideas from the timeline into a paragraph to create a summary of McCourt's life.

Dreams Never Die 15

USING *NORTHSTAR* IN SECONDARY CLASSES

Each unit of the *Teacher's Manual* offers a set of strategies that provide opportunities for greater differentiation in a typical mixed classroom to meet the needs of multi-level secondary students. These strategies are equally beneficial in academic and adult classes. The scaffolded instruction enables teachers to facilitate student mastery of complex skills and ideas. Repeated exposure to concepts helps accelerate English language learning.

Reading/Listening Strategies give teachers additional support to guide students who have limited experience with basic reading/listening skills as they learn to explore and understand academic content. Suggestions are given to help students understand how to predict, determine main idea and supporting details, navigate and comprehend a text, monitor their understanding, and organize information.

Reaching All Students are activity suggestions for two levels of language proficiency, intended to assist less proficient students and challenge students with higher proficiencies. These are generally included in the Reading/Listening section to help teachers to modify reading/listening activities.

Critical Thinking suggestions focus on a hierarchy of questions using Bloom's taxonomy. These are designed specifically to scaffold questions to move students from knowledge-based questions to higher order thinking.

Vocabulary Expansion builds upon vocabulary introduced in each unit to help students further integrate vocabulary. They are offered as word analysis or as vocabulary strategies to reinforce vocabulary skills and provide opportunities for review.

COURSE PLANNERS

Each unit contains approximately eight hours of classroom material, plus expansion, homework, and support material, including MyNorthStarLab. Teachers can customize the units by assigning some exercises for homework and/or eliminating others. To help teachers customize the units for their specific teaching situation, the unit-by-unit teaching suggestions in the *Teacher's Manual* include 1, 2, or 3 stars to indicate the relative importance of each section or exercise as follows:

✪✪✪ **Essential:** Predict, Background and Vocabulary, Reading One, Read for Main Ideas, Read for Details, Make Inferences, Express Opinions, Reading Two, Integrate Readings One and Two, Prepare to Write, Write, Revise, Edit
✪✪ **Recommended:** Share Information, Expand, Grammar
✪ **Optional:** Review, Create, Writing Topics, Research Topics

Class time available per unit	Sections to complete
8 hours or more	Essential (✪✪✪), Recommended (✪✪), Optional (✪)
6 hours	Essential (✪✪✪), Recommended (✪✪)
4 hours	Essential (✪✪✪) only

For more detailed, downloadable unit-by-unit course planners, visit www.mynorthstarlab.com or www.longman.com/northstar.

ACHIEVEMENT TESTS

The reproducible Achievement Tests allow teachers to evaluate students' progress and to identify areas where students might have problems developing their reading and writing skills. The Achievement Tests should be given upon completion of the corresponding unit.

Description

There are four parts for every test:

Parts 1 and **2** test students' receptive skills. Part 1 assesses students' mastery of reading comprehension. Part 2 assesses the knowledge of the vocabulary introduced in the unit. **Parts 3** and **4** test students' productive skills. Part 3 assesses students' knowledge of the grammar and style introduced in the unit. Part 4 is a writing test related to the content of the unit.

Administration

All parts of each test should be taken in class and students should not be allowed access to any *NorthStar* materials or to their dictionaries. Students should be able to complete Parts 1–3 within 30 minutes and Part 4 within 20 minutes.

Teachers can decide how to incorporate Part 4 (the writing task) into their testing situations. Some teachers will assign each writing task immediately after students complete Parts 1–3; others may decide to set aside another time to complete it.

Scoring the Parts

Parts 1–3: Individual test items are worth one point, for a maximum total of 30 points per test. A student's raw score can be obtained by adding together the number of correct items, or by subtracting the total number of incorrect items from 30. To convert the raw score to a percentage score, multiply it by 3.33.

Part 4: The writing tasks are evaluated holistically using scoring rubrics. The scale ranges from 0–5 and includes information from the reading and coherence/connectedness, paragraph development, structures and vocabulary from the unit, and errors.

Combining scores from Parts 1–3 and Part 4: To get a total Achievement Test score, multiply the writing test score by 2. Then, add the writing score to the score in Parts 1–3. Multiply this new score by 2.5 to get a percentage score.

Example 1	Example 2
Score on Test Parts 1–3 = 30	Score on Parts 1–3 = 23
Score on Part 4 = 5	Score on Part 4 = 3
Multiply 5 x 2	Multiply 3 x 2
Add 10 to 30	Add 6 to 23
Multiply 40 x 2.5	Multiply 29 by 2.5
Total score = 100%	Total score = 72.5%

Using the Scoring Rubrics

The *NorthStar Reading and Writing* rubrics are adapted from the integrated writing rubric of TOEFL iBT. Whereas the TOEFL iBT scoring rubric is intended to distinguish levels of English proficiency among candidates to colleges and universities, the *NorthStar* scoring rubrics are intended to show progress in students' writing at each of the five *NorthStar* levels. Therefore, *NorthStar* scoring bands make finer distinctions than TOEFL iBT's scoring band. In this way, students at each level will be able to both see improvement in their scores and receive high marks. The detailed scoring rubric is included in the Achievement Tests Answer Key.

Relationship between TOEFL iBT Rubric and *NorthStar 4* Integrated Writing Rubric		
TOEFL iBT	⟷	*NorthStar 4*
4–5	⟷	5
4	⟷	4
3	⟷	3
3	⟷	2
2	⟷	1
1–2	⟷	0
0	⟷	

OTHER NorthStar COMPONENTS

EXAMVIEW

NorthStar ExamView is a stand-alone CD-ROM that allows teachers to **create and customize** their own *NorthStar* tests.

DVD

The *NorthStar* DVD has **engaging, authentic video clips**, including animation, documentaries, interviews, and biographies, that correspond to the themes in *NorthStar*. Each theme contains a three- to five-minute segment that can be used with either the *Reading and Writing* strand or the *Listening and Speaking* strand. The video clips can also be viewed in MyNorthStarLab.

COMPANION WEBSITE

The companion website, www.longman.com/northstar, includes resources for teachers, such as the **scope and sequence, correlations** to other Longman products and to state standards, and **podcasts** from the *NorthStar* authors and series editors.

UNIT 1 Untruth and Consequences

OVERVIEW

Theme: Media

This unit focuses on sensational tabloid journalism and how it affects people's lives. Students confront questions about journalistic responsibility and what makes news newsworthy. Students discuss their opinions concerning celebrity tabloid journalism and other news media.

Reading One: *Peeping Tom Journalism* discusses the responsibility journalists have in reporting what they deem newsworthy.

Reading Two: *Focus on Bomb Suspect Brings Tears and a Plea* deals with how reporters victimized Richard Jewell after the bombing in Centennial Olympic Park in 1996.

Critical Thinking

Interpret a photograph
Recognize how details support main ideas
Use examples to support answers

Classify information
Draw conclusions
Hypothesize another's point of view

Reading

Interpret quotations
Make predictions
Categorize main ideas

Scan for supporting details
Make inferences about author's viewpoint
Form and express opinions based on a text

Writing

Develop topic sentences
Paraphrase
Write a letter to a newspaper editor
Write an opinion paragraph

Compose topic sentences
Brainstorm ideas using a web organizer
Use time transitions

Vocabulary	Grammar
Categorize vocabulary words Use context clues to find meaning Use idiomatic expressions	Passive and active voice

 MyNorthStarLab
Readiness Check, Background and Vocabulary, Readings One and Two, Notetaking and Academic Skills Practice, Vocabulary and Grammar, Writing the Final Draft, Achievement Test

 NorthStar: Listening and Speaking 4
Unit 1 focuses on the positive and negative content of the news and individuals who choose to limit the amount of news in their lives.

Go to www.mynorthstarlab.com for the MyNorthStarLab *Readiness Check*.

① FOCUS ON THE TOPIC

◀ SKILLS

Predict the content of the unit based on the photograph and the title of the unit; activate prior knowledge; identify opinions; practice paraphrasing skills; infer the meaning of new vocabulary from context.

✪✪✪ Ⓐ PREDICT

Suggested Time: 10 minutes

1. Check that students are familiar with Princess Diana and that they know what country she was princess of. Ask if any of the students know when she died and anything about the circumstances of her death.

2. Check students' comprehension of the words *untruth* and *consequences*. Ask students how they think these terms might relate to the topic of news, and more specifically, to Princess Diana. Put students in pairs to discuss the discussion questions.

✪✪ Ⓑ SHARE INFORMATION

Suggested Time: 15 minutes

1. Have students look at the first two quotes and decide on the answers individually before getting into groups to compare and justify their answers.

2. Have students work together in their groups to write their own interpretations of quotations 3 and 4. Circulate and ask questions, providing help with vocabulary where necessary.

✪✪✪ Ⓒ BACKGROUND AND VOCABULARY

Go to www.mynorthstarlab.com for *Background and Vocabulary*.

Suggested Time: 20 minutes

1. Have students read the instructions for **Exercise 1**. Emphasize that the purpose of the reading is both to provide more background on the topic of "news" and to provide a context for new vocabulary words.

2. Suggest that students read the text all the way to the end first without worrying about new vocabulary items. Then have them reread the text attempting to understand the boldfaced vocabulary items from the context.

3. Put students in pairs to discuss the following (or alternatively, assign these questions for homework): What functions of the news are mentioned in paragraph 1? What makes the news not necessarily "unquestionably true" in paragraph 2? What are some examples of news stories that are "high-interest"?

4. Have students do **Exercise 2** in pairs or individually before going over the answers as a class. Have students point out the phrases in the text that helped them ascertain the correct meanings.

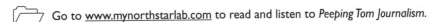 Go to www.mynorthstarlab.com for additional *Background and Vocabulary* practice.

 FOCUS ON READING

◖SKILLS

Differentiate between main ideas and details; make inferences about the author's point of view; express opinions; make predictions about the content of a reading.

✸✸✸Ⓐ READING ONE: Peeping Tom Journalism

 Go to www.mynorthstarlab.com to read and listen to *Peeping Tom Journalism.*

Suggested Time: 25 minutes

Reading One is a book excerpt in which students read about the consequences of indiscriminate journalism. The article should get students thinking about the effects of sensational tabloid journalism and how news in various media is gathered, reported, and interpreted.

1. Ask students to look at the illustration and the title of the excerpt. Explain the term "peeping Tom" (a person who secretly watches others). Ask students to say how the term relates to the news today.

2. Have students read the first three paragraphs. Put them in pairs or groups to discuss the questions in paragraph three. Have pairs or groups share their answers with the class or with other pairs/groups.

3. Have students read paragraph 4. Ask them if the answers in the article to the questions posed in paragraph 3 are the same as their own answers. Then have students read the remainder of the article independently. The reading can be assigned as homework or lab work using MyNorthStarLab. You can also choose to play the recording of the reading and have students listen as they read.

1. Tell students that anecdotes are small stories, and many writers rely on them to illustrate their point. When they begin to distinguish these anecdotes from main ideas/topic sentences and explanations, they will be better readers—and better writers.

2. Have students work with the anecdotes in this text. Ask them to work in small groups to identify the people and the events for the four stories that are discussed in this text. Provide story maps or charts if students need them. Then have each group retell one of the stories to the class, ensuring that all stories are adequately recounted.

✪✪✪ READ FOR MAIN IDEAS   Suggested Time: 15 minutes

Have students complete the exercise. Go over the answers as a class. If there is any disagreement, ask students to point to the appropriate facts in the text.

REACHING ALL STUDENTS: Read for Main Ideas

• **Less Proficient:** Tell students to read the introduction (first paragraph) to locate the main idea. Then copy the title and main idea. Are they similar?	• **More Proficient:** In the exercise for Main Ideas, ask students to write the four headings (main ideas) in complete sentences and then use the outline to write a summary.

✪✪✪ READ FOR DETAILS   Suggested Time: 15 minutes

1. Elicit the difference between main ideas and details. Explain that details support the main ideas of a text.

2. Have students scan the text again to find the supporting details for each of the main ideas listed in the chart.

3. Divide the class into pairs (of mixed abilities if possible) and have students compare their charts. Then go over the answers with the whole class. Ask individual students to read the details they listed.

✪✪✪ MAKE INFERENCES   Suggested Time: 10 minutes

1. Have students read the instructions. Give them an example by making a statement and then asking students why you might have said it. For example, say "I wish we had an extra 15 minutes to this class." Then ask students why you might have said that, to elicit that you have too much to do in the allotted time. Show students that that is the inference they can make from your statement.

2. Tell students to read the statements and then to refer to the text to find the answers. Put students in pairs to discuss their answers.

✿✿✿ EXPRESS OPINIONS

Suggested Time: 15 minutes

Tell students that it is now their turn to express their own opinions about the topic of what is newsworthy and the amount of privacy people in the news should be entitled to. Divide the class into pairs and assign each pair one of the three questions to discuss.

CRITICAL THINKING

Give students the following questions for discussion in small groups before discussing as a whole class:

1. According to the article, how did journalists in the past differ from those today?

   Answer: They didn't report on the negative aspects of the personal lives of celebrities.

2. If you were a reporter who had a personal story about a celebrity that would hurt his/her family, would you report it? Explain.

   Answers will vary, but students should support their choice with convincing reasons.

3. Would you report it if you knew that another reporter also had the story?

   Answers will vary, but students should support their choice with convincing reasons.

4. If we do something that is newsworthy, do we have a right to privacy?

   Answers will vary, but students should support their choice with convincing reasons based on the text and their own knowledge.

 Link to *NorthStar: Listening and Speaking 4*
Students who are also using the companion text can extend the discussion to include the positive and negative content of the news and individuals who choose to limit the amount of news in their lives.

✦✦✦ B | READING TWO: Focus on Bomb Suspect Brings Tears and a Plea

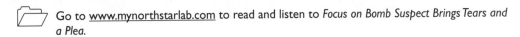

Go to www.mynorthstarlab.com to read and listen to *Focus on Bomb Suspect Brings Tears and a Plea.*

Suggested Time: 20 minutes

In Reading Two, students read an article from *The New York Times* about the consequences of reporting news before having all the facts.

1. Ask students if they can remember a time when they jumped to a conclusion about something or someone only to find they were wrong later. Ask them to reflect on how they felt after they discovered they were wrong.

2. Have students read the background information about the Richard Jewell case, and then in small groups, discuss the answers to the questions in **Exercise 1**. Then have students read the text individually. You can also choose to play the recording of the reading and have students listen as they read.

3. Have students complete the charts in **Exercise 2**, working either alone or in groups. Go over the answers as a class.

✦✦✦Ⓒ INTEGRATE READINGS ONE AND TWO

◖ SKILLS

Organize the main ideas of the reading into categories; integrate and synthesize the information in two texts, and form opinions as a reader using this information.

STEP 1: Organize   Suggested Time: 15 minutes

1. Check students' comprehension of some of the phrases in the chart by either having students use the phrases in conjunction with the people in the two readings or with other people or celebrities currently in the news.

2. Have students complete the exercise in pairs or individually and then compare answers.

3. Go over the answers with the entire class.

STEP 2: Synthesize   Suggested Time: 15 minutes

1. Read the instructions with the class. Emphasize the importance of supporting their answers with examples from the readings and from the chart students filled out.

2. Have students decide whether they agree or disagree with the statements and find examples to support their opinions. You might have them discuss their opinions with a partner.

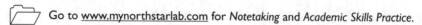 Go to www.mynorthstarlab.com for *Notetaking* and *Academic Skills Practice*.

③ FOCUS ON WRITING

Ⓐ VOCABULARY

◀ SKILLS

Review vocabulary and idioms from Readings One and Two; expand vocabulary by identifying idioms; use new vocabulary creatively in a written assignment.

✪ REVIEW   **Suggested Time: 10 minutes**

  Go to www.mynorthstarlab.com for *Review*.

1. Have students read the background information for the imaginary letter. Ask students what they think the focus of the letter will be. Check students' comprehension of the vocabulary items.

2. Have students work individually. Suggest that students read each paragraph to the end before attempting to fill in the blanks. Also suggest that students think of what kind of word they would fill the blank with before reviewing the choices. As students finish, pair them up to compare their answers.

 Link to *NorthStar: Listening and Speaking 4*
If students are also using the companion text, you can repeat the exercise for homework using vocabulary from the *Listening and Speaking* strand.

✪✪ EXPAND   **Suggested Time: 20 minutes**

1. Check students' comprehension of the term *idiom*. Elicit from them other idioms they know and write these on the board, showing them how the meaning is different from the meaning of the separate words.

2. Put students in groups to complete **Exercise 1**. Then go over the answers with the class.

3. Read the instructions for **Exercise 2** with students and review who the people listed are and their feelings about their individual situations. Then put students in groups or pairs to complete the exercise. Have students give reasons for their decisions. Go over the answers with the class.

VOCABULARY EXPANSION: Roots

1. Remind students that many English words contain Greek or Latin roots and understanding the meaning of those roots will help them to know the meaning of many words.

(continued on next page)

---

2. Provide this list of roots: *spec, legis/leg, act, bio, chron/chrono, form, geo, graph, log/logy, multi, phono, scribe/script,* and *sphere.* Then have them work in groups to list as many words as they can think of for each root word. Have groups share their lists and then come to a conclusion as to the meaning of each root word. Students can check meanings in a dictionary, and then add the root, meanings, and examples to a section titled "Roots" in their personal dictionaries.

Expansion/Homework

Have students research online one person from Exercise 2 to find out the last time they appeared in the news. Have students return to class ready to share what they found and the circumstances of the most recent news stories.

✪ CREATE
Suggested Time: 20 minutes

Have students read the reporter's comments and then put them in pairs to brainstorm their reactions. Then have students write their responses individually, or have them write them for homework. Suggest students write their response first without thinking about the vocabulary or idiom items to be used, and then fit the five items in during a revision, or with a partner after having exchanged papers.

🗁 Go to www.mynorthstarlab.com for additional *Vocabulary* practice.

✪✪ B GRAMMAR: Passive Voice

🗁 Go to www.mynorthstarlab.com for *Grammar Chart* and *Exercise 2.*

◖ SKILLS

Learn the difference in use and form between the passive and active voices and use each one appropriately.

Suggested Time: 25 minutes

1. Have students work in pairs to examine the sets of sentences in **Exercise 1** and answer the questions that follow. Go over the answers as a class, putting the answers to question number 1, especially, on the board.

2. Ask students to read the grammar explanation silently while you circulate to answer individual questions. Check that they are clear on the uses of the passive voice in the different forms of the past and present.

3. Read the instructions for **Exercise 2** and check that students understand why the first one is in the active voice. Have students complete the exercise individually. Review answers and address questions and problems as a class.

4. Read the instructions for **Exercise 3** with the class. Check that students understand they are focusing on form as well as whether or not the agent is important and should be mentioned. Have students do the exercise

individually or in pairs, justifying to one another why the agent should or should not be included. Go over the answers together as a class.

Expansion/Homework

(1) Have students decide which sentences in Exercise 3 can be written in the active. Students can complete the exercises at home and then go over the answers in class. (2) For further practice, offer exercises from *Focus on Grammar 4, 3rd Edition* and Azar's *Understanding and Using English Grammar, 3rd Edition*. See the Grammar Book References on page 267 of the student book for specific units and chapters.

 Go to www.mynorthstarlab.com for additional *Grammar* practice.

C WRITING

If you wish to assign a different writing task than the one in this section, see page 24. The Alternative Writing Topics can also be assigned as additional writing topics for homework. The alternative topics relate to the theme of the unit, but may not target the same grammar or rhetorical structures taught in the unit.

SKILLS

Brainstorm ideas; use time transitions; identify and practice writing topic sentences; integrate the concepts, vocabulary, grammar, and rhetorical structures from the unit to write a summary paragraph.

✪✪✪ PREPARE TO WRITE: Group Brainstorming

Suggested Time: 10 minutes

Put the students in groups to brainstorm. You might want to suggest that only one student writes the ideas so that everyone is working together, and that afterwards, the other students in the group copy the list into their own books. Then have students choose a story to write about.

✪✪✪ WRITE: A Summary Paragraph

Suggested Time: 30 minutes

1. Have students read the background information on paragraphs and check that they understand the differences between topics, main ideas, and controlling ideas.

2. Have students read the paragraph in **Exercise 1**. Then put students in pairs to discuss their answers to the questions that follow. Go over the answers as a class, referring back to the information in the Topic Sentence box as needed.

3. Have students complete **Exercise 2** individually and then compare their answers with those of a partner. Tell students to discuss why the other two choices are not effective. Go over the answers as a class.

4. Read the instructions for **Exercise 3** with the class. Have students say what the topic, the main idea, and the controlling idea for the first paragraph is.

5. Have students complete the exercise individually. As they finish, put them in pairs to compare their answers.

6. Read the instructions for **Exercise 4** with students. Review or elicit the purpose and structure of a summary paragraph and write the key components on the board. Have students complete the organizer while you move around the room to answer any individual questions about vocabulary.

7. Have students write their first drafts. You can also assign writing the first draft as homework.

✪✪✪ REVISE: Using Time Transitions

Suggested Time: 20 minutes

1. Go over the information on time transitions, paying particular attention to the fact that they are not usually used in topic sentences. Note that for most students this will be a review rather than a new presentation.

2. Have students read the paragraph in **Exercise 1** first without attempting to fill in the blanks, and then reread it and complete the exercise. Go over the answers as a class asking students to share any variations they have.

3. For **Exercise 2**, have students review their own drafts. Move around the room and make comments where appropriate.

✪✪✪ EDIT: Writing the Final Draft

Suggested Time: 25 minutes

Have students write the final draft of their paragraphs. Encourage them to use language and grammar from the unit. Make sure they go through the checklist before submitting their final drafts. Collect the paragraphs and correct them before the next class.

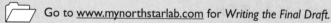 Go to www.mynorthstarlab.com for *Writing the Final Draft.*

✪ ALTERNATIVE WRITING TOPICS

These topics give students an alternative opportunity to explore and write about issues related to the unit theme.

✪ RESEARCH TOPICS

Suggested Time: 30 minutes in class

1. Have students turn to page 259. Review the instructions for the activity with the class. Brainstorm with students the names of newspapers and magazines to choose from.

2. Have students look at the chart. Discuss with the class the different categories and what types of articles would make money for the newspaper or magazine.

3. Have students present their findings to the class or in small groups. Compare the various sources the students have used and, as a class, decide which is the most newsworthy.

 Link to *NorthStar: Listening and Speaking 4*

Have students write an essay on the role news plays in their lives using examples from Unit 1: Information Overload.

 Go to www.mynorthstarlab.com for *Student Writing Models, Integrated Task, Video Activity, Internet Activity,* and *Unit 1 Achievement Test.*

UNIT 2 Dreams Never Die

OVERVIEW

Theme: Overcoming obstacles

This unit focuses on people who have faced and overcome obstacles and suffering in their lives and how those obstacles have shaped them. Students reflect on their own personal stories and describe their own thoughts on personal suffering and overcoming challenges.

Reading One: *The Education of Frank McCourt* by Frank McCourt describes how the author overcame extreme poverty to become a loved and respected teacher, and a successful writer.

Reading Two: *The Miracle*, from *Time*, tells the story of Diane Schuur, a woman who overcame blindness to become a jazz musician.

Critical Thinking

Infer word meaning from context
Interpret meaning of a text
Evaluate the role of obstacles and character in personal success

Interpret quotations
Differentiate between main ideas and details
Support answers with information from a text

Reading

Scan for information
Identify chronology in a text by using a timeline
Find correlations between two texts

Organize and synthesize information in different texts
Form and express opinions based on a text

Writing

Write a compare and contrast paragraph
Use a list as a pre-writing device
Write supporting sentences using transitional expressions

Write concluding sentences
Recognize sentences that do not support main ideas
Summarize research in a report

Vocabulary	Grammar
Find and use synonyms Categorize vocabulary words Use context clues to find meaning Use idiomatic expressions	Gerunds and infinitives
MyNorthStarLab Readiness Check, Background and Vocabulary, Readings One and Two, Notetaking and Academic Skills Practice, Vocabulary and Grammar, Writing the Final Draft, Achievement Test	**NorthStar: Listening and Speaking 4** Unit 2 focuses on disabled people who have overcome obstacles in order to meet challenges.

1 FOCUS ON THE TOPIC

◖ SKILLS

Predict the content of the unit; activate prior knowledge; express opinions; infer the meaning of new vocabulary words from context.

✱✱✱ Ⓐ PREDICT

Suggested Time: 15 minutes

1. Have students look at the picture and the title. Ask students what this young woman is doing with her hands. Have students read the caption and explain that Helen Keller was blind, deaf, and mute. Ask students if they know ways in which people become blind or deaf. Ask if students know any blind or deaf people personally.

2. Have students read the background information on Helen Keller and the quote, and then read the discussion questions, giving them a few minutes to develop their own thoughts. Then have students discuss the questions in pairs.

✱✱ Ⓑ SHARE INFORMATION

Suggested Time: 15 minutes

1. Have students look at the pictures and say what they know about each person.

2. Have students read the listed obstacles and match them to the pictures.

3. Put students in pairs to compare their answers and then answer questions 2 and 3.

Expansion/Homework
Have pairs of students list different types of obstacles and put this list on the board. For homework, students could write a sentence or two about which types of obstacles they think they personally might find the hardest to overcome and why.

📁 Go to www.mynorthstarlab.com for *Background and Vocabulary*.

Suggested Time: 20 minutes

1. Have students read the instructions for **Exercise 1**. Ask students if any of them have ever heard of Frank McCourt. If not, tell them that they will find out through the reading, but elicit from them that he must be someone who also overcame obstacles.

2. Suggest that students read the text all the way to the end first without worrying about new vocabulary items. Then have them reread the text attempting to understand the boldfaced vocabulary items from the context.

3. Put students in pairs to discuss the questions in **Exercise 2**. Go over question 3 with the class, checking that they understand what it means to "reinvent" his past.

4. Have students complete **Exercise 3** in pairs or individually before going over the answers as a class.

Expansion/Homework

You may want to assign these exercises as homework and use class time to check answers.

 Link to *NorthStar: Listening and Speaking 4*

If students are also using the companion text, you may want to list vocabulary from Background and Vocabulary in Unit 2 on the board and see if students can find synonyms for those words in the background passage.

📁 Go to www.mynorthstarlab.com for additional *Background and Vocabulary* practice.

② FOCUS ON READING

◖ SKILLS

Make predictions about the content of the article; differentiate between main ideas and details; make a timeline; make inferences and support them with evidence from the text; scan the article for specific information; express opinions.

📁 Go to www.mynorthstarlab.com to read and listen to *The Education of Frank McCourt.*

Suggested Time: 25 minutes

In Reading One, students read about Frank McCourt and how becoming a teacher "educated" him in many ways. The article should get students thinking more about the different ways in which people look at their specific obstacles and the different ways they strive to overcome them.

1. Have students work individually to read the first two paragraphs, and as students finish reading, put them in pairs to discuss the three questions. Go over the questions as a class. Ask students to predict what the rest of the article is going to be about.

2. Have students read the rest of the article independently. The reading can be assigned as homework or lab work using MyNorthStarLab. You can also choose to play the recording of the reading and have students listen as they read.

Expansion/Homework
Have students research Frank McCourt online and find out if he has written any other books since *Angela's Ashes*.

READING STRATEGY: Flashback

1. Tell students that writers sometimes use a technique called a flashback to provide information from the past. Often this is given as a memory or a dream.

2. To help students see this clearly, have them read paragraphs 1, 2, 34, 35, 36, and 37. Then have them work in small groups to retell that story to each other (setting, character, and events) until they have a clear sense of the present time in the narrative. Then have students find the sentence that sets up the flashback in this article (He let his mind wander . . .). Once they have this piece, they can approach the rest of the article and the stories within this frame as coming from Frank McCourt's memory.

✪✪✪ READ FOR MAIN IDEAS   **Suggested Time: 15 minutes**

Have students work individually to scan the reading to fill in the timeline with the events of Frank McCourt's life. Then go over the answers as a class.

Expansion/Homework
This is a good opportunity to work with students on highlighting strategies. Ask students to highlight the main events in Frank McCourt's life. Also, have students put the ideas from the timeline into a paragraph to create a summary of McCourt's life.

✪✪✪ READ FOR DETAILS

1. Have students look at the chart and point out that the event timeline in the left column are the main ideas of the article, or the main events in this man's life, and the details students will put in the right side of the chart are the details of this man's life explaining why things happened and what the results were.

2. Have students scan the text again to find the supporting details for each of the main events listed. Then divide the class into pairs or small groups and have students compare their charts. Finally, go over the students' charts with the whole class. Ask individual students to read the details they listed.

REACHING ALL STUDENTS: Read for Details

- **Less Proficient:** Provide these paragraph numbers: 1, 3, 17, 19, 20, 24, 29, 33, and ask students to list dates/places/events in chronological order in a 3-column chart.

- **More Proficient:** Have students list dates/places/events in chronological order in a 3-column chart.

Date	Place	Event

✪✪✪ MAKE INFERENCES

1. Have students read the instructions. Remind them what inferences are—conclusions the reader makes based on information in the text that is not explicitly stated.

2. Tell students to read the statements, and then scan the text to find the paragraph in which the statements appear. Tell students to use the information surrounding the statement to help them make their inferences.

3. Put students in pairs to discuss their answers. If students disagree, tell them to go back to the text to point out specific details to support their decisions; however, reiterate that an inference is more informed than a guess.

✪✪✪ EXPRESS OPINIONS

1. Have students read the first question. Tell them to think about the list of Frank McCourt's obstacles that they made in Background and Vocabulary. Have them choose the obstacle they thought was the greatest.

2. Put students in pairs or small groups to compare the challenge they chose and to give reasons for their choice. Have them also say how Frank McCourt overcame that challenge. Then have students read the second question and discuss their opinions in their pairs or groups.

CRITICAL THINKING

Give students the following questions for discussion in small groups before discussing as a whole class:

1. According to information in the article, how did Frank McCourt feel about his education and background? What paragraphs provide this information?

   Answer: He was embarrassed and afraid to reveal the information (see paragraphs 5, 6, and 12).

2. How was his poverty similar to or different than his students'?

   Answer: Though the poverty was similar, there appeared to be more loneliness and less family companionship in his students' lives.

3. Do you think anyone can become successful in the United States? Explain.

   Answers will vary, but students should support their ideas with clear explanations and examples.

4. Why does he say that his students gave him lessons in courage?

   Answers will vary, but might include his students' willingness to tell their stories and their encouragement for him to tell his.

 Link to *NorthStar: Listening and Speaking 4*
Students who are also using the companion text can extend the discussion to include disabled people and their challenges.

✦✦✦ B READING TWO: The Miracle

 Go to www.mynorthstarlab.com to read and listen to *The Miracle*.

Suggested Time: 20 minutes

In Reading Two, students read a *Time* magazine article about a blind jazz singer, Diane Schuur. The purpose of this article is to expand students' understanding of the topic of suffering and the people who have overcome their suffering.

1. Have students read the background information about Diane Schuur individually, and then read the two discussion questions in **Exercise 1**. Check students' comprehension of *remapped* and *boundaries of sight and sense*. Put students in pairs to discuss the answers to the two questions.

2. Have students read the article individually. You can also choose to play the recording of the reading and have students listen as they read.

3. Have students read the questions in **Exercise 2** and check that they understand them. Check especially that students understand what Diane Schuur means by "touched." Ask students the different ways a person can be touched, eliciting both physically and emotionally. Then have students answer the questions individually, in class, or for homework.

◖ SKILLS

Organize information from the readings in a chart; synthesize information in a writing assignment.

STEP 1: Organize   Suggested Time: 15 minutes

1. Have students read the four topics that they are going to compare in the chart and check their comprehension of all the key items.

2. Have students think about the information they would like to include, checking back in the texts as necessary. Have students complete the exercise in pairs or individually. Then go over the answers with the entire class.

 Link to *NorthStar: Listening and Speaking 4*
For students who are also using the companion text, you may want to have them include Richard Van Ornum and the Achilles Track Club on the chart for comparison.

STEP 2: Synthesize   Suggested Time: 15 minutes

Read the instructions with students. Emphasize the importance of supporting their statements with examples from the readings and from the chart they filled out in Step 1. Then have students write a short comparison paragraph either in class or for homework.

🗁 Go to www.mynorthstarlab.com for *Notetaking* and *Academic Skills Practice.*

 3 FOCUS ON WRITING

A VOCABULARY

◖ SKILLS

Review vocabulary from Readings One and Two; expand understanding of vocabulary by categorizing; use new vocabulary creatively in a writing assignment.

✪ REVIEW   Suggested Time: 10 minutes

🗁 Go to www.mynorthstarlab.com for *Review.*

1. Read the background information on the three stages of overcoming obstacles with the class. Ask students to explain in their own words what they think each

stage means. Then have students look at the diagram and check their understanding of how the chain works.

2. Have students work individually while you circulate to offer assistance with vocabulary items. Remind students that some terms can appear in more than one circle.

3. Go over the chart as a class. Check answers by having students read the words they've assigned to each stage. If students have different opinions about placement, have them support their choices.

Expansion/Homework
Ask students to think of another way to diagram the progress of overcoming obstacles, to bring their new diagram to class, and to be prepared to explain how it works.

○○ EXPAND   Suggested Time: 15 minutes

1. Put a simple analogy on the board, for example, black : white = night : _____. Ask students what word goes in the blank, eliciting *day*. Explain that this is an analogy. Ask students what relationship the words have to each other, eliciting that they are antonyms.

2. Read the instructions with the class. Go over the example with students. Put them in pairs to complete the activity. Tell students to try to put the words in sentences to help clarify the meanings for them and to discuss their answers. Then bring the class together and go over the answers.

VOCABULARY EXPANSION: Draw the Word

Provide definitions and large chart paper and ask students to work with a partner to draw five of the words. Encourage students to use stick figures, smiley/sad faces, and simple drawings to illustrate the meanings. Have students share their drawings with the class and then have students select drawings to use in their Personal Dictionaries or on flash cards.

○ CREATE   Suggested Time: 20 minutes

1. Explain to students that they will be writing a letter to either Helen Keller or Frank McCourt. Have students select the situation they would prefer to write about. Give them time to freewrite their ideas individually.

2. Have students write their letters in class or at home, reminding them to use the words and phrases from Review and Expand.

Go to www.mynorthstarlab.com for additional *Vocabulary* practice.

✪✪ B GRAMMAR: Gerunds and Infinitives

📁 Go to www.mynorthstarlab.com for *Grammar Chart* and *Exercise 2*.

◀ SKILLS

Learn the difference in use and form between gerunds and infinitives and use each one appropriately.

Suggested Time: 30 minutes

1. Remind students of the function of a sentence's subject and object by putting the following sentence on the board: Frank McCourt loved teaching.

2. Put the gerund *teaching* in the sentence *Teaching is fun,* and the infinitive *to teach* on the board and go over the meaning of each one very briefly. Then have students work in pairs to examine the sentences in **Exercise 1** and answer the questions that follow. Tell students to pay attention to the words in boldface.

3. Go over the grammar chart with the class.

4. Read the instructions for **Exercise 2**. You might want to have students read the sentences and underline the gerunds and infinitives before completing the exercise as written. Then have students complete the exercise individually. Review answers and address questions and problems as a class.

5. Read the instructions for **Exercise 3** with the class. Check that students understand they are not combining sentences but rather paraphrasing or rewording each situation. Have students complete the exercise individually or in pairs. Go over the answers together as a class. Note that the parts of the sentence that are not the gerund or infinitive may vary.

Expansion/Homework
For further practice, offer exercises from *Focus on Grammar 4, 3rd Edition* and Azar's *Understanding and Using English Grammar, 3rd Edition*. See the Grammar Book References on page 267 of the student book for specific units and chapters.

 Go to www.mynorthstarlab.com for additional *Grammar* practice.

ⓒ WRITING

If you wish to assign a different writing task than the one in this section, see page 46. The Alternative Writing Topics can also be assigned as additional writing topics for homework. The alternative topics relate to the theme of the unit, but may not target the same grammar or rhetorical structures taught in the unit.

◖ SKILLS

Use a list as a pre-writing strategy; practice choosing appropriate supporting details; integrate the concepts, vocabulary, grammar, and rhetorical structures from the unit to write a cohesive biographical paragraph.

✪✪✪ PREPARE TO WRITE: Listing

Suggested Time: 10 minutes

1. Read the instructions and the information about the writing topic with students. Brainstorm some typical types of obstacles students might be willing to write about.

2. Have students read about listing, explaining that it is another type of brainstorming and that it is useful as a way to draw out their ideas.

3. Have students complete the listing exercise individually before putting them in pairs to compare charts.

4. Have students choose an obstacle that they or a friend of theirs overcame to write about.

✪✪✪ WRITE: A Biographical Paragraph

Suggested Time: 30 minutes

1. Have students read the background information on the three parts of a paragraph, and the explanation of topic sentences, supporting sentences, and concluding sentences in the box.

2. Have students read the paragraph about Greg Barton and then discuss their answers to the questions that follow in **Exercise 1** with a partner. Then put students in pairs to discuss their answers to the questions that follow.

3. Have students complete **Exercise 2** individually. Have them write their paragraphs. You can also assign writing the first draft as homework.

✪✪✪ REVISE: Choosing Appropriate Support

Suggested Time: 20 minutes

1. Go over the information on supporting sentences, paying particular attention to the different forms they can have: examples, details, and facts, and that they are not useful unless they support the topic sentence.

2. Have students complete **Exercises 1** and **2** individually after going over the examples together.

3. For **Exercise 3**, have students review their own drafts. Move around the room and make comments where appropriate.

EDIT: Writing the Final Draft

Suggested Time: 25 minutes

Have students write the final draft of their paragraphs. Encourage them to use language and grammar from the unit. Make sure they go through the checklist before submitting their final drafts. Collect the paragraphs and correct them before the next class.

 Link to *NorthStar: Listening and Speaking 4*

If students are also using the companion text, have them refer to the list of devices to help disabled people, choose one of the devices, and write a short paragraph describing how that device would help Diane Schuur (or a person with another disability) in everyday life.

> Go to www.mynorthstarlab.com for *Writing the Final Draft.*

○ ALTERNATIVE WRITING TOPICS

These topics give students an alternative opportunity to explore and write about issues related to the unit theme.

○ RESEARCH TOPICS

Suggested Time: 30 minutes in class

1. Have students turn to pages 259–260. Review the instructions for the activity with the class. Read the list of questions with the class. Encourage students to ask additional questions.

2. Look over the list of famous people and have students choose a person who they are interested in researching. Have students do their research on the Internet or in a library, using the questions as an outline for their biography.

3. Have students present their biographies to the class or in small groups.

> Go to www.mynorthstarlab.com for *Student Writing Models, Integrated Task, Video Activity, Internet Activity,* and *Unit 2 Achievement Test.*

UNIT 3 Dying for Their Beliefs

OVERVIEW

Theme: Medicine

This unit focuses on alternative medical treatments, religious constraints concerning traditional medical treatments, and legal consequences. Students consider the question of individuals' rights regarding their own and their children's health, their own beliefs concerning alternative and conventional medical treatments, and some extreme religious beliefs about medicine.

Reading One: *Dying for Their Beliefs: Christian Scientist Parents on Trial in Girl's Death* discusses a case in which a young girl died because her parents, following their religion's doctrines, denied her medical care.

Reading Two: *Norman Cousins's Laugh Therapy* describes how this well-known writer cured himself of a serious disease by using an alternative form of treatment.

Critical Thinking

Draw logical conclusions	Categorize information
Support answers with information from a text	Re-evaluate assumptions
Research medical treatments	Analyze the development of an argument

Reading

Make predictions	Identify philosophical rationale for a text
Summarize main ideas	Paraphrase
Identify details	Make inferences
Relate texts to personal values and experiences	Use Venn diagrams as a note-taking device

Writing

Write an opinion essay	Develop an opinion in outline form
Use tree mapping as a pre-writing device	Support an opinion with evidence
Write hooks	Develop a classroom survey

Vocabulary	Grammar
Find analogies	Past unreal conditionals
Compare and contrast word meanings	

 MyNorthStarLab
Readiness Check, Background and Vocabulary, Readings One and Two, Notetaking and Academic Skills Practice, Vocabulary and Grammar, Writing the Final Draft, Achievement Test

 NorthStar: Listening and Speaking 4
Unit 3 focuses on an examination of modern sleep habits.

①FOCUS ON THE TOPIC

◀ SKILLS

Predict the content of the unit based on the photograph and the title of the unit; activate prior knowledge; identify opinions; practice paraphrasing skills; infer the meaning of new vocabulary from context.

✸✸✸Ⓐ PREDICT

Suggested Time: 10 minutes

1. With the class, read the title of the unit and have students look at the photographs. Elicit from students the names of the objects in the photographs and the differences between the contents of the two photos. Write on the board the words *conventional* and *nonconventional*. Elicit from students some forms of nonconventional treatments they may be familiar with.

2. Read the questions with students and then put them in pairs to discuss the questions.

✸✸Ⓑ SHARE INFORMATION

Suggested Time: 20 minutes

1. Ask students to read the statements about medicine and to decide whether or not they agree with them. Clarify vocabulary or the meaning of the statements if necessary.

2. Put students in groups of three to discuss their opinions. Remind them to give reasons for their opinions. Tell groups to chart their agreement or disagreement with each statement, and then prepare their summary of their discussion using the chart. Then have groups report to the class.

✸✸✸Ⓒ BACKGROUND AND VOCABULARY

 Go to www.mynorthstarlab.com for *Background and Vocabulary*.

Suggested Time: 20 minutes

1. Have students read the instructions for **Exercise 1**. Emphasize that the purpose of the reading is both to provide more background on the topic of one particular religion's beliefs concerning medicine and to provide a context for new vocabulary words.

2. Suggest that students read the text all the way to the end first without worrying about new vocabulary items. Then have them reread the text attempting to use the context to understand the boldfaced vocabulary items.

3. Have students read the definitions in **Exercise 2**. Check their comprehension of them. Then have students complete the exercise in pairs or individually before going over the answers as a class. It is useful to have students point out the parts of the text that helped them ascertain the meanings of the boldface words.

Expansion/Homework

Ask students to answer the following questions on the reading: (1) Why did Eddy believe all sickness was mental as opposed to physical? (2) How do Christian Scientists heal their "sick"? (3) What do Christian Scientists feel they should be able to decide on their own?

 Link to *NorthStar: Listening and Speaking 4*

If students are also using the companion text, you may want to list vocabulary from Background and Vocabulary, pages 48–50, on the board and see if students can find synonyms for those words in the background passage.

 Go to www.mynorthstarlab.com for additional *Background and Vocabulary* practice.

FOCUS ON READING

◖ SKILLS

Differentiate between main ideas and details; make inferences about the author's point of view; make inferences by connecting statements to different speakers; organize the main ideas of the reading into categories.

✪✪✪ Ⓐ READING ONE: Dying for Their Beliefs

Go to www.mynorthstarlab.com to read and listen to *Dying for Their Beliefs*.

Suggested Time: 20 minutes

Reading One is an article about one particular case of a sick child and her parents' decision about her treatment. The article should get students thinking about the rights of the individual to make health care decisions and the role of the state in such decisions.

1. Have students read the three questions. Then have them work individually to read the first three paragraphs. Have students write the answers to the questions.

2. Go over the questions as a class. Ask students to predict what the rest of the article is going to be about.

3. Have students read the rest of the article independently. The reading can be assigned as homework or lab work using MyNorthStarLab. You can also choose to play the recording of the reading and have students listen as they read.

READING STRATEGY: Non-linear Text Structure

1. Tell students that many newspaper articles intertwine several stories, which can be confusing for people who are learning English. One of the strategies that can be helpful is to use a graphic organizer to separate these stories to better define the various people and events.

2. Have students draw a 3-column chart and label as follows: Amy, Amy's Parents, Legal Information. Then have them work in small groups to sort out each separate piece of information. Suggest that they use 5Ws (*who, when, where, what, why*) for each column. Then have students retell or summarize the information they have in each column as if it were a separate story/article.

✪✪✪ READ FOR MAIN IDEAS   Suggested Time: 15 minutes

1. Have students work individually to complete the main idea sentences.

2. Put students in pairs to compare their sentences. Encourage them to find evidence in the text to support their answers. Then go over the answers as a class.

Expansion/Homework
Ask students to highlight or underline the sections where the main ideas are found. Then have them share their highlighting or underlining in groups or as a class.

✪✪✪ READ FOR DETAILS   Suggested Time: 15 minutes

Have students work individually to read the statements. Then tell them to reread the article and find the paragraphs in which the information they need can be found. Have them write the number of the paragraph number as well as *true* or *false*. Finally, go over the answers with the whole class. If time allows, ask students to say how the details support the main ideas.

Expansion/Homework
Have students rewrite the false statements as true ones either in pairs in class, or for homework.

REACHING ALL STUDENTS: Read for Details

• **Less Proficient:** Provide paragraph numbers to help students locate the correct statements.	• **More Proficient:** Have pairs of students find five details and write true-false statements for other students to answer.

✪✪✪ MAKE INFERENCES

1. Have students read the instructions. Check that students understand that these statements weren't made in the text, but that their understanding of each of the characters should help them to say whether or not a character could have said each one.

2. Read the statements as a class and clarify meaning if needed. Then put students in groups to identify the speakers of the statements. Remind students to refer to the text to support their point of view.

✪✪✪ EXPRESS OPINIONS

Suggested Time: 15 minutes

Tell students that it is now their turn to express their own opinions about the topic of parents having the right to determine health care solutions for their children and freedom of religion in this matter. Divide the class into small groups and assign each group one of the two questions to discuss.

Link to NorthStar: Listening and Speaking 4
Students who are also using the companion text can extend the discussion to include sleep habits.

CRITICAL THINKING

Give students the following questions for discussion in small groups before discussing as a whole class:

1. According to the article, why didn't Amy's parents take her to a doctor?

   Answer: As Christian Scientists, they believed she could be cured through prayer.

2. Do you think that only the parents have the right to make a decision about the health of their children or should the government have responsibility, too?

   Answers will vary, but students should use the information in the text and their own knowledge and experience to support their position.

3. Should Amy's parents go to prison?

   Answers will vary, but students should support their opinion with convincing reasons from the text and their own knowledge.

4. If you saw a parent beating a child, what would you do?

   Answers will vary, but students should support their ideas from their own experience and knowledge.

✪✪✪ B READING TWO: Norman Cousins's Laugh Therapy

Go to www.mynorthstarlab.com to read and listen to *Norman Cousins's Laugh Therapy*.

Suggested Time: 20 minutes

In Reading Two, students read about how Norman Cousins, a well-known writer and editor, used laugh therapy to help cure a serious case of arthritis. The reading expands students' understanding of how personal beliefs influence medical decisions.

1. For **Exercise 1**, have students look at the photo of Charlie Chaplin. Then elicit from students what they know about Charlie Chaplin.

2. Check students' comprehension of the title of the article. Then have them read the background text individually. Put students in pairs to discuss the two questions. Draw a picture of a glass half full of liquid on the board and write on one side, "half full" and on the other, "half empty." Ask students to discuss with a partner which of the phrases they think describes the glass. Then ask them to say which of the phrases describes a positive attitude and which describes a negative attitude.

3. Have students read the article in class, for homework, or lab work using MyNorthStarLab. You can also choose to play the recording of the reading and have students listen as they read. Then have them complete **Exercise 2**.

 Link to *NorthStar: Listening and Speaking 4*
Students who are using the companion text could discuss whether sleep deprivation warrants conventional or nonconventional treatment. If they talk about nonconventional treatments, ask them to be specific about what types of treatments they would suggest.

✣✣✣ C INTEGRATE READINGS ONE AND TWO

◀ SKILLS

Organize information from both readings in a Venn diagram; synthesize the content from the readings in a short paragraph.

STEP 1: Organize   Suggested Time: 15 minutes

1. Go over the instructions with the class. Make sure students understand the task. Tell students to first try to fill in the diagram with what they remember first, and then have them scan the two articles to complete the diagram.

2. Put students in pairs or groups to compare their diagrams before going over them as a class.

STEP 2: Synthesize   Suggested Time: 15 minutes

1. Read the instructions with students. Emphasize the importance of supporting their answers with examples from the readings and from the Venn diagram in Step 1.

2. Have students write a short paragraph using their inferences and the information in their Venn diagrams. You could have them do this in pairs or individually, in class, or for homework.

Go to www.mynorthstarlab.com for *Notetaking* and *Academic Skills Practice*.

③ FOCUS ON WRITING

Ⓐ VOCABULARY

◖ SKILLS

Review vocabulary and idioms from Readings One and Two; expand vocabulary by identifying analogies; use new vocabulary creatively in a writing assignment.

✪ REVIEW   Suggested Time: 10 minutes

 Go to www.mynorthstarlab.com for *Review*.

1. Read the words aloud and have students practice pronouncing them.

2. Have students complete the exercise. Tell students to scan the articles for the words and their contexts if they aren't sure of the meanings. Go over the answers as a class. For the words they decided had different meanings, have students say what the differences are.

✪✪ EXPAND   Suggested Time: 15 minutes

1. Read the information about analogies with the class and answer any questions.

2. Look at the first item and elicit from the students the relationship between the words; for example, arthritis is a diagnosis and achiness is a symptom of arthritis.

3. Have students work in pairs to complete the analogies. Remind pairs to describe the relationship between the words before circling the correct term.

VOCABULARY EXPANSION: Word Map

1. There are many variations to this strategy, but all contain the following elements: the word in a center circle or square, 2–3 circles on one side for synonyms, 2–3 circles on the other side for antonyms, a circle or square for the definition, and another for a sentence.

2. Have students create word maps for five of the vocabulary words in this unit that they personally feel will be helpful for them to know. Then ask them to add those words to their personal dictionaries, either in the form of their word maps, or with boxes that contain the same information as the word maps.

CREATE   **Suggested Time: 20 minutes**

Read the instructions with students. Ask them to decide who they would prefer to interview. Put students in pairs. Tell them to brainstorm together what they would like to ask in their interview and to make a list. Remind students to use the boxed words in their questions. Then have students write their questions.

 Link to NorthStar: Listening and Speaking 4
Students who are also using the companion text could create interview questions for one of the experts interviewed in Listening One or Dr. Walsleben from Listening Two. Partners could role-play the interviews, with one student taking the part of the interviewer and the other taking the part of the interviewee.

Go to www.mynorthstarlab.com for additional *Vocabulary* practice.

B GRAMMAR: Past Unreal Conditionals

Go to www.mynorthstarlab.com for *Grammar Chart* and *Exercise 2*.

SKILLS

Understand, identify, and use the past unreal conditional.

Suggested Time: 25 minutes

1. Read the instructions for **Exercise 1** with students and have them work in pairs to examine the sentences and decide if the statements that follow are true or false. Go over the answers as a class.

2. Go over the grammar chart with the class.

3. Have students work individually, either in class or for homework, to complete **Exercises 2** and **3** after going over the examples of each. Review answers as a class.

Expansion/Homework

1. You might find it useful to review the three different types of conditionals at this time by putting the following on the board and discussing the differences in meaning and form of each one:

   If you take your medicine, you'll get better.

   If you took your medicine, you would get better.

   If you'd taken your medicine, you would have gotten better.

2. For further practice, offer exercises from *Focus on Grammar 4, 3rd Edition* and Azar's *Understanding and Using English Grammar, 3rd Edition*. See the Grammar Book References on page 267 of the student book for specific units and chapters.

 Go to www.mynorthstarlab.com for additional *Grammar* practice.

If you wish to assign a different writing task than the one in this section, see page 66. The Alternative Writing Topics can also be assigned as additional writing topics for homework. The alternative topics relate to the theme of the unit, but may not target the same grammar or rhetorical structures taught in the unit.

◖ SKILLS

Use tree mapping as a pre-writing strategy; write introductions and hooks; integrate the concepts, vocabulary, grammar, and rhetorical structures from the unit to write a three-part opinion essay with an introduction, body, and conclusion.

✿✿✿ PREPARE TO WRITE: Tree Mapping

Suggested Time: 10 minutes

1. Read the paragraph about William and Christine Hermanson aloud to students and check their comprehension of *suspended sentence, probation,* and *initial verdict.* Ask students where they think an opinion essay on this matter might be found, eliciting *a newspaper.*

2. Have students look at the tree map and explain that this is just another way of organizing one's ideas before writing about them.

3. Have students complete the tree map individually. Put students in pairs as they finish their tree maps to compare and discuss their trees.

✿✿✿ WRITE: An Opinion Essay

Suggested Time: 30 minutes

1. Have students read the background information on three-part opinion essays and the explanation that follows.

2. Have students read the essay in **Exercise 1** and complete the essay organizer individually. Then put students in pairs or small groups to compare their organizers. Go over the essay organizer as a class, referring back to the information on page 62.

3. Have students work individually to complete **Exercise 2** using the information they tree mapped. With a partner, have students exchange outlines and give each other feedback.

4. For **Exercise 3**, have students write the first draft of their opinion essays either in class or for homework.

Expansion/Homework
Bring in the Op Ed section of the local newspaper, and have students identify the topics being written about. Then have students suggest additional current topics that lend themselves to an Op Ed section of a newspaper. Write all the topics on the

board. Finally, have students work individually or in pairs to write an article on one of the topics.

✪✪✪ REVISE: Writing Introductions and Hooks

Suggested Time: 20 minutes

1. Have students look at the picture and say what they see. Then go over the information on introductions and hooks. Ask students to say the significance of the illustration.

2. Have students look at the hook in the essay on page 63. Have them discuss their opinions of the hook in pairs before going over it as a class.

3. Have students complete **Exercise 2** individually before comparing and discussing their answers in pairs.

4. For **Exercise 3**, have students review their own introductions. Move around the room and make comments where appropriate.

✪✪✪ EDIT: Writing the Final Draft

Suggested Time: 25 minutes

Have students write the final draft of their essays. Encourage them to use language and grammar from the unit. Make sure they go through the checklist before submitting their final drafts. Collect the essays and correct them before the next class.

Expansion/Homework
(1) You may want to use samples of student writing to review grammar. You can create an error-correction exercise from sentences in which students misuse the past unreal conditional. (2) In addition to submitting the final draft to you, volunteers may wish to share their writing with the class.

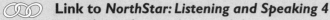 **Link to *NorthStar: Listening and Speaking 4***
Have the students write an opinion essay on some aspect of sleep deprivation using information from Unit 3: Early to Bed, Early to Rise . . .

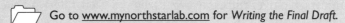 Go to www.mynorthstarlab.com for *Writing the Final Draft.*

✪ ALTERNATIVE WRITING TOPICS

These topics give students an alternative opportunity to explore and write about issues related to the unit theme.

✪ RESEARCH TOPICS

Suggested Time: 25 minutes in class

1. Have students turn to pages 260–261. Review the instructions for the activity with the class. Discuss the questions that students would ask each other in order to complete the survey.

2. Discuss the results of the surveys with the class. Encourage students to describe any treatments that they are personally familiar with.

3. Have students work in small groups to decide which treatment each student is researching and where to find information about the treatment.

4. After the groups have completed their research and shared their findings, have the groups present their reports to the class.

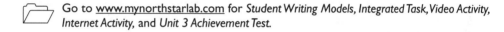 Go to www.mynorthstarlab.com for *Student Writing Models, Integrated Task, Video Activity, Internet Activity,* and *Unit 3 Achievement Test.*

UNIT 4

Animal Intelligence:
Instinct or Intellect?

OVERVIEW

Theme: Animal intelligence

This unit focuses on the intelligence of animals, and more specifically, how to evaluate that intelligence. Students question whether or not animals act more intelligently than expected based on intelligence, on instinct, or are just performing for rewards.

Reading One: *How Smart Is Smart?*, a book excerpt, talks about the development of scientific thinking concerning animal intelligence and how to evaluate it.

Reading Two: *Extreme Perception and Animal Intelligence* discusses the idea that there are some animals who have exhibited behaviors which seem to be born from an intelligence that is similar to human intelligence.

Critical Thinking

Infer word meaning from context
Interpret meaning of a text
Recognize how details support main ideas

Find correlations between two texts
Interpret animals' behavior

Reading

Make predictions
Identify main ideas
Scan for supporting details
Make inferences
Identify chronology in a text

Form and express opinions based on a text
Organize and synthesize information in different texts
Use a sequence organizer as a note-taking device

Writing

Write a summarizing essay
Use *wh-* questions to summarize

Paraphrase

Vocabulary	Grammar
Find and use synonyms Identify word roots Use context clues to find meaning	Identifying adjective clauses

📁 *MyNorthStarLab*
Readiness Check, Background and Vocabulary, Readings One and Two, Notetaking and Academic Skills Practice, Vocabulary and Grammar, Writing the Final Draft, Achievement Test

⊘⊘ *NorthStar: Listening and Speaking 4*
Unit 4 focuses on comparisons between human and animal behavior and intelligence.

① FOCUS ON THE TOPIC

◖ SKILLS

Predict the content of the unit; express opinions; infer the meaning of new vocabulary from context.

✪✪✪ Ⓐ PREDICT

Suggested Time: 10 minutes

1. Have students look at the picture, the caption, and the unit title. Check students' comprehension of the word *instinct* eliciting examples, such as animals being afraid of fire, mothers wanting to take care of their young, etc.

2. Elicit from students what they already know about pigs. Ask students to guess what they think the pig might have done to save her owner. Either put students in pairs to discuss their guesses or elicit their guesses as a class.

3. Have students read the paragraph on Lulu and how she saved her owner, and read the questions. Then put students in pairs to discuss the questions.

✪✪ Ⓑ SHARE INFORMATION

Suggested Time: 20 minutes

1. Have students get into groups to discuss their thoughts on animal intelligence and examples they have either experienced or heard about. Tell them to rank their examples in order of intelligence exhibited.

2. Have the groups complete the chart in **Exercise 1**. Then regroup students to compare their charts with another group.

3. Have students read the discussion questions in **Exercise 2** individually. Then put students back in their groups to discuss the questions.

Expansion/Homework
Ask students to bring in pictures from magazines or the Internet showing animals behaving in what appears to be an intelligent manner.

BACKGROUND AND VOCABULARY

📁   Go to www.mynorthstarlab.com for *Background and Vocabulary*.

Suggested Time: 20 minutes

1. Have students read the instructions and the list of words in the right-hand column. You might want to have students highlight the words that are new to them.

2. Review with students the parts of speech and their functions. Then suggest that students think about which parts of speech fit into each blank before searching for the right choice. Have students complete the exercise individually before putting them in pairs to compare their answers.

3. Go over the answers as a class, checking their comprehension of the vocabulary words.

📁   Go to www.mynorthstarlab.com for additional *Background and Vocabulary* practice.

FOCUS ON READING

SKILLS

Make predictions about the content of the article; differentiate between main ideas and details; make inferences and support them with evidence from the text; express opinions; scan the article for specific information.

READING ONE: How Smart Is Smart?

📁   Go to www.mynorthstarlab.com to read and listen to *How Smart Is Smart?*

Suggested Time: 20 minutes

In Reading One, students read about common perceptions about animal intelligence and the challenges involved in evaluating animal intelligence. The article should get students thinking more about intelligence in general, and how animal intelligence might differ from human intelligence.

1. Have students work individually to read the first paragraph, and as students finish reading, put them in pairs to summarize and discuss what they read.

2. Go over the questions as a class. Ask students to look at the subheadings of the article and make predictions about what the rest of the article is going to be about.

3. Have students read the rest of the article independently. The reading can be assigned as homework or lab work using MyNorthStarLab. You can also choose to play the recording of the reading and have students listen as they read.

Expansion/Homework

Have students research the Ken-l Ration Dog Hero Award online, choosing one more dog to read about and report on in class.

READING STRATEGY: DRTA

1. Directed Reading Thinking Activity (DRTA) is a process originally developed by Dr. Russell Stauffer, which helps students to read actively by predicting and then verifying their predictions as they read. (Stauffer, R. G. *Directing reading maturity as a cognitive process.* New York: Harper & Row, 1969.)

2. Ask students to begin by surveying title and subtitles. Then have them talk with their partner, predict what the selection will be about, and indicate the information they read that caused them to make this prediction. Ask them to record their predictions and then read the first section to confirm or revise their first prediction(s), citing evidence from the text. Next, have them make a new prediction and repeat the process in the second section of text, and again in the third section.

✪✪✪ READ FOR MAIN IDEAS

Suggested Time: 15 minutes

Have students work individually to scan the reading to match the main ideas to specific paragraphs before going over the answers as a class.

REACHING ALL STUDENTS: Read for Main Ideas

• **Less Proficient:** Suggest that students read to locate three examples of animals' intelligence and compare information with a partner's.
• **More Proficient:** Read "What Is Intelligence" to determine different areas of intelligence and give an example of each.

✪✪✪ READ FOR DETAILS

Suggested Time: 20 minutes

1. Have students read the instructions. Remind them of the difference between main ideas and details, reiterating that details support the main ideas of a text.

2. Have students scan the text again to find the supporting details/information for each of the main ideas listed, using the paragraph numbers they chose for the Read for Main Ideas exercise.

Expansion/Homework

The Read for Main Ideas and/or Read for Details activities could be assigned for homework. The answers could then be discussed in class, first in pairs and then as a whole class.

✪✪✪ MAKE INFERENCES

1. Have students look at the pictures of the animals. Elicit from students what they already know or think about each of the three animals. Have students read the instructions.

2. Tell students to read the animals' stories, and then skim the given paragraphs from the reading to find the information that helps them to make their inferences. Tell students they should be prepared to defend their decisions, using information from the reading.

✪✪✪ EXPRESS OPINIONS

1. Have students read the two questions. Have them first review how Pfungst proved that Hans was "reading" the movements of his questioners and not actually solving math problems.

2. Put students in pairs to discuss the two questions. You might suggest that students review the vocabulary in Background and Vocabulary and try to use some of the words in their discussion.

CRITICAL THINKING

Give students the following questions for discussion in small groups before discussing as a whole class:

1. How did Villa demonstrate thinking?

    Answer: Villa followed a sequence of steps to rescue Andrea from the snowdrift.

2. What evidence can you give from the article to support that animals do or do not think?

    Answers will vary, but might include Villa's actions, the details of the animals in paragraph 4, the information on Clever Hans, and information on how we define intelligence.

3. How would you define intelligence in an animal (for example, obedience, communication, instinct) based on the information in the text?

    Answers will vary, but students should be encouraged to add their own ideas to the information in the text to produce creative answers.

4. Is animal instinct as valuable as human intelligence?

    Answers will vary, but students should be able to give reasons and examples to support their opinions.

B   READING TWO: Extreme Perception and Animal Intelligence

Go to www.mynorthstarlab.com to read and listen to *Extreme Perception and Animal Intelligence*.

Suggested Time: 20 minutes

In Reading Two, students read an article about animals that appear to have extreme perception and high levels of animal intelligence. The purpose of this article is to further challenge students to decide whether animal behavior is in fact driven by intelligence or not.

1. Ask students to read the title of the article. Ask students if they know what extreme perception is. Have them read the first paragraph to check that they understand the concept.

2. Put students in small groups to discuss the two questions in **Exercise 1**. Then have students read the article individually. You can also choose to play the recording of the reading and have students listen as they read.

3. Have students read the statements in **Exercise 2**. Clarify that the statements can't be found in the reading, but rather are summarizing statements about the information in the reading. Then have students complete the statements individually, in class, or for homework.

C   INTEGRATE READINGS ONE AND TWO

SKILLS

Organize, compare, and synthesize information from two texts and form opinions as a reader using this information; use a sequence organizer as a comprehension and note-taking device.

STEP 1: Organize   **Suggested Time: 15 minutes**

1. Have students read the instructions and then look at the sequence organizer. Explain that it is a flow chart pointing out to students the arrows connecting the seven boxes.

2. Explain that students will want to scan the two readings for the relevant information. You might have students make note of the reading and paragraph in which they found their answers. Have students complete the exercise in pairs or individually.

3. Have students compare answers with another student's.

4. Go over the answers with the entire class.

STEP 2: Synthesize   Suggested Time: 20 minutes

Read the instructions with students. Emphasize the importance of supporting their
statements with examples from the readings and from the chart they filled out in
Step 1. Have students write a short summary paragraph either in class or for
homework.

 Link to *NorthStar: Listening and Speaking 4*
For students who are also using the companion text, you may want to have them
include information from the listenings for comparison.

 # ③ FOCUS ON WRITING

 ## A VOCABULARY

◀ SKILLS

Review vocabulary from Readings One and Two; expand understanding of
vocabulary by thinking about the larger meaning groups in which they fit; use new
vocabulary creatively in a cohesive piece of writing.

✪ REVIEW   Suggested Time: 10 minutes

📂 Go to www.mynorthstarlab.com for *Review*.

1. Have students look at the rows and check their understanding of the task. Go
   over the first one with students and have them say why *signal* doesn't belong in
   that group.

2. Check students' comprehension of the vocabulary items listed. If the meaning
   of a word is unclear, students should scan the readings to find the context of
   the item.

3. Have students work individually to complete the exercise. Then go over the
   exercise as a class. If students have different answers, suggest that they try to
   make sentences with the terms in dispute.

✪✪ EXPAND   Suggested Time: 15 minutes

1. Go over the background information on roots with the class. You may want to
   elicit other words students are sure to know with Latin or Greek roots such as
   anti in the word *antibiotic* or *deca* in *decade*.

2. Read the instructions with students and go over the example. Check that
   students understand that the root does not necessarily come at the beginning
   of the word.

3. Bring the class together and go over the answers.

VOCABULARY EXPANSION: I'm Thinking of a Word

1. To review vocabulary for the first four units, play I'm Thinking of a Word. This activity allows the teacher to demonstrate various strategies for learning a word, while helping students to narrow the possibilities in order to guess the word.

2. To play, the teacher will give clues leading to the meaning of the word which might include: the original context/unit of study, examples/non-examples, antonyms, synonyms, parts of speech, etc. Students will guess after each clue is offered. Clues become more detailed as they are added.

✪ CREATE   Suggested Time: 20 minutes

1. Explain to the students that they will be further exploring the Clever Hans story. You might want to put them in pairs to brainstorm topics.

2. Have students write their questions in class or at home, reminding them to use the words and phrases from Review and Expand and to look back at the readings to help them. Then put students in pairs to exchange papers and answer each other's questions.

Expansion/Homework
Ask students to research the Clever Hans story in Wikipedia and find the current use of the story in popular culture.

Go to www.mynorthstarlab.com for additional *Vocabulary* practice.

✪✪ B GRAMMAR: Identifying Adjective Clauses

Go to www.mynorthstarlab.com for *Grammar Chart* and *Exercise 2*.

◖ SKILLS

Learn the form of identifying adjective clauses and use them appropriately.

Suggested Time: 25 minutes

1. Have students work in pairs to examine the sentences in **Exercise 1** and answer the questions that follow before going over their answers as a class. Make sure students understand that the boldface phrases qualify or describe the nouns that precede them.

2. Go over the grammar chart with the class. Have students look at the incorrect example and correct it together. Check that students understand that *the horse* at the end of the sentence is redundant because the relative pronoun *that* refers to the horse, making it unnecessary (and grammatically incorrect) to repeat.

3. Read the instructions for **Exercise 2**. Check that students understand that there are two tasks to do with each one. Have students complete the exercise individually. Put them in pairs to compare their answers as they finish.

4. Read the instructions for **Exercise 3** with students. Go over the two examples together. Then have students complete the exercise individually or in pairs. Go over the answers together as a class. Note that some of the answers will vary depending on the relative pronoun chosen. Make sure to elicit all the alternatives from students.

Expansion/Homework

(**1**) Exercises 2 and 3 could be completed at home and then reviewed in class.
(**2**) For further practice, offer exercises from *Focus on Grammar 4, 3rd Edition* and Azar's *Understanding and Using English Grammar, 3rd Edition*. See the Grammar Book References on page 267 of the student book for specific units and chapters.

 Go to www.mynorthstarlab.com for additional *Grammar* practice.

ⓒ WRITING

If you wish to assign a different writing task than the one in this section, see page 90. The Alternative Writing Topics can also be assigned as additional writing topics for homework. The alternative topics relate to the theme of the unit, but may not target the same grammar or rhetorical structures taught in the unit.

◖ SKILLS

Ask and answer *wh-* questions; summarize information; paraphrase; integrate the concepts, vocabulary, grammar, and rhetorical structures from the unit to write a summary of an article by paraphrasing the information.

✪✪✪ PREPARE TO WRITE: Asking and Answering *Wh-* Questions

Suggested Time: 10 minutes

1. Read the instructions and the information about summarizing with the class.

2. Have students write *wh-* questions individually before getting together in pairs to compare and answer their questions.

✪✪✪ WRITE: A Summary

Suggested Time: 30 minutes

1. Have the students read the background information on summaries and the important process points.

2. Have students read the summary of the first reading and answer the questions in **Exercise 1** individually. Go over the answers as a class, referring back to the information in the box as needed.

3. Go over the instructions for **Exercise 2** with students. Have them complete the exercise individually either at home or in class before putting them in pairs to compare their answers.

4. Have students complete **Exercise 3** individually in class or at home. You may want to have them compare their paragraphs with those of a partner.

✪✪✪ REVISE: Paraphrasing

Suggested Time: 20 minutes

1. Go over the boxed information on paraphrasing, paying particular attention to the way the paraphrased texts are reworded.

2. Have students complete **Exercise 1** individually. Then put students in pairs or groups to compare their answers.

3. For **Exercise 2**, have students review their own drafts. Move around the room and make comments where appropriate.

✪✪✪ EDIT: Writing the Final Draft

Suggested Time: 25 minutes

Have students write the final draft of their summaries. Encourage students to use language and grammar from the unit. Make sure they go through the checklist before submitting their final drafts. Collect the summaries and correct them before the next class.

Expansion/Homework
Choose some of the student summaries to illustrate good examples of paraphrasing. You can also choose to use student summaries to illustrate previous unit writing points such as topic and concluding sentences or supporting sentences.

Link to *NorthStar: Listening and Speaking 4*
Have students write a summary on some aspect of what they learned about animal intelligence in Unit 4 of the *Listening and Speaking* strand.

Go to www.mynorthstarlab.com for *Writing the Final Draft.*

○ ALTERNATIVE WRITING TOPICS

These topics give students an alternative opportunity to explore and write about issues related to the unit theme.

○ RESEARCH TOPICS

Suggested Time: 20 minutes in class

1. Have students turn to page 261. Review the instructions for the activity with the class.

2. Have students look at the list of animals and choose one they want to research. Tell students to use a search engine to look for the specific animals in the list. Before students begin their research, have them make a list of questions that they want to find answers to.

3. As students prepare their summaries, remind them that they need to write a conclusion explaining whether or not they think the animal is intelligent.

 Go to www.mynorthstarlab.com for *Student Writing Models, Integrated Task, Video Activity, Internet Activity*, and *Unit 4 Achievement Test*.

UNIT 5

Longevity: Too Much of a Good Thing?

OVERVIEW

Theme: Longevity
This unit focuses on the potential of science to prolong our life spans and the resulting consequences to how we live our lives. Students reflect on the concept of immortality, the benefits of prolonged life spans, and how living significantly longer would change their lives.

Reading One: An excerpt from the short story *Death Do Us Part* deals with the perspectives of a man who is 300 years old compared with those of his new 30-year-old wife.

Reading Two: *Toward Immortality: The Social Burden of Longer Lives* discusses realistic expectations concerning longer life spans and the costs to society, marriage, and our work lives.

Critical Thinking

Interpret a cartoon
Compare observations on living longer lives
Infer word meaning from context
Extract logical arguments from a text

Establish cause and effect relationships
Evaluate advantages and disadvantages of living
   longer

Reading

Make predictions
Compare characters' views to real world views
Scan for details
Make inferences based on a text

Form and express opinions based on a text
Identify cause and effect in a text
Identify connecting themes between texts
Draw a cause and effect diagram

Writing

Develop descriptive writing skills
Write a descriptive essay
Write cause and effect sentences

Use figurative language
Use an idea web as a pre-writing device
Summarize research in a report

Vocabulary	Grammar
Categorize vocabulary Use context clues to find meaning Learn adjective suffixes	Contrasting the simple past, present perfect, and present perfect continuous

MyNorthStarLab	*NorthStar: Listening and Speaking 4*
Readiness Check, Background and Vocabulary, Readings One and Two, Notetaking and Academic Skills Practice, Vocabulary and Grammar, Writing the Final Draft, Achievement Test	Unit 5 focuses on the social aspects of aging and the consequences of having a larger gray population.

1 FOCUS ON THE TOPIC

◖ SKILLS

Predict the content of the unit; activate prior knowledge; express opinions; infer the meaning of new vocabulary from context.

✪✪✪ A PREDICT

Suggested Time: 10 minutes

1. Before opening the book, write *Ponce de Leon* on the board and elicit from students what they know about him (he was a Spanish explorer) and his quest for the alleged fountain of youth. Also write *immortality* on the board and ask students to say what it means. To follow from previous work on roots, ask students to break down the word into *im-* and *-mort* and see if they can figure out what it means (living for an infinite period of time).

2. Have students look at the cartoon, the caption, and the unit title. Check students' comprehension of the word *longevity*. Then have students discuss the questions either as a class or in groups.

✪✪ B SHARE INFORMATION

Suggested Time: 15 minutes

Have students read the background information on immortality and current life spans. Then put students in pairs or small groups to discuss the two questions.

Expansion/Homework
Ask students to research common life spans in different parts of the world at the moment as compared with 50 and 100 years ago.

✪✪✪ C BACKGROUND AND VOCABULARY

 Go to www.mynorthstarlab.com for *Background and Vocabulary*.

Suggested Time: 20 minutes

1. Have students read the instructions and scan the boldfaced words. You might want to have students check or highlight the words that are new to them.

2. Suggest that students read the letter all the way through once without worrying about the words they don't know to get the general idea of the context. Then have them reread the letter and complete the exercise.

3. Go over the answers as a class. Suggest that students think about which parts of speech fit into each blank before searching for the right choice.

Expansion/Homework

You may want to assign the reading again now that students know the meanings of the boldfaced words. Tell them to answer the following questions: How old do you think Susannah is? Do you think Susannah is married, and if so, to a man of what age? How many positive and negative qualities of Leo does Marilisa mention? Which of the qualities mentioned do you think is the most important to Marilisa?

 Link to *NorthStar: Listening and Speaking 4*

If students are also using the companion text, you may want to list vocabulary from Background and Vocabulary in Unit 5 on the board and see if students can find synonyms for those words in the background passage.

 Go to www.mynorthstarlab.com for additional *Background and Vocabulary* practice.

② FOCUS ON READING

◀ SKILLS

Make predictions about the content of the article; differentiate between main ideas and details; make inferences; scan for specific information.

 **✪✪✪ Ⓐ READING ONE: Death Do Us Part**

 Go to www.mynorthstarlab.com to read and listen to *Death Do Us Part*.

Suggested Time: 25 minutes

In Reading One, students read an excerpt from a short story that takes place in the future at a time when life spans have been prolonged, possibly indefinitely. The excerpt should get students thinking more about the effects of such a phenomenon on various facets of everyday life, such as work, family, and marriage.

1. Ask students what they know about science fiction as a literary or film genre. Elicit examples of common science-fiction titles, such as *Star Wars, Star Trek, Dune*, etc., and write them on the board. Ask students to say what they think makes this genre particularly appealing to some people.

2. Have students work individually to read the first two paragraphs, and as students finish reading, put them in pairs to discuss the questions. Encourage students to take notes as they read.

3. Go over the questions as a class. Then have students read the rest of the article independently. The reading can be assigned as homework or lab work using MyNorthStarLab. You can also choose to play the recording of the reading and have students listen as they read.

READING STRATEGY: Character Analysis

1. Since this narrative involves two characters, students can use a comparison web to record the descriptions of both characters. Students can record similarities and differences while retaining the qualities of a web in recording character attributes.

2. Provide index cards for student pairs. On one card, have them write *Marilisa*. On another card, have them write *Leo*. Then have them write details on the other cards and arrange them around the two characters. Cards with attributes common to both Marilisa and Leo will be arranged between the two. Then have them glue or tape the cards onto large chart paper and draw lines to connect them.

❂❂❂ READ FOR MAIN IDEAS   Suggested Time: 15 minutes

1. Read the instructions with the class. Then read the present day societal views and ask students if they agree with them.

2. Have students work individually to complete the exercise. Go over the answers as a class.

Expansion/Homework
For homework, or in class, have students look back at the story to find the paragraphs or sentences which provide the answers to the exercise.

❂❂❂ READ FOR DETAILS   Suggested Time: 15 minutes

1. Have students read the instructions. Remind them of the difference between main ideas and details, reiterating that details support the main ideas of a text.

2. Have students scan the text again to find the supporting details for each of the "perspectives" listed. Then go over students' charts with the whole class.

❂❂❂ MAKE INFERENCES   Suggested Time: 10 minutes

1. Have students read the instructions. Then have them read the seven statements, checking their comprehension of each one.

2. Tell students to complete the exercise individually, noting down the paragraph or line number they got their supporting evidence from. Go over the answers as a class. Welcome disagreement, telling students to go back to the text to point out specific details to support their decisions.

- **Less Proficient:** Scaffold by providing evidence for items 1–4 to help students see the implied information. Check and discuss those; then have students complete items 5–7 with a partner.

- **More Proficient:** Have students add explicit statements that would fit the text and provide appropriate evidence for the inference statement (for example, "When yet another son appeared, Marilisa demanded to know the total number of children. 'Only 42,' said Leo.")

✪✪✪ EXPRESS OPINIONS   Suggested Time: 15 minutes

Have students read the four questions and give them a few minutes to gather their thoughts about them. Then put students in pairs to discuss their thoughts. You might suggest that students review the vocabulary in Section C Background and Vocabulary and try to use some of the words in their discussion.

Link to *NorthStar: Listening and Speaking 4*
Students who are also using the companion text can extend the discussion to include aging.

CRITICAL THINKING

Give students the following questions for discussion in small groups before discussing as a whole class:

1. What is Marilisa and Leo's age difference?

   Answer: He is 331 years older than she is.

2. How does their difference in age affect their views on marriage?

   Answer: She expects to have many husbands; he intends that she will be his last wife.

3. What facts tell you that Leo is probably wealthy?

   Answer: Their honeymoon, sky house, vacation in Capri, that he lives on interest from investments, his careers.

4. According to the story, in what ways would lives improve by extending our life spans?

   Answer: There is more time for study, for multiple careers, to develop many interests, to see many things, to have many relationships—or to focus intensely on only a few things. Students might extend the logic to say that this would increase opportunities for knowledge and progress because scientists, doctors, researchers, etc. would have more time and experience to pursue knowledge.

✱✱✱ B | READING TWO: Toward Immortality: The Social Burden of Longer Lives

📁 Go to www.mynorthstarlab.com to read and listen to *Toward Immortality: The Social Burden of Longer Lives*.

Suggested Time: 20 minutes

Reading Two is an article about current thinking on how long science might be able to prolong our lives and the repercussions of having longer life spans. Students are challenged to consider the problems inherent in living longer.

1. Ask students to read the title of the article. Ask students to consider the phrase "social burden" and have them list examples of current social burdens where they live, for example, homeless people.

2. Have students read the background paragraph on longer life spans. Then put them in pairs to discuss the answer to the question in **Exercise 1**.

3. Have students first preview the article by reading the subheadings and then read the article individually. You can also choose to play the recording of the reading and have students listen as they read.

4. Have students read the statements in **Exercise 2** and say whether or not they agree.

✱✱✱ C | INTEGRATE READINGS ONE AND TWO

◖ SKILLS

Organize information from the readings in a cause and effect diagram; synthesize information to form opinions.

STEP 1: Organize   **Suggested Time: 15 minutes**

1. Have students read the instructions and then look at the cause and effect diagram. Check students' comprehension of the *prolonged life span* being both a cause and an effect.

2. Remind students that they will need to scan the two readings for the relevant information. You might have students make a note of the paragraph with the relevant information within each reading. Have students complete the exercise in pairs or individually.

STEP 2: Synthesize   **Suggested Time: 20 minutes**

1. Check students' comprehension of *bioethicist*. To discuss the meaning, it could be useful to divide the word into its root and prefix and suffix.

2. Read the instructions with the class. Before writing, you might want to have students discuss whether or not they agree and the main reasons for their

agreement or disagreement. Then they could list their reasons and go back to the chart in Step 1 to support their reasons.

3. Have students write a short summary paragraph either in class or for homework. Remind them to pay special attention to the cause and effect relationships in their reasons.

 Go to www.mynorthstarlab.com for *Notetaking* and *Academic Skills Practice*.

③ FOCUS ON WRITING

Ⓐ VOCABULARY

◖ SKILLS

Review vocabulary from Readings One and Two; expand understanding of vocabulary by thinking about the larger meaning groups in which they fit; use new vocabulary creatively in a cohesive piece of writing.

✪ REVIEW   Suggested Time: 10 minutes

 Go to www.mynorthstarlab.com for *Review*.

1. Have students read the instructions and review with them the role of adjectives (to describe nouns) and adverbs (to describe verbs and adjectives). You might want to have students determine whether or not the words are adjectives or adverbs first.

2. Put students in pairs to do the exercise. Remind them to scan the readings for the words to see them in context if they aren't sure about the meanings and/or to look back at Section C Background and Vocabulary.

3. As students finish the exercise, have them discuss their choices.

4. Go over the answers as a class.

✪✪ EXPAND   Suggested Time: 20 minutes

1. Go over the background information on suffixes with the class. Ask students what noun the adjectives in the examples are describing.

2. Go over the common adjective suffixes box with students, making sure they can pronounce them all. You might want to try to elicit examples of adjectives with these suffixes from students.

3. Read the instructions with students and go over the example. Have students complete the exercise in class, getting together in pairs or groups to compare their answers when they are finished.

VOCABULARY EXPANSION: Match the Root and Suffix

Have students make one set of index cards that have a base word on each card, and another set of cards that have adjective suffixes. Then they will play a game that is similar to *Concentration*, except that instead of matching duplicate words, they will match a base word and a suffix to create a word.

✪ CREATE

Suggested Time: 20 minutes

1. Review with students the expressed opinions of Daniel Callahan and Gregory Stock from Reading Two.

2. Have students write their questions in class or at home, reminding them to use the words and phrases from Review and Expand and to look back at the readings for help.

3. Review with students Leo's apparent feelings about his life. Put students in pairs to exchange questions. Have students answer each other's questions as if they were Leo.

Expansion/Homework
Put students in groups of three to role-play the situation of Daniel Callahan and Gregory Stock interviewing Leo. After giving them time to practice their role play, ask for volunteers to perform their role play for the class.

 Go to www.mynorthstarlab.com for additional *Vocabulary* practice.

✪✪ B GRAMMAR: Contrasting the Simple Past, Present Perfect, and Present Perfect Continuous

 Go to www.mynorthstarlab.com for *Grammar Chart* and *Exercise 2*.

◖ SKILLS

Recognize the differences between the simple past, the present perfect, and the present perfect continuous tenses in form and meaning; use these tenses correctly.

Suggested Time: 25 minutes

1. Have students work in pairs to examine the sentences and answer the questions that follow in **Exercise 1** before going over their answers as a class. Tell students to notice which example sentences have time phrases and what they are.

2. Ask students to read the grammar explanation silently. Move around the room while students read the grammar explanation to answer individual questions.

3. You may want to put a timeline on the board with a point in the middle labeled *now*. Have students come up to the board to draw arrows indicating the time frame each sentence is about.

4. Read the instructions in **Exercise 2**. Tell students that they are reading an imaginary interview. Explain that they should look for time words or phrases to help them know what tense to use. Suggest that they underline or highlight the relevant time phrases. Then have students complete the exercise individually. Put them in pairs to compare their answers as they finish. Finally, review the answers and address questions and problems as a class.

5. Read the instructions in **Exercise 3** with students. Have them complete the exercise individually or in pairs. Go over the answers together as a class, eliciting all the possibilities for the ones that have more than one answer.

Expansion/Homework

For further practice, offer exercises from *Focus on Grammar, High Intermediate* and Azar's *Understanding and Using English Grammar*. See the Grammar Book References on page 267 of the student book for specific units and chapters.

 Go to www.mynorthstarlab.com for additional *Grammar* practice.

ⓒ WRITING

If you wish to assign a different writing task than the one in this section, see page 114. The Alternative Writing Topics can also be assigned as additional writing topics for homework. The alternative topics relate to the theme of the unit, but may not target the same grammar or rhetorical structures taught in the unit.

◖ SKILLS

Use an idea web as a note-taking device; use figurative language; integrate the concepts, vocabulary, grammar, and rhetorical structures from the unit to write an imaginary descriptive essay of how life is in the next century.

✿✿✿ PREPARE TO WRITE: Using an Idea Web

Suggested Time: 15 minutes

1. Read the instructions and the questions for students to answer in their essays. Have them read about idea webs. Look at the examples in the idea web together.

2. Have students complete the exercise as suggested. Then put them in pairs to discuss details they put in each circle. Suggest that they attempt to ascertain from each other's idea webs whether or not their partner thinks immortality is more of a positive or negative phenomenon.

✪✪✪ WRITE: A Descriptive Essay

Suggested Time: 25 minutes

1. Have students read the background information on descriptive essays and the boxed points on what to include. You might want to have students practice creating sensory images for each sense in pairs or groups and then share them with the class.

2. Have students read the introductory paragraph and answer the questions in **Exercise 1** individually. Put students in pairs to discuss their answers. Then go over the answers as a class, referring back to the information in the boxed points as needed.

3. Go over the instructions in **Exercise 2** with students. Have them write their first drafts either at home or in class. You might suggest that they think about writing individual paragraphs for the information they put in different circles in their idea web.

Expansion/Homework
Have students exchange drafts with each other. Tell students to check their partner's drafts especially for the inclusion of an introduction, body paragraphs, and a conclusion. Also, they could check each other's essays for correct use of tenses.

✪✪✪ REVISE: Using Figurative Language

Suggested Time: 20 minutes

1. Go over the boxed information on similes, metaphors, and personification.

2. Have students find the examples individually or in pairs, going over them together as a class.

3. Have students look at their own drafts for figurative language. Have them add figurative language where possible. Move around the room and make comments or help with vocabulary or general language questions where appropriate.

✪✪✪ EDIT: Writing the Final Draft

Suggested Time: 25 minutes

Have students write the final draft of their essays. Encourage students to use language and grammar from the unit. Make sure they go through the checklist before submitting their final drafts. Collect the essays and correct them before the next class.

Expansion/Homework
Choose some of the students' descriptive essays or parts of essays to illustrate good examples. You can also choose to use student descriptive essays to illustrate previous unit writing points such as topic and concluding sentences or supporting sentences. Make sure, however, to use different students' papers in each class, whenever possible.

Link to *Northstar: Listening and Speaking 4*
Have the students write an essay on some aspect of aging using examples from Unit 5 of the *Listening and Speaking* strand.

 Go to www.mynorthstarlab.com for *Writing the Final Draft.*

✪ ALTERNATIVE WRITING TOPICS

These topics give students an alternative opportunity to explore and write about issues related to the unit theme.

✪ RESEARCH TOPICS

Suggested Time: 25 minutes in class

1. Have students turn to pages 261–262. Review the instructions for the activity with the class. Tell students to use a search engine to look for parts of the world where people have long life spans.

2. With the class, brainstorm questions that would help with your research, for example, What kind of lifestyle do these people lead? What kinds of food do they eat or avoid eating?

3. As students present the results of their research, the rest of the class should think of questions they might still have about the area or people being presented.

4. Discuss with the class the results of all of the presentations. Are there any common factors? Have students summarize the presentations.

 Go to www.mynorthstarlab.com for *Student Writing Models, Integrated Task, Video Activity, Internet Activity,* and *Unit 5 Achievement Test.*

OVERVIEW

Theme: Philanthropy

This unit focuses on philanthropy and the benefits that volunteers receive from donating their time and energy to a charity. Students think about what actually motivates people to volunteer and whether or not volunteering should be mandatory for young people.

Reading One: *Justin Lebo*, from the book *It's Our World, Too* by Phillip Hoose, is the story of a young boy who volunteers his own time, energy, and money to help others in a unique way.

Reading Two: *Some Take the Time Gladly* and *Mandatory Volunteering for High School Diploma Not a Good Idea* are two opposing editorials about mandatory volunteering for young people as a requirement for high school graduation.

Critical Thinking

Re-evaluate personal attitudes and values
Infer information not explicit in a text
Identify an author's opinions
Identify motivations of characters

Hypothesize another's point of view
Relate specific examples to broad themes
Analyze concessive language

Reading

Make predictions
Paraphrase main ideas
Scan for supporting details
Identify contrasting arguments in a text

Make inferences
Express opinions
Complete a chart as a note-taking device

Writing

Use commas, semicolons, colons, and dashes
Write a persuasive essay
Use concession clauses

Use T-charts as a pre-writing device
Practice writing introductions and conclusions

Vocabulary	Grammar
Find and use synonyms Recognize word forms Use context clues to find meaning	Concessions

📁 *MyNorthStarLab* Readiness Check, Background and Vocabulary, Readings One and Two, Notetaking and Academic Skills Practice, Vocabulary and Grammar, Writing the Final Draft, Achievement Test	🔗 *NorthStar: Listening and Speaking 4* Unit 6 focuses on the motivations of people who give their own money to charity.

Go to www.mynorthstarlab.com for the MyNorthStarLab *Readiness Check.*

FOCUS ON THE TOPIC

◖ SKILLS

Predict the content of the unit; activate prior knowledge; express opinions; infer the meaning of new vocabulary from context.

✱✱✱ Ⓐ PREDICT

Suggested Time: 10 minutes

1. Have students look at the photographs and say what they know about each person.

2. Read the definition of philanthropy to the class. Elicit questions or comments. Give students a few minutes to read the title and write what they think it means. Ask them to share their ideas with the class.

3. Have students match the people to their descriptions and then put them in pairs to discuss the questions. Ask them to write their answers and share them with the class.

Expansion/Homework

For homework, have students look through current newspapers or magazines to find an example of philanthropic individuals or organizations. Have them write who or what is being helped and in what way.

 Link to NorthStar: Listening and Speaking 4

If students are using the companion text, ask them to discuss the questions as they relate to the people they heard about who volunteer time or donate money to charity.

✱✱ Ⓑ SHARE INFORMATION

Suggested Time: 15 minutes

1. As a class, read the quotations. Check students' comprehension of the word *bestows.*

2. Put students in small groups to answer the two questions about the quotations before having them share their ideas with the class.

📁 Go to www.mynorthstarlab.com for *Background and Vocabulary.*

Suggested Time: 20 minutes

1. As a class, read the vocabulary words and have students practice their pronunciation. Clarify that students are looking for the one word that doesn't belong in the group.

2. Have students work individually to complete **Exercise 1**. Put students in pairs or small groups to compare their answers.

3. Have students read the background information on volunteer programs and the reasons why people choose to volunteer. Then have them read the instructions in **Exercise 2**. Check that students realize there are two tasks to do for each one and that the reasons can be used more than once.

4. Do the first item together as a class. Tell students that if they aren't sure of the meaning of a word, to look back at the synonyms in Exercise 1.

5. Give students time to complete the exercise individually. Put students in groups as they finish the exercise to compare and discuss their answers.

📁 Go to www.mynorthstarlab.com for additional *Background and Vocabulary* practice.

②FOCUS ON READING

◖ SKILLS

Make predictions about the content of the article; differentiate between main ideas and details; make inferences and support them with evidence from the text; express opinions; scan the article for specific information.

✹✹✹ A **READING ONE:** Justin Lebo

📁 Go to www.mynorthstarlab.com to read and listen to *Justin Lebo.*

Suggested Time: 25 minutes

In Reading One, students read about a young man and his efforts to help others. The article should get students thinking about what motivates people to volunteer their time to help others.

1. Have students look at the photograph of Justin Lebo and say how old they think he might be. Then have students read the first two paragraphs individually, and answer the questions.

2. Go over the questions as a class. Ask students to write down their predictions about what Justin is going to do with the bicycle to refer back to later.

3. Have students read the rest of the article independently, either in class or for homework. You can also choose to play the recording of the reading and have students listen as they read.

READING STRATEGY: Retell

1. Tell students that retelling events in a text can help them to more fully understand the story or article. It's helpful if students begin to retell in sections rather than to take on the entire article. Suggest that they read the story once and then divide it into 6–8 sections. A change in setting (time or place) can be a good place for division. Then have students read the first section and retell that part to his/her partner. Both partners should retell, but they should alternate who will go first in each section. Once they've completed the retelling, they should have a good idea of how an article can be a series of linking stories and how each of those can contribute to an overall summary.

2. Then have students retell the entire piece to their partner before writing a 1–2-paragraph summary. Students should note that the summary will not be a detailed retelling of each section, but a concise retelling of the entire piece.

✪✪✪ READ FOR MAIN IDEAS   Suggested Time: 15 minutes

1. Read the six statements with students. Have students work individually to decide which three are the main ideas.

2. Put students in pairs to compare and discuss their answers. If there are disagreements, encourage students to go back to the story for evidence to support their answers.

REACHING ALL STUDENTS: Read for Main Ideas

- **Less Proficient:** Help students see the difference in general (main idea) and specific (facts and details) by showing them the general or specific word or phrase in each statement (bikes/first bike/first BMX bike).

- **More Proficient:** Write each statement as a more general statement. Note that specifics add details and general statements often will remove details.

✪✪✪ READ FOR DETAILS   Suggested Time: 15 minutes

1. Before students complete the exercise, check their comprehension of *benefit* (something that helps you or has a good/positive effect). Read the benefits and the first example.

2. Have students scan the text to find the examples for each of the benefits listed individually before putting them in pairs or small groups to compare and discuss their answers.

3. Go over students' charts with the whole class. Ask individual students to read the examples they listed.

✪✪✪ MAKE INFERENCES

Suggested Time: 15 minutes

1. Read the instructions with students. Suggest that they attempt to find the best answer before looking back at the story for support.

2. Have students work individually to complete the exercise. Pair them with another student to compare answers as they finish. Go over students' choices and their reasons together as a class.

✪✪✪ EXPRESS OPINIONS

Suggested Time: 15 minutes

1. Read the questions with the class. Give students a few minutes to think about the questions individually before putting them in pairs to discuss them.

2. Have pairs share summaries of their discussions with the class. Alternatively, have pairs choose one of the questions to share with the class. Then have them practice what they are going to say before presenting it.

 Link to *NorthStar: Listening and Speaking 4*
Students who are also using the companion text can extend the discussion to include people's motivation for giving their own money to charity.

CRITICAL THINKING

Give students the following questions for discussion in small groups before discussing as a whole class:

1. What is a good word to describe Justin?

   Answers will vary, but students should use information from the article to support their choices.

2. How do Justin's parents feel about what he is doing?

   Answer: His parents are supportive of his efforts, and they are proud of him.

3. What kinds of future activities would you predict for Justin?

   Answer: Because he likes giving to others, he will probably do more charity work; because he has academic interests, he will probably have more education.

4. What information supports that Justin is probably a good student?

   Answer: Information in paragraph 23.

**✪✪✪ B READING TWO: Some Take the Time Gladly /
Mandatory Volunteering**

📁 Go to www.mynorthstarlab.com to read and listen to *Some Take the Time Gladly / Mandatory Volunteering*.

Suggested Time: 20 minutes

In Reading Two, students read two opposing editorial articles about mandatory volunteering. Students decide whether or not it is fair to have mandatory volunteering, and whether or not it is the best way to get young people to volunteer.

1. Ask students to read the titles of the two articles. Explain that they are editorial articles from different newspapers. Check students' comprehension of *mandatory*, and explain that in an editorial an opinion is expressed. Ask students if they can tell what opinions are going to be expressed in the two editorials. Then read and discuss the introductory information with the class.

2. Put students in pairs to discuss the question. Tell them to write their answers and then share their answers with the class.

3. Have students read the two editorials individually and write their opinions in the chart that follows. Have students share their charts with the class. You can also choose to play the recording and have students listen as they read.

✪✪✪ C INTEGRATE READINGS ONE AND TWO

❮ SKILLS

Organize information from the readings in a chart; synthesize information in a letter.

STEP 1: Organize   **Suggested Time: 15 minutes**

1. Have students read the instructions and then look at the chart. Go over the four different issues, checking students' comprehension of each.

2. Explain that students will want to scan the two readings for the relevant information. You might have students note from which reading and which paragraph they found their answers. Have students complete the exercise in pairs or individually.

3. Have students compare answers with another student or another pair. Then go over the answers with the entire class.

STEP 2: Synthesize   Suggested Time: 20 minutes

1. Read the instructions with the class. Elicit ideas from students about Justin's opinion and write them on the board. You may want to put students in pairs or groups to discuss their opinions of what Justin would say.

2. Suggest that students scan the first reading to find supporting quotes or information concerning Justin's opinions. Then have students write letters individually to share with the class. Remind them to also use the reasons they wrote in the two previous charts.

 Link to NorthStar: Listening and Speaking 4
For students who are also using the companion text, you may want to have them include the information they heard in Listenings One and Two for comparison.

 Go to www.mynorthstarlab.com for *Notetaking* and *Academic Skills Practice*.

③ FOCUS ON WRITING

Ⓐ VOCABULARY

◖ SKILLS

Review vocabulary from Readings One and Two; expand understanding of vocabulary through knowledge of word forms; apply understanding of the vocabulary and language from both texts in responses to questions.

✪ REVIEW   Suggested Time: 10 minutes

 Go to www.mynorthstarlab.com for *Review*.

1. Have students look at the word chart in **Exercise 1**, pointing out that not all words have four forms.

2. Go over the instructions in **Exercise 2**. Suggest that they think first about what word form is needed before changing the word in parentheses.

3. Have students complete the exercise individually, pairing them up as they finish to compare answers.

✪✪ EXPAND   Suggested Time: 15 minutes

1. Read the instructions with the class. Put on the board the phrasal verbs *look for, look at*, and *look over* and ask students to say the meaning for each one.

2. Put students in small groups to complete the exercise.

3. Bring the class together and go over the answers.

Remind students that many word endings change the form or part of speech of a word. Have students select the vocabulary words with suffixes *-ed, -ly, -ion/-tion, -ing*. Have them determine the part of speech according to the use of the word in context and/or the change in tense and create a chart to record the suffix, the word, and the part of speech.

✪ CREATE
Suggested Time: 20 minutes

1. Explain to students that they will be further exploring the concept of volunteering by imagining they are reporters interviewing people from the readings and asking them questions. Encourage students to write statements that reflect the attitudes of the people in the readings. They may want to scan the readings for ideas.

2. Go over the example with the class. Then have students write their questions in class or at home. Then put students in pairs to compare answers. You might have students check each other's word forms and tenses in the responses.

Expansion/Homework
Pair students. Ask them to choose one of the people in items 1–6 and expand upon the given question by writing a dialogue between a newsreporter and that person.

 Go to www.mynorthstarlab.com for additional *Vocabulary* practice.

✪✪ B GRAMMAR: Concessions

 Go to www.mynorthstarlab.com for *Grammar Chart* and *Exercise 2*.

◀ SKILLS

Learn to form and use concessions appropriately; present opinions by including opposing viewpoints using concession clauses.

Suggested Time: 25 minutes

1. Have students work in pairs to examine the sentences in **Exercise 1** and answer the questions that follow before going over their answers as a class. Make sure students understand that the boldface phrases introduce concession clauses.

2. Go over each point in the chart, eliciting more examples and writing them on the board.

3. Read the instructions in **Exercise 2**. Check that students understand that there are two tasks to do with each item: first to combine the sentences, and then to determine whether or not they are supporting or opposing mandatory volunteering. Go over the example with students.

4. Have students complete the exercise individually. Put them in pairs to compare their answers as they finish. Then review answers and address questions and problems as a class.

5. Read the instructions in **Exercise 3** with students. Go over the example together. Tell students to first decide what their opinion is and then to choose the appropriate concession phrase.

6. Have students complete the exercise individually. Move around the room to offer individual help with vocabulary and structure. Weaker students may want to use sentences in Exercise 2 as models where possible. Put students in pairs or small groups as they finish to compare and discuss their answers. Encourage them to expand on their answers in their discussions.

Expansion/Homework
(1) Exercises 2 and 3 could be completed at home and then reviewed in class.
(2) For further practice, offer exercises from *Focus on Grammar 4, 3rd Edition* and Azar's *Understanding and Using English Grammar, 3rd Edition*. See the Grammar Book References on page 268 of the student book for specific units and chapters.

 Go to www.mynorthstarlab.com for additional *Grammar* practice.

C WRITING

If you wish to assign a different writing task than the one in this section, see page 144. The Alternative Writing Topics can also be assigned as additional writing topics for homework. The alternative topics relate to the theme of the unit, but may not target the same grammar or rhetorical structures taught in the unit.

◖ SKILLS

Use a T-chart as a pre-writing device; write introductions and conclusions; integrate the concepts, vocabulary, grammar, and style focus from the unit in a persuasive essay.

✪✪✪ PREPARE TO WRITE: Using a T-Chart

Suggested Time: 10 minutes

1. Read the situation about which students are going to write their persuasive essays. Read the explanation of a T-chart.

2. Have students complete the T-chart in small groups. Suggest that they attempt to complete the chart from their memory and their understanding of the readings before referring back to the articles. This will show them how much they understood and help to transition them to forming their own opinions.

3. Have students use their T-charts to decide what they want to write about and to write a thesis statement stating their opinions. You might suggest to students that this thesis statement be considered provisional: often as students write their first drafts, they find their ideas change and thesis statements may need to change accordingly.

✪✪✪ WRITE: A Persuasive Essay

Suggested Time: 30 minutes

1. Have students read the background information on persuasive essays and the boxed important points to consider and include.

2. Have students read the persuasive essay in **Exercise 1** and answer the questions. Put students in pairs to discuss their answers. Then go over the answers as a class, referring back to the information in the box as needed.

3. Go over the instructions for **Exercise 2** with students. Have them complete the brace map individually either at home or in class. You may want to move around the room to help them with individual language and vocabulary questions.

4. Go over the instructions for **Exercise 3** together. You may want to have students look back at the essay in Exercise 1 to discuss the clarity and strength of each opposing argument. Point out that a strong refuting statement addresses the issue mentioned in the opposing statement directly, not the general concept.

5. You might want to have students circle either *for* or *against*. Then have students complete the charts individually. You may want to have them discuss their charts in pairs or small groups either with others who agree with them or students who don't. Also, have students check that their counter arguments refute the main points from the arguments for or against on the other side of the chart.

6. Read the instructions for **Exercise 4** and have students write their first drafts either in class or at home. Note that some students may want to write the introduction first. For those students, suggest that they write a rough draft of their introductions, but that they consider them as provisional, and just as a step to get them into the body of their essays.

✪✪✪ REVISE: Writing Introductions and Conclusions

Suggested Time: 25 minutes

1. Read the background information on introductions with the class.

2. Have students work in pairs to complete **Exercise 1** before going over the answers as a class. Make sure students understand that there are two tasks to do.

3. For **Exercise 2**, have students write their introductions.

4. Have students work in pairs or individually to complete **Exercise 3** before going over the answers as a class. Make sure students understand that there are two tasks to do.

5. For **Exercise 4**, have students write their conclusions.

Expansion/Homework
You may want to have the students rate the introductions in Exercise 1 for their ability to promote readers' interest in their opinions. Also, students could look back at the other essays in this unit to label the introductions accordingly and to underline the thesis statements.

 EDIT: Writing the Final Draft

Suggested Time: 25 minutes

Have students write the final draft of their essays. Encourage them to use language and grammar from the unit. Make sure they go through the checklist before submitting their final drafts. Collect the essays and correct them before the next class.

Expansion/Homework
Choose some of the better student persuasive essays to illustrate good examples of concessions and introductions and conclusions.

 Link to *NorthStar: Listening and Speaking 4*
Have students write a persuasive essay on some aspect of philanthropy and volunteerism using examples from *Giving to Others: Why Do We Do It?*

Go to www.mynorthstarlab.com for *Writing the Final Draft*.

❂ ALTERNATIVE WRITING TOPICS

These topics give students an alternative opportunity to explore and write about issues related to the unit theme.

❂ RESEARCH TOPICS

Suggested Time: 25 minutes in class

1. Have students turn to page 262. Review the instructions for the activity with the class. With the class, brainstorm a list of community centers or community work being done in your area. Discuss the types of service they provide.

2. Work in small groups or individually and research the community organization. Review the chart to help you find the information to organize the report.

3. Have students present their reports to the class. The other students could take notes or make a list of questions for the presenters.

 Go to www.mynorthstarlab.com for *Student Writing Models, Integrated Task, Video Activity, Internet Activity*, and *Unit 6 Achievement Test*.

UNIT 7

Homing in on Education

Theme: Education

This unit focuses on education, specifically the popularity of homeschooling. Students consider their own feelings about school and the benefits and disadvantages of homeschooling.

Reading One: *The Satisfied Learner: How Families Homeschool Their Teens* discusses why people homeschool and the ongoing debate on homeschooling versus traditional education.

Reading Two: *The Fun They Had* is an excerpt from a science-fiction novel that gives an account of schools in the future. It shows how the social benefits and enjoyable aspects of traditional school could get lost in the effort to make education more efficient and individualized.

Critical Thinking

Re-evaluate personal assumptions
Evaluate and classify information
Compare and contrast models of education

Infer information not explicit in a text
Relate specific situations to broad themes
Hypothesize another's point of view

Reading

Predict content
Read and interpret bar graphs
Paraphrase main ideas in a reading
Scan for details

Compare the content of two texts
Use a chart as a note-taking device
View ideas from the perspectives of the voices
Express opinions

Writing

Write a classification essay
Use parallel sentence structure

Classify information as a pre-writing device

Vocabulary

Find and use synonyms
Use context clues to find meaning
Identify word forms

Grammar

Direct and indirect speech

MyNorthStarLab
Readiness Check, Background and Vocabulary, Readings One and Two, Notetaking and Academic Skills Practice, Vocabulary and Grammar, Writing the Final Draft, Achievement Test

NorthStar: Listening and Speaking 4
Unit 7 focuses on the advantages and problems of having a lot of homework.

Go to www.mynorthstarlab.com for the MyNorthStarLab *Readiness Check*.

FOCUS ON THE TOPIC

◀ SKILLS

Predict the content of the unit; activate prior knowledge; express opinions; read and interpret graphs and tables; infer the meaning of new vocabulary from context.

✱✱✱ A PREDICT

Suggested Time: 10 minutes

1. Have students read the cartoon. Check students' comprehension of the word *postpone* and the meaning of the father's reply "Welcome to the world," eliciting from students that the father is implying that in life one often has to postpone what you want to do and do what you have to do instead.

2. Have students read the unit title. Put students in pairs to discuss the questions before going over their answers as a class.

✱✱ B SHARE INFORMATION

Suggested Time: 15 minutes

1. Read the definition of the term *homeschooling* with the class. Have students look at the graph and the map and their respective captions. Ask students if they are surprised by the information in the graphs.

2. Put students in groups to discuss the three questions. Have them either choose one question to report on to the class, or have them prepare brief reports on all the questions. You may want to have the groups select a reporter, a recorder/secretary, and a discussion leader within each group.

Expansion/Homework
Ask students to research online the phenomenon of homeschooling in their own countries, or one of the countries not included on the map, to find if it happens there and if so, to what extent.

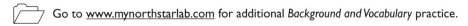

BACKGROUND AND VOCABULARY

Go to www.mynorthstarlab.com for *Background and Vocabulary.*

Suggested Time: 20 minutes

1. Have students read the text all the way through so that they understand the general meaning before having them reread the text to understand the boldfaced words.

2. Have students complete the exercise individually before putting them in pairs to compare their answers. Go over the answers as a class. You might want to elicit other sentences for the words that cause particular difficulties.

Go to www.mynorthstarlab.com for additional *Background and Vocabulary* practice.

②FOCUS ON READING

◀ SKILLS

Make predictions about the content of the article; differentiate between main ideas and details; make inferences and support them with evidence from the text; express opinions; scan the article for specific information.

READING ONE: The Satisfied Learner: How Families Homeschool Their Teens

Go to www.mynorthstarlab.com to read and listen to *The Satisfied Learner: How Families Homeschool Their Teens.*

Suggested Time: 20 minutes

In Reading One, students read about common perceptions and misconceptions about homeschooling and three examples of successful homeschooling situations. The article should get students thinking about their own education and questioning their own assumptions about how students are best educated.

1. Have students work individually to read the first paragraph, and look at the subheadings of the article and say how many examples are given. Ask them to predict from the title if they think that all of the examples are going to illustrate positive experiences or if one or more of them might not. Put students in pairs to answer the questions. Review the answers with the class.

2. Have students read the rest of the article independently, either in class, for homework, or lab work using MyNorthStarLab. You can also choose to play the recording of the reading and have students listen as they read.

Expansion/Homework

For homework, or in class, have students decide if their own feelings about school paralleled any of those of the teens in the reading passage, and if so, how. Have them discuss this in groups.

READING STRATEGY: Reaction Pyramid

1. To help students respond to the reading, have them complete a reaction pyramid as follows: one-word reaction, two-word reaction, three-word reaction, etc. Model Nikki's story to give students an idea.

interesting
faster learning
more free time
work on your own
it is a little expensive
you can usually graduate much faster

2. Note that these are their own thoughts and reactions, not paraphrases. Have students continue by offering their thoughts to add to the pyramid. Then have them work with a partner to complete a reaction pyramid for David's story. Students will enjoy reacting to the reading by expanding their pyramids. Caution them to use their own ideas rather than copying from the text.

✪✪✪ READ FOR MAIN IDEAS   Suggested Time: 15 minutes

1. Have students work individually to determine whether or not the statements are true and to change the false ones to make them true.

2. Go over the answers as a class, pointing out that the changed false statements are now main ideas.

REACHING ALL STUDENTS: Read for Main Ideas

• **Less Proficient:** Have students locate two details about each student, write them in their notebook, and then compare with their partner's.	• **More Proficient:** Chart each student according to type of schooling, location, studies, and activities.

✪✪✪ READ FOR DETAILS   Suggested Time: 15 minutes

Have students read the instructions. Tell them to scan the text again to find the answers. Then put students in pairs or small groups as they finish to compare their answers before going over them as a class.

✪✪✪ MAKE INFERENCES   Suggested Time: 15 minutes

1. Read the instructions in **Exercise 1** with students and do the first one together as an example. Tell students to read the quotes, underlining the specific words or phrases which convey positive or negative feelings.

2. Put students in pairs to compare and discuss their answers. If students disagree, tell them to go back to the text to point out specific details to support their decisions. However, emphasize that there is only one correct answer.

3. Give students a few moments to think about the answers to the questions in **Exercise 2** individually before putting them in pairs to discuss them.

4. Point out to students that knowing an author's purpose and opinion or attitude about their subject always assists comprehension and helps students to comprehend on a deeper level. Tell students they should always be looking out for purpose and opinion/attitude when they read, where applicable.

✪✪✪ EXPRESS OPINIONS   Suggested Time: 15 minutes

1. Have students read the three questions. You might want to have students first summarize Nikki, David, and Andy's stories before discussing the questions. Then put students in small groups to discuss the questions.

2. If time allows, have groups or pairs share their thoughts with the class to one or all of the questions.

 Link to *NorthStar: Listening and Speaking 4*
Students who are also using the companion text can extend the discussion to include the issues surrounding homework.

CRITICAL THINKING

Give students the following questions for discussion in small groups before discussing as a whole class:

1. How is the schooling of these students different than yours?

Answers will vary depending on students' areas of focus, but generally will illustrate that public school is more fixed in terms of schedules, more social, and more traditional.

2. Do you think these three students are receiving a better education?

Answers will vary, but students should support their opinions from the text and their own experience.

3. Do you agree or disagree with criticisms of public schools?

Answers will vary, but students should provide reasons to support their opinions from the text and their own experience.

4. If you could be homeschooled, would you choose that over public school?

Answers will vary, but students should support their choice with information from the text and their own knowledge and experience.

✪✪✪ B | READING TWO: The Fun They Had

📁 Go to www.mynorthstarlab.com to read and listen to *The Fun They Had*.

Suggested Time: 25 minutes

In Reading Two, students read a short science-fiction story about education in the future as predicted in 1951. The purpose of this article is to further challenge students to think about some of the benefits of traditional classroom education as seen from the eyes of a child.

1. Read the pre-reading question in **Exercise 1** with students and put them in pairs to discuss it.

2. Have students read the story. You can also choose to play the recording of the reading and have students listen as they read.

3. Put students in small groups to discuss the questions in **Exercise 2** before discussing the answers as a class.

Expansion/Homework
After having read the story, have students make a list of the things Margie thinks she would have preferred about traditional school. Then have them compare that list with the list they wrote in Exercise 1. They could also make a list of the things they remember enjoying from their own school days.

✪✪✪ C | INTEGRATE READINGS ONE AND TWO

◖ SKILLS

Organize information from the readings in a chart; view the ideas from the perspective of the people in the texts.

STEP 1: Organize   **Suggested Time: 15 minutes**

1. Have students read the instructions and then read the questions in the chart. You might have students make a note of the paragraphs they found their answers in. Have students complete the exercise in pairs or individually.

2. Go over the answers with the entire class.

Expansion/Homework
Have students use their charts to write a paragraph describing the similarities and differences between the types of homeschooling described in Reading One and the homeschooling Asimov describes in Reading Two.

STEP 2: Synthesize   Suggested Time: 20 minutes

1. Read the instructions with students. Emphasize the importance of supporting their responses with examples from the readings and from the chart they filled out in Step 1. You may want to have students discuss possible replies in pairs or groups before they start to write.

2. Have students write their responses either in class or for homework.

Expansion/Homework
You might want to divide the class into Nikki and David supporters, and Margie and Tommy supporters and have an in-class debate.

 Go to www.mynorthstarlab.com for *Notetaking* and *Academic Skills Practice*.

③ FOCUS ON WRITING

A VOCABULARY

◖ SKILLS

Review vocabulary from Readings One and Two; expand understanding of vocabulary through knowledge of word forms and usage; use new vocabulary creatively in a cohesive piece of writing.

✪ REVIEW   Suggested Time: 15 minutes

 Go to www.mynorthstarlab.com for *Review*.

1. Have students look at the vocabulary items in the boxes and check their comprehension of them. Either have them check back at the contexts of the words in the reading to review them, or have them explain them to each other in groups or pairs.

2. Have students work individually while you circulate to offer assistance with the changes some words require. As students finish the exercise, pair them up to compare and discuss their answers. Then go over the exercise as a class.

Expansion/Homework
Students could be asked to write sentences or a short paragraph with selected terms.

✪✪ EXPAND   Suggested Time: 15 minutes

1. Read the instructions and review the function of the different word forms with students. Then go over the example with the class.

2. Have students work individually to complete the chart of word forms, using a dictionary if needed before bringing the class together to go over the answers.

1. Remind students that writers often help us to understand unfamiliar words. They give clues, provide synonyms, antonyms, definitions, and examples.

2. Give students these vocabulary words and have them locate them in context: *misconceptions, ambition,* and *eclectic.* Have them find the word, sentence(s), or paragraph(s) that help them to understand the meaning. Then ask them to work with their partner to decide what kind of clue they were given (synonym, antonym, general clues, definition, or example). After volunteers share results, have students choose three words from the article and add information to create a sentence with a context that would help others to understand it.

✪ CREATE
Suggested Time: 20 minutes

1. Explain to students that they will be further exploring the ideas of the people detailed in the two readings. Read the example with students. Point out how David says not only what he does but why he does it.

2. Have students read each situation and the boxed vocabulary items and check their comprehension. Have students complete the exercise individually in class or at home. Encourage them to refer to the readings to get the opinions of the people.

Expansion/Homework
Once students have completed the activity, ask volunteers to write their sentences on the board so that you have one student reply for each question. Go over these replies and elicit additions from students.

📁 Go to www.mynorthstarlab.com for additional *Vocabulary* practice.

✺✺ B GRAMMAR: Direct and Indirect Speech

📁 Go to www.mynorthstarlab.com for *Grammar Chart* and *Exercise 2.*

◖ SKILLS

Identify direct and indirect speech in reading and use it in writing with correct use of punctuation, verb tense, time and location phrases, pronouns, and possessives.

Suggested Time: 25 minutes

1. Before doing **Exercise 1**, remind students what direct and indirect speech are, by asking a student a question such as, *How much time did you spend on your homework last night?* Start to write the answer on the board but act like you didn't hear exactly what he said. Then turn to another student and ask what the first student's reply was. Write the second student's answer on the board, prompting him/her to answer with appropriate grammar. Then point out to the students that what the second student said was *indirect speech* because

he/she was telling you what another student had said. Write the original quote on the board and point out that this is called *direct speech*.

2. Put students in pairs to examine the sentences and answer the two questions that follow before going over the answers as a class. Make sure students understand that only the form changes, not the meaning and not the time referred to.

3. Go over each point in the chart eliciting more examples and writing them on the board.

4. Read the instructions for **Exercise 2**. Go over the example with students. Remind students to pay special attention to tense changes between the indirect and direct speech. Have students complete the exercise individually. Put them in pairs to compare their answers as they finish.

5. Read the instructions for **Exercise 3** with students. Go over the example together. Have students complete the exercise individually or in pairs. Go over the answers together as a class.

Expansion/Homework

(**1**) Exercises 2 and 3 can be completed at home and then reviewed in class. You could have students go back to the reading *Justin Lebo* on pages 119–122 from Unit 6 to write the direct speech (quotations) as indirect speech. (**2**) For further practice, offer exercises from *Focus on Grammar 4, 3rd Edition*, and Azar's *Understanding and Using English Grammar, 3rd Edition*. See the Grammar Book References on page 268 of the student book for specific units and chapters.

 Link to NorthStar: Listening and Speaking 4
If students are also using the companion text, have them change three or four of the direct quotations on page 142 into indirect speech.

 Go to www.mynorthstarlab.com for additional *Grammar* practice.

Ⓒ WRITING

If you wish to assign a different writing task than the one in this section, see page 174. The Alternative Writing Topics can also be assigned as additional writing topics for homework. The alternative topics relate to the theme of the unit, but may not target the same grammar or rhetorical structures taught in the unit.

◖ SKILLS

Classify information as a pre-writing device; use parallel structures; integrate the concepts, vocabulary, grammar, and style focus from the unit to write a classification essay on education.

✪✪✪ PREPARE TO WRITE: Classifying

Suggested Time: 10 minutes

1. Read the introductory material on choices with students. You could put them in groups or pairs to brainstorm important choices they made while in school.

2. To review the idea of classifying and categorizing, put labels in a line across the board, for example, furniture, food, and transportation. Then elicit a few categories that fit into each of the major categories, for example, for furniture put office, bedroom, living room; for food put vegetables, sweet, dairy; and for transportation put public and private. Then have students suggest further items that might go into each of the smaller categories.

3. Read the information about classifying and categorizing with students. Go over the boxed categories together.

4. Have students choose a topic about education and start their charts. Then put them in pairs to brainstorm categories to put into the chart.

✪✪✪ WRITE: A Classification Essay

Suggested Time: 25 minutes

1. Have students read the background information on classification essays and the numbered points.

2. Have students read the outline and answer the questions in **Exercise 1** individually. Put students in pairs to discuss their answers. Then go over the answers as a class.

3. Go over the instructions for **Exercise 2** with students. Have them complete the exercise individually either at home or in class.

4. Have students write their first drafts in class or at home.

✪✪✪ REVISE: Using Parallel Structure

Suggested Time: 25 minutes

1. Go over the bulleted points on parallel structures. You might want to rewrite each of the sentences with one or two of the listed items in a structure that is not parallel so the students can "hear" how it sounds, for example, *Nikki was not interested in being a cheerleader, fund-raisers, or dancing.* Elicit the different ways of making the listed items parallel in each sentence.

2. Go over the instructions for **Exercise 1** with students, checking that they comprehend all the tasks required. Go over the example and correct the incorrect part of speech together. Have students complete the exercise individually. Put students in pairs or groups to compare their answers and their corrected parallel structures.

3. Have students complete the sentences in **Exercise 2** individually for homework. Then go over their answers as a class, eliciting all the various possibilities.

4. Have students review their own drafts (**Exercise 3**) for incorrect parallel structures. Move around the room and make comments where appropriate.

 ### EDIT: Writing the Final Draft

Suggested Time: 25 minutes

Have students write the final draft of their essays. Encourage them to use language and grammar from the unit. Make sure they go through the checklist before submitting their final drafts. Collect the essays and correct them before the next class.

 Link to *Northstar: Listening and Speaking 4*
If students are also using the companion text, have them write a classification essay on homework using information from Unit 7 of the *Listening and Speaking* strand.

Go to www.mynorthstarlab.com for *Writing the Final Draft.*

✪ ALTERNATIVE WRITING TOPICS

These topics give students an alternative opportunity to explore and write about issues related to the unit theme.

✪ RESEARCH TOPICS

Suggested Time: 25 minutes in class

1. Have students turn to page 263. Review the instructions for the activity with the class. In small groups, have students brainstorm a list of questions about homeschooling. Then discuss as a class.

2. Tell students to use a search engine to look for homeschooling organizations. Divide the list of questions among the members of the group.

3. Have students share the results of their research with their group and then write a report cooperatively.

4. Have students present their reports to the class.

 Go to www.mynorthstarlab.com for *Student Writing Models, Integrated Task, Video Activity, Internet Activity,* and *Unit 7 Achievement Test.*

Eat to Live or Live to Eat?

OVERVIEW

Theme: Food

This unit focuses on attitudes toward food. Students consider their own feelings about food and how intertwined our attitudes about food are with our cultural beliefs.

Reading One: An excerpt from *The Chinese Kitchen* by Eileen Yin-Fei Lo describes cooking and food traditions in a Chinese family and illustrates the importance of food to Chinese culture and Chinese families.

Reading Two: *"Slow Food" Movement Aims at Restoring the Joy of Eating* by Cathy Heiner from *USA Today* introduces this international group that celebrates "the joy of the table."

Critical Thinking

Re-evaluate personal attitudes and values	Support opinions with information from a text
Compare and contrast information	Analyze techniques in narrative voice
Infer meaning not explicit in a text	Identify connecting themes between texts
Identify different perspectives within one text	

Reading

Make predictions	Express opinions
Restate main ideas	Organize and synthesize information in different
Scan for specific details in a text	texts
Relate the text to personal culinary experiences	Use a chart to compare and contrast beliefs

Writing

Write a narrative essay	Take notes to organize information
Evaluate a classmate's narrative using a rubric	Write sentences with varying sentence lengths
Practice parallel structures and sentence variation	Use chronological sequencing showing how events relate to each other in time

Vocabulary	Grammar
Use context clues to find meaning Find and use synonyms	Phrasal verbs

MyNorthStarLab Readiness Check, Background and Vocabulary, Readings One and Two, Notetaking and Academic Skills Practice, Vocabulary and Grammar, Writing the Final Draft, Achievement Test	*NorthStar: Listening and Speaking 4* Unit 8 focuses on eating trends and habits.

1 FOCUS ON THE TOPIC

◖ SKILLS

Predict the content of the unit; activate prior knowledge; express opinions; infer the meaning of new vocabulary words from context.

✿✿✿ A PREDICT

Suggested Time: 10 minutes

Have students look at the photographs and the unit title. Put students in pairs to compare the photographs and discuss the questions before going over their responses as a class.

Expansion/Homework
Have students research on the Internet other eating or food expressions to share when they return to class. You could put them in groups to compare and discuss them, possibly discussing the relevance to their own cultures of each expression.

✿✿ B SHARE INFORMATION

Suggested Time: 25 minutes

1. For **Exercise 1**, have students read the instructions. Check students' comprehension of the word *memorable*. You might want to put them in pairs to brainstorm together prior to interviewing one another. Then have them all stand up and wander around the room interviewing one another and completing the chart.

2. Have students look at their charts and try to find some commonalities, or alternatively, something surprising or unexpected. Explain that in **Exercise 2**, they need to be able to summarize some part of their chart.

3. Have students share the interesting part of their charts with the class or in larger groups.

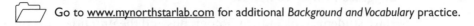

✪✪✪ C BACKGROUND AND VOCABULARY

📁 Go to www.mynorthstarlab.com for *Background and Vocabulary*.

Suggested Time: 20 minutes

1. Have students read the instructions, checking that they realize there are two definitions to circle for each word. Check students' comprehension of all the definitions. Then have students read the restaurant review all the way through so that they understand the general meaning before having them reread the text to understand the boldfaced words.

2. Have students complete the exercise individually before putting them in pairs to compare their answers.

3. Go over the answers as a class. You might want to elicit other sentences for the words that cause particular difficulties.

📁 Go to www.mynorthstarlab.com for additional *Background and Vocabulary* practice.

②FOCUS ON READING

◖ SKILLS

Make predictions about the content of the article; recognize how details support main ideas; make inferences and support them with evidence from the text; express opinions; scan the article for specific information.

✪✪✪ A READING ONE: The Chinese Kitchen

📁 Go to www.mynorthstarlab.com to read and listen to *The Chinese Kitchen*.

Suggested Time: 20 minutes

Reading One is an excerpt from the book *The Chinese Kitchen*, in which students read about cooking and food traditions in a Chinese family. The reading should make students aware of the relationships between food and culture and make them think about their own attitudes toward cooking and eating.

1. Have students read the first paragraph, and then put them in pairs to summarize and discuss what they read.

2. Have students write three questions either in pairs or individually that the remainder of the reading might discuss.

3. Have students read the rest of the article independently, either in class, as homework, or as lab work using MyNorthStarLab. You can also choose to play the recording of the reading and have students listen as they read.

Expansion/Homework

For homework, or in class, have students decide if their own experiences with eating and cooking in their childhood homes paralleled any of those in the reading passage, and if so, how. Have them discuss this in groups.

READING STRATEGY: Inference and Conclusions

1. Introduce students to the process of making inferences and drawing conclusions. Provide magazine advertisements with people engaged in an activity. Have students describe the pictures and then ask questions similar to these: What are the people doing? How do they feel? What are they probably going to do next? Where are they going? What does the advertiser want us to think about their product? Students must support their conclusions with specific evidence from the text (for example, they are going to work because they're wearing suits, carrying briefcases, and getting on an elevator).

2. After students have worked with ads, have students discuss these questions about Reading One in small groups: What did the father value in life? What did the mother's advice reveal about her? What is a good word to describe the grandmother; the writer? Have the groups write answers and evidence on large chart paper to present to the class.

✪✪✪ READ FOR MAIN IDEAS
Suggested Time: 15 minutes

1. Have students work individually to complete each statement in **Exercise 1**. Remind students to refer back to the passage for evidence to support their answers. Go over the answers as a class.

2. Read the instructions for **Exercise 2**. Have students work individually or in pairs or small groups to answer this question.

REACHING ALL STUDENTS: Read for Main Ideas

- **Less Proficient:** Have students read to locate one piece of cooking advice in each of these paragraphs: 6, 7, 8, 9, 10, 11, 14.

- **More Proficient:** Have students list the cooking advice given to Eileen by her parents and grandmother.

✪✪✪ READ FOR DETAILS
Suggested Time: 15 minutes

1. Have students decide whether each sentence in **Exercise 1** is true or false. Be sure students note the paragraph where they found the necessary information.

2. Put students in pairs as they finish the sentences to compare and discuss their answers. Note that there will be different ways to correct the false sentences.

3. Go over the corrected false statements as a class, eliciting all of the possible variations.

4. Have students work individually to complete the chart in **Exercise 2**. As they finish, pair students to compare answers.

Expansion/Homework

Have students fill out a similar chart, where possible, for cooking and eating traditions in their own cultures. Then have them write a paragraph, using the information in the chart.

✪✪✪ MAKE INFERENCES   Suggested Time: 15 minutes

1. Read the instructions with students. You might want to do the first one together as an example.

2. Tell students to read the quotes, checking back in the text for the larger context to make their inferences. Put students in pairs to compare and discuss their answers.

✪✪✪ EXPRESS OPINIONS   Suggested Time: 15 minutes

Have the students read the first question. You might want to have students first discuss what Eileen Yin-Fei Lo means by *manners, form, tradition,* and *history,* looking back in the text to find examples before discussing the question. Then put students in pairs to discuss the remaining questions.

CRITICAL THINKING

Give students the following questions for discussion in small groups before discussing as a whole class:

1. What did Eileen's father teach her about life and cooking?

   Students can give specifics from the story or make inferences using the information in the text (for example, that her father taught her to respect tradition, but to be open-minded in her approach to cooking and life).

2. What information tells you that her mother was practical?

   Answer: Her mother tells her: "If you are wealthy and know how to cook, then servants cannot take advantage of you. If you are poor and know how to cook, you will be able to create wonderful meals with few resources."

3. What was her grandmother's advice for behavior in the kitchen? Do you agree with this advice? Give reasons to support your opinion.

   Answers will vary, but students should have clear reasons that support their opinion.

4. How is food linked with manners, tradition, and history in your culture?

   Students will answer from their own experience, but they might use the information in the text to guide their responses.

Expansion/Homework

Have students ask an older relative, such as a grandparent, the discussion questions to see how the perspectives of another generation compare to their own and possibly write a paragraph about those comparisons.

Link to *NorthStar: Listening and Speaking 4*
Students who are also using the companion text can extend the discussion to include more recent food and eating trends.

 B **READING TWO: "Slow Food" Movement Aims at Restoring the Joy of Eating**

Go to www.mynorthstarlab.com to read and listen to *"Slow Food" Movement Aims at Restoring the Joy of Eating.*

Suggested Time: 25 minutes

In Reading Two, students read a newspaper article about a movement to make people rethink the way they handle food and eating. The purpose of the movement is to get people to take food preparation and eating in general more seriously, and when possible, to slow down and appreciate food and all the social aspects of eating more than is commonly done. The article further challenges students to rethink and possibly even change their attitudes about food preparation and eating.

1. You may want to start out by asking students how many of them have eaten fast food in the last 48 hours, or to think about how often they eat fast-food a week on average. Put them in pairs or groups to compare their fast-food eating habits.

2. Read the introductory information about the Slow Food movement as a class. Have students work in pairs to discuss the questions and report their answers to the class.

3. Have students read the article individually, either in class or for homework. You can also choose to play the recording of the reading and have students listen as they read. Finally, have students write answers to the questions, getting into pairs to compare and discuss their answers.

C **INTEGRATE READINGS ONE AND TWO**

◀ **SKILLS**

Organize information from the readings in a chart; view the ideas from the perspective of the people in the texts.

STEP 1: Organize   **Suggested Time: 15 minutes**

1. Have students read the instructions and then read the categories of the chart. Read the example in "Eileen Yin-Fei Lo's Food Traditions" column. Discuss how the two boxes are similar and how Eileen Yin-Fei Lo's experiences with cooking relate to the ideas of the Slow Food movement's beliefs about cooking.

2. Have students complete the chart either individually or in pairs. Remind students to scan the first reading if needed for helpful information.

3. Have students compare answers with another student's before going over the answers with the entire class.

STEP 2: Synthesize   Suggested Time: 20 minutes

1. Read the instructions with students. Emphasize the importance of supporting their ideas with examples from the readings and from the chart they filled out in Step 1. You may want to have students discuss possible ideas in pairs or groups before they start to write.

2. Have students write their responses either in class or for homework.

 Link to NorthStar: Listening and Speaking 4
Students who are also using the companion text can add another column to the chart headed: "French people." Based on the information in Unit 8 of the *Listening and Speaking* strand, ask them to complete the column with information on how current eating trends in France would fit the Slow Food movement's beliefs.

. Go to www.mynorthstarlab.com for *Notetaking* and *Academic Skills Practice*.

③ FOCUS ON WRITING

Ⓐ VOCABULARY

◖ SKILLS

Review vocabulary from Readings One and Two; expand understanding of vocabulary through knowledge of word forms and usage; use new vocabulary creatively in a cohesive piece of writing.

✪ REVIEW   Suggested Time: 10 minutes

 Go to www.mynorthstarlab.com for *Review*.

1. Have students look at the vocabulary items in the boxes and check their comprehension of them. Either have students look back at the contexts of the words in the readings to review the words, or have them explain the meaning of each word to each other in groups or pairs.

2. Tell students to read each sentence to the end before rereading it to choose the correct vocabulary item. Have students work individually while you move around the room to offer assistance.

3. Go over the answers as a class.

✪✪ EXPAND

1. Read the instructions with the class. You may want to explain that the meaning of phrasal verbs is different than the meaning of the individual words added together as a preview to the grammar section in which phrasal verbs are more thoroughly examined.

2. Read the instructions and have students work in small groups. It might be useful for students to find some of these phrasal verbs in a monolingual learner's dictionary to practice which of the words to look up (the verb usually) and to see how the dictionary indicates a phrasal verb.

3. Go over the answers with the class.

VOCABULARY EXPANSION: Pantomime the Verb

1. Remind students that words with an *-ed* suffix are the past tense forms of regular verbs. Then have students revisit the text to determine how each of these words is used: *insisted, linked, specified, necessitated, declined.* Add these words from Units 5–7: *determined, inspired, thrilled, dictate, adjust, dispute, disappoint.* Then ask students to draw one of the words from a bowl and work with a small group to show the action through pantomime.

2. As other groups guess, a spokesperson from the actors will tell the group if its guess is hot, warm, cold, or freezing. Proceed, giving each group a guess, until groups reach a correct response.

✪ CREATE

1. Read the introductory information together, and then divide the class into two groups—Group A, the students who are in favor of building a fast-food restaurant, and Group B, the students who are against it.

2. Have each group read only the instructions for their group. Then have students brainstorm ideas together before they write six ideas for their position. Move around the room to offer individual help as needed.

3. Pair Group A students with Group B students. Have them read and respond (in writing) to each other's reasons. Remind students to try to use the words and phrases in the box, or any others from the unit.

Expansion/Homework

For homework, have students write their ideas in the form of a letter to the editor either for or against building the fast-food restaurant.

📁 Go to www.mynorthstarlab.com for additional *Vocabulary* practice.

B **GRAMMAR: Phrasal Verbs**

Go to www.mynorthstarlab.com for *Grammar Chart* and *Exercise 2*.

◀ **SKILLS**

Examine and identify phrasal verbs in reading and use them in writing with correct use of particles and word positioning in the sentence.

Suggested Time: 30 minutes

1. Have students work in pairs to examine the sentences in **Exercise 1** and answer the questions that follow.

2. Go over each point in the chart, eliciting more examples and writing them on the board.

3. Read the instructions for **Exercise 2**. Go over the example. Put students in small groups to complete the exercise. Then review answers and address questions and problems as a class.

4. Read the instructions for **Exercise 3** with the class. Suggest that students read the complete text to get the gist before rereading it to complete the exercise.

5. Have students complete the exercise individually. Go over the answers together as a class.

Expansion/Homework
(1) Have students listen to native English speakers outside of class, on the radio, or on TV, and write examples of phrasal verbs that they hear. Have them share any new phrasal verbs with the class. (2) For further practice, offer exercises from *Focus on Grammar 4, 3rd Edition* and Azar's *Understanding and Using English Grammar, 3rd Edition*. See the Grammar Book References on page 268 of the student book for specific units and chapters.

 Go to www.mynorthstarlab.com for additional *Grammar* practice.

C **WRITING**

If you wish to assign a different writing task than the one in this section, see page 200. The Alternative Writing Topics can also be assigned as additional writing topics for homework. The alternative topics relate to the theme of the unit, but may not target the same grammar or rhetorical structures taught in the unit.

◖ SKILLS

Practice notetaking as a pre-writing device; write sentences with varying sentence lengths; integrate the concepts, vocabulary, grammar, and style focus from the unit to write a narrative essay on a memorable meal.

✱✱✱ PREPARE TO WRITE: Notetaking

Suggested Time: 10 minutes

1. Read the introductory material and the background information on notetaking with the class. Go over the organizer together in class. Have students complete the organizer individually as you circulate to help with individual vocabulary questions.

2. Put students in pairs to share and discuss their ideas.

✱✱✱ WRITE: A Narrative Essay

Suggested Time: 30 minutes

1. Have students read the background information on narrative essays and the four points. You may want to bring to class some examples of narrative essays either from a book of essays, such as *Chicken Soup for the Soul* or the human interest section of a newspaper or magazine, and have students find the numbered points in the essays.

2. Have students read the narrative essay and answer the questions in **Exercise 1** individually. You might put students in pairs to discuss their answers before going over them as a class.

3. Go over the instructions in **Exercise 2** with the students. Have students write their first drafts in class or at home.

✱✱✱ REVISE: Varying Sentence Length

Suggested Time: 20 minutes

1. Go over the background information of using sentences of varying length.

2. Go over the instructions for **Exercise 1** with students, checking that they comprehend all the tasks required. Have students complete the exercise individually.

3. Have students complete **Exercises 2** and **3** individually for homework. Then go over their answers as a class, eliciting all the various possibilities.

4. For **Exercise 4**, have students review their own drafts for varying sentence length.

EDIT: Writing the Final Draft

Suggested Time: 25 minutes

Have students write the final draft of their essays. Encourage students to use language and grammar from the unit. Make sure they go through the checklist before submitting their final drafts. Collect the essays and correct them before the next class.

Link to *Northstar: Listening and Speaking 4*
Have the students write an essay on food trends using examples from Unit 8 of the *Listening and Speaking* strand.

Go to www.mynorthstarlab.com for *Writing the Final Draft.*

✪ ALTERNATIVE WRITING TOPICS

These topics give students an alternative opportunity to explore and write about issues related to the unit theme.

✪ RESEARCH TOPICS

Suggested Time: 25 minutes in class

1. Have students turn to page 264. Review the instructions for the activity with the class. Have students look over the chart and the questions and points that they may need to research for the food or drink that they choose. Tell students to use a search engine to look for the history or origin of their food or drink.

2. Have students complete their charts after they have done their research. Have students write their reports in class or for homework, using their chart to help organize their report.

3. Have students present their reports to the class or in small groups.

 Go to www.mynorthstarlab.com for *Student Writing Models, Integrated Task, Video Activity, Internet Activity,* and *Unit 8 Achievement Test.*

UNIT 9

The Grass Is Always Greener . . .

OVERVIEW

Theme: Immigration

This unit focuses on immigration and the feelings the experience evokes. Students think about the losses as well as the benefits of immigration and consider their own feelings about an event that changed their own lives.

Reading One: *Poor Visitor*, an excerpt from the novel *Lucy* by Jamaica Kincaid, is the story of a girl who left her homeland, Antigua, to immigrate to the United States and describes the conflicted and confused feelings this 16-year-old girl has upon her arrival.

Reading Two: *Nostalgia*, a poem by Virgilio Dávila, a well-known Puerto Rican poet, describes Dávila's nostalgia for his homeland after his immigration to New York City.

Critical Thinking

Classify observations and life experiences
Identify similarities in three different life histories
Interpret imagery in a text

Compare and contrast imagery in a text
Hypothesize another's point of view
Support answers with information from a text

Reading

Make predictions
Scan for information
Identify main ideas
Relate text to personal experiences
Make inferences

Interpret a poem
Organize and synthesize information in different texts
Express opinions
Complete a chart

Writing

Write a comparison and contrast essay
Use transitional expressions and subordinating conjunctions to combine sentences

Write comparison and contrast statements
Organize ideas in different frameworks
Make a comparison and contrast chart

Vocabulary

Find multiple definitions of words
Use context clues to find meaning
Understand and use analogies

Grammar

Past perfect

 MyNorthStarLab
Readiness Check, Background and Vocabulary, Readings One and Two, Notetaking and Academic Skills Practice, Vocabulary and Grammar, Writing the Final Draft, Achievement Test

 NorthStar: Listening and Speaking 4
Unit 9 focuses on the experiences of young people who immigrate.

①FOCUS ON THE TOPIC

◀ SKILLS

Predict the content of the unit; activate prior knowledge; express opinions; infer the meaning of new vocabulary from context.

✪✪✪Ⓐ PREDICT

Suggested Time: 10 minutes

1. Have students look at the photographs and the accompanying information. Ask students which of the people pictured they know and to say what else they know about them. Ask students if they know of any other famous immigrants to the United States. Then have students read the unit title.

2. Put students in pairs to discuss the questions before going over their responses as a class.

Expansion/Homework

Have students research online information about immigration patterns to the United States over the years. You could assign groups of students certain periods of time to research, such as the late 1800's, the early 1900's, post World War I, post World War II, and the present, telling them to note who the immigrants were and how many there were in their assigned period. When they return to class, they could compare and contrast the immigration patterns of their time periods.

✪✪Ⓑ SHARE INFORMATION

Suggested Time: 15 minutes

1. Have students read the instructions. You might want to discuss what the economic, political, and personal reasons to do something might be.

2. Put students in small groups to complete the chart together. Then have students share their lists while you construct a master chart on the board.

 Link to NorthStar: Listening and Speaking 4
If students are also using the companion text, they can use the questions from Share Information, in Unit 9, as a guide to write their paragraphs. Ask students to read their paragraphs to the class.

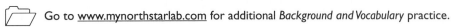

C BACKGROUND AND VOCABULARY

Go to www.mynorthstarlab.com for *Background and Vocabulary*.

Suggested Time: 20 minutes

1. Have students read the instructions for **Exercise 1**. Then have students read the narrative all the way through so that they understand the general meaning before having them reread the text to understand the boldfaced words.

2. Have students complete **Exercise 2** individually before putting them in pairs to compare their answers. Go over the answers as a class. You might want to elicit other sentences for the words that cause particular difficulties.

Expansion/Homework

You may want to have students work in groups to write an original sentence for both of the meanings of all the words in Exercise 2. Then have the groups play against each other as teams. A student from one team reads a sentence and a student from the other team gives the correct definition of the vocabulary word.

Go to www.mynorthstarlab.com for additional *Background and Vocabulary* practice.

2 FOCUS ON READING

◖ SKILLS

Make predictions about the content of the article; differentiate between main ideas and details; make inferences about the main characters' intentions and feelings; express opinions; scan the article for specific information.

A READING ONE: Poor Visitor

Go to www.mynorthstarlab.com to read and listen to *Poor Visitor*.

Suggested Time: 20 minutes

Reading One is an excerpt from the book *Lucy*, in which students read about a young girl's first day in the United States and her feelings about finally realizing her "dream." The article should make students aware of the negative aspects of immigration for the immigrant and the difficulties of leaving one's home.

1. Have students work individually to read the first paragraph and write their answers to the two questions. Then put students in pairs to share and discuss their answers. Have some volunteers share their answers, possibly writing them on the board or on an overhead transparency to be referred to later.

2. Have students read the rest of the text independently. You can assign the reading for homework or lab work using MyNorthStarLab. You can also choose to play the recording of the reading and have students listen as they read.

Expansion/Homework

You could have students research Antigua and meet in groups during the next class to share what they found out to better understand the author's experiences and feelings.

✪✪✪ READ FOR MAIN IDEAS
Suggested Time: 15 minutes

1. Have students work individually to decide whether or not each statement is true or false. Encourage students to refer back to the passage for evidence to support their answers. Also remind them that there is more than one way to make the false statements true.

2. Go over the corrected statements as a class, pointing out that the changed false statements are now main ideas.

READING STRATEGY: Similes and Metaphors

1. Have students draw a two-column chart. Give an example of a simile and a metaphor and model how the comparisons could be listed on the chart, with the thing being compared in the first column and the metaphor or simile in the second. Provide these comparisons from the text and have students work with a partner to chart them:
   - These places were lifeboats to my small drowning soul.
   - I was no longer in a tropical zone, and this realization now entered my life like a flow of water dividing formerly dry and solid ground,
   - creating two banks, one of which was my past ... the other my future, a gray blank, an overcast seascape on which rain was falling and no boats were in sight.
   - Oh, I had imagined that with my one swift act—leaving home and coming to this new place—I could leave behind me, as if it were an old garment never to be worn again, my sad thoughts, my sad feelings, and my discontent with life in general ...

2. After students complete this activity, have them write a simile and a metaphor to describe something in their own life.

✪✪✪ READ FOR DETAILS
Suggested Time: 20 minutes

1. Go over the instructions with students, pointing out that there are two tasks to do. Then have students read the letter and underline the incorrect information individually. You may want to have students make a note of the paragraphs in which they found the information referred to in the sentences with the factual errors.

2. Put students in pairs as they finish the sentences to compare and discuss their underlined errors and corrections. Note that there may be different ways to correct the errors. Go over the corrected false statements as a class, eliciting all of the possible variations.

Expansion/Homework
Have students rewrite the letter to include the correct information in class or for homework.

REACHING ALL STUDENTS: Read for Details	
• **Less Proficient:** Help students with details of the story by having them list Lucy's experiences in each paragraph. Begin with her first night, leaving the airport.	• **More Proficient:** Have students create a sentence outline for the story.

✪✪✪ MAKE INFERENCES

Suggested Time: 15 minutes

1. Read the instructions with students. You might want to do the first one together as an example. Tell students to read the quotes, checking back in the text for the larger context to choose the best inference option.

2. You might put students in pairs to compare and discuss their answers before going over the answers as a class.

 Link to *NorthStar: Listening and Speaking 4*
Students who are also using the companion text can discuss the problems Esteban faced in his new country.

✪✪✪ EXPRESS OPINIONS

Suggested Time: 20 minutes

Have students read each quote. It might be useful for students to discuss in pairs the meaning of each quote before relating them to experiences and feelings of their own. You might also suggest that students review the vocabulary in Section C Background and Vocabulary and try to use some of the words in their discussion.

 Link to *NorthStar: Listening and Speaking 4*
Students who are also using the companion text can extend the discussion to include the experiences of younger immigrants.

CRITICAL THINKING

Give students the following questions for discussion in small groups before discussing as a whole class:

1. Describe the author's disappointment with her new city.

   Answer: She says: "I only knew it felt a little like sadness but heavier than that. Now that I saw these places, they looked ordinary, dirty, worn down by so many people entering and leaving them in real life."

2. What evidence is there of her homesickness?

   Answer: She talks about drawing a picture of her future as "black, blacker, blackest; she longed to go back to the familiar; she felt cold inside and out."

(continued on next page)

3. Why is the cold, sunny day upsetting to her?

Answer: It was completely unexpected and served as a sharp reminder that she was in a completely new environment.

4. How do her experiences and feelings compare with yours?

Answers will vary, but students should provide information from the text and from their own experience.

✪✪✪ B READING TWO: Nostalgia

Go to www.mynorthstarlab.com to read and listen to *Nostalgia*.

Suggested Time: 20 minutes

In Reading Two, students read a poem expressing an immigrant's nostalgia for his homeland. The poem further challenges the students to think about the negative side of immigration, but this time from an older person's perspective.

1. Have students read the background information on Virgilio Dávila and the meaning of nostalgia. You might want to elicit from students things they get nostalgic for at times.

2. Have students read the two pre-reading questions in **Exercise 1**. Then have them read the first stanza of the poem and answer the questions. Put them in pairs to share and discuss their ideas.

3. Have students read the poem individually. You can also choose to play the recording of the reading and have students listen as they read. After students finish reading, you might want to read the poem aloud for the students while they read along silently, explaining to them that a lot of poetry is meant to be "heard" as well as read.

4. For **Exercise 2**, have students individually write down four things mentioned in the poem. Have individuals share their answers with the class.

✪✪✪ C INTEGRATE READINGS ONE AND TWO

◀ SKILLS

Organize information from the readings and form opinions as a reader using this information; view the ideas from the perspective of the people in the texts.

STEP 1: Organize   **Suggested Time: 15 minutes**

1. Look at the chart with the class. You may want to elicit examples for the first topic, weather, together as a class.

2. Have students complete the chart individually, and then compare their examples with a partner's. You might want to put a larger chart on the board, and use students' examples to fill in your chart.

Link to *NorthStar: Listening and Speaking 4*

Students who are also using the companion text can add another column to the chart headed: "New Students at the International High School." Based on the information in the unit, ask them to complete the column with information on how the experiences of the new students would compare with those of Lucy and Virgilio Dávila.

STEP 2: Synthesize   Suggested Time: 20 minutes

1. Read the instructions with students. Emphasize the importance of supporting their ideas with examples from the readings and from the chart they filled out in Step 1. You may want to have the students discuss possible ideas in pairs or groups before they start to write.

2. Have students write their paragraphs either in class or for homework.

Expansion/Homework

Split the class into pairs to role-play the situation of Dávila and Lucy talking together about their feelings. Have students practice their role plays and then have volunteers perform them for the group.

③ FOCUS ON WRITING

Ⓐ VOCABULARY

❰ SKILLS

Review vocabulary from Readings One and Two; expand understanding of vocabulary through knowledge of word forms and usage; expand vocabulary through study of analogies; use new vocabulary creatively in a cohesive piece of writing.

✪ REVIEW   Suggested Time: 15 minutes

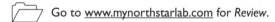 Go to www.mynorthstarlab.com for *Review*.

1. Read the vocabulary words in **Exercise 1** as a class. Discuss which words are associated with positive feelings and which with negative ones.

2. Have students assign the words from the list to the appropriate boxes individually. Remind students to check back at the contexts of the words in the readings to review the words when needed.

3. Read the instructions for **Exercise 2** with students. Have them compare and discuss their charts in pairs or small groups.

4. Check answers as a class by making a "master" chart on the board. Go over the meaning of particularly problematic words.

✪✪ EXPAND

1. Read the instructions and the analogy review information with students. Go over the example as a class. Put students in pairs to complete the activity. Tell students to try to put the words in sentences to help clarify the meanings for them and to discuss their answers.

2. Bring the class together and go over the answers.

> ### VOCABULARY EXPANSION: Create a Comic
>
> 1. Have students use the vocabulary words to create their own comic book story. Tell them to work with a partner and select 8 of the vocabulary words to use in balloons above their characters' heads. Remind students that they do not have to be artists to complete this activity. Simple stick figures or smiley faces are sufficient, but they should feel free to add setting/background to their comics if it helps to better define the word they are using.
>
> 2. After comics are drawn, circulate the comics to share with all members of the class.

✪ CREATE

1. Read the instructions and have students decide whom they would prefer to write a letter to. You might want to put students in pairs or groups with others who decided to write the same person to brainstorm things they might say.

2. Have students write their letters to either Lucy or Virgilio Dávila in class or for homework. Remind them to keep the vocabulary words from the previous two exercises in mind.

 Go to www.mynorthstarlab.com for additional *Vocabulary* practice.

✪✪ B GRAMMAR: Past Perfect

Go to www.mynorthstarlab.com for *Grammar Chart* and *Exercise 2*.

Suggested Time: 25 minutes

◖ SKILLS

Examine and identify sentences written in the past perfect in reading and use them in writing with correct use of the past participle, the auxiliary verb, and the correct time phrases in the sentence.

1. Have students work in pairs to examine the sentences in **Exercise 1** and answer the questions that follow.

2. Go over each point in the chart, eliciting more examples and writing them on the board.

3. Read the instructions for **Exercise 2**. Go over the example. Have students work individually to complete the exercise before comparing and discussing their answers in pairs or small groups. Then review answers and address questions and problems as a class.

4. Read the instructions for **Exercise 3** with the class. Suggest that students read the complete timeline before attempting to complete the sentences. Then have students complete the exercise individually. Go over the answers together as a class.

Expansion/Homework

(**1**) Students can complete the exercises at home and then go over the answers in class. You could also have students use the sentences and timeline in Exercise 3 to write a paragraph. (**2**) For further practice, offer exercises from *Focus on Grammar 4, 3rd Edition* and Azar's *Understanding and Using English Grammar, 3rd Edition*. See the Grammar Book References on page 268 of the student book for specific units and chapters.

 Go to www.mynorthstarlab.com for additional *Grammar* practice.

C WRITING

If you wish to assign a different writing task than the one in this section, see page 226. The Alternative Writing Topics can also be assigned as additional writing topics for homework. The alternative topics relate to the theme of the unit, but may not target the same grammar or rhetorical structures taught in the unit.

◖ SKILLS

Use charting as a pre-writing device; use subordinations and transitions; integrate the concepts, vocabulary, grammar, and style focus from the unit to write a comparison and contrast essay.

✪✪✪ PREPARE TO WRITE: Charting

Suggested Time: 15 minutes

1. Read the introductory material on change with students. You could put them into groups or pairs to brainstorm life-changing events they've had to each other as a pre-writing technique.

2. Read the background information on charting. For **Exercise 1**, put students in pairs to discuss the life-changing event and resulting feelings together.

3. Go over the example chart in **Exercise 2** together in class. You might have students make sentences using the past perfect to discuss what they are reading in the chart together in pairs or as a class.

4. Read the instructions for **Exercise 3** with the class. Have students make their own charts about the things that were affected by the life-changing event they have chosen to write about. Move around the room to help with individual vocabulary questions.

✪✪✪ WRITE: A Comparison and Contrast Essay

Suggested Time: 25 minutes

1. Have students read the background information on comparison and contrast essays and the six important points. Then have them read the explanation of the two main ways to organize a comparison and contrast essay.

2. Have students read the two outlines in **Exercise 1** and discuss them in pairs. Tell students to look for whether or not all the same information is included and how the points to be compared and contrasted are ordered.

3. Go over the instructions for **Exercise 2** with students. Have them read the essay excerpts in class or for homework.

4. For **Exercise 3**, have students make their outlines while you move around the room to offer individual help. Then have them discuss the outlines with a partner to decide which outline best fits their topic.

5. Go over the instructions in **Exercise 4** with students. Have them write their first drafts in class or at home.

✪✪✪ REVISE: Using Subordinators and Transitions

Suggested Time: 25 minutes

1. Go over the background information on using signal words.

2. Go over the instructions for **Exercise 1** with students. Have them read the paragraph and answer the questions individually.

3. Put students in pairs to compare their answers to the questions and reflect on the usage of the signal words.

4. Have students read the boxed information on comparisons and contrasts and the corresponding signal words often used with them.

5. Have students complete **Exercise 2** individually at home for homework. Tell them to pay special attention to the punctuation used with each term or phrase. Then go over their answers as a class, eliciting all the various possibilities.

6. Go over the instructions for **Exercise 3** with students. You might suggest that they look for the places where transitions and subordinators would go in each paragraph before deciding on the one they want to use.

7. Have students complete the exercise individually at home for homework. Then go over their answers as a class, eliciting all the various possibilities.

8. For **Exercise 4**, have students review their own drafts for comparison and contrast transitions and subordinators, adding them as needed.

 EDIT: Writing the Final Draft

Suggested Time: 25 minutes

Have students write the final draft of their essays. Encourage them to use language and grammar from the unit. Make sure they go through the checklist before submitting their final drafts. Collect the essays and correct them before the next class.

Expansion/Homework
Choose some of the student essays to illustrate good examples of comparison and contrast essays, past perfect, and subordinators and transitions. You can also choose to use student essays to illustrate the topics in the final draft checklist.

 Link to *NorthStar: Listening and Speaking 4*
If students are also using the companion text, have them write a comparison and contrast essay on older and younger immigrants using examples from Unit 9 of the *Listening and Speaking* strand.

Go to www.mynorthstarlab.com for *Writing the Final Draft.*

✪ ALTERNATIVE WRITING TOPICS

These topics give students an alternative opportunity to explore and write about issues related to the unit theme.

✪ RESEARCH TOPICS

Suggested Time: 25 minutes in class

1. Have students turn to pages 264–265. Review the instructions for the activity with the class. Have students work in small groups reviewing the list of famous U.S. immigrants.

2. Review the questions with students. Tell them they will use this list to organize their reports. Tell students to use a search engine to research the immigrant they have chosen. If students choose someone they know, they should arrange an interview with that person.

3. Have students write their report, answering the questions given and any other additional questions they might have about the immigrant. Finally, have students present their reports to the class or in small groups.

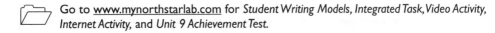 Go to www.mynorthstarlab.com for *Student Writing Models, Integrated Task, Video Activity, Internet Activity,* and *Unit 9 Achievement Test.*

UNIT 10 Take It or Leave It

OVERVIEW

Theme: Technology
> This unit focuses on both the positive and the negative impacts of technology on our everyday lives. Students consider the benefits and the losses of living in a high-tech world.

Reading One *Inside the House*, an excerpt from *The Road Ahead*, by Bill Gates, outlines how technology will enhance our living environment and will also improve our social lives as opposed to isolating us more as some believe.

Reading Two *Thoreau's Home*, an excerpt from Henry David Thoreau's *Walden* describes the simple pleasure of the house he built in the woods.

Critical Thinking

Interpret a cartoon
Compare and contrast concepts of technology
Evaluate personal standards in technology
Infer word meaning from context

Hypothesize another's point of view
Classify information
Support answers with examples from a text
Recognize organization of a text

Reading

Make predictions
Summarize main ideas
Locate examples and details in a text
Make inferences

Express opinions
Organize and synthesize information in different texts
Relate text to personal values

Writing

Write a cause and effect essay
Take notes in outline form
Develop an essay from an outline
Use signal words

Brainstorm ideas using a graphic organizer
Write and respond to interview questions
Use a flow chart as a pre-writing device

Vocabulary	Grammar
Find and use synonyms Use context clues to find meaning Recognize word forms	Future progressive

📁 ***MyNorthStarLab*** Readiness Check, Background and Vocabulary, Readings One and Two, Notetaking and Academic Skills Practice, Vocabulary and Grammar, Writing the Final Draft, Achievement Test	***NorthStar: Listening and Speaking 4*** Unit 10 focuses on noise pollution and cell phone etiquette.

①FOCUS ON THE TOPIC

◖ SKILLS

Predict the content of the unit; interpret a cartoon; activate prior knowledge; express opinions; infer the meaning of new vocabulary from context.

✺✺✺Ⓐ PREDICT

Suggested Time: 10 minutes

1. Have students read the cartoon together. Ask students to say what happened in the cartoon.

2. Put students in pairs to discuss the cartoon, their own feelings about technology, and the title before going over their thoughts and responses to the question as a class.

Link to *NorthStar: Listening and Speaking 4*
If students are also using the companion text, have them look at the cartoon on page 193 and compare it with the cartoon in this unit. Ask: *Is the message similar or different? How?*

✺✺Ⓑ SHARE INFORMATION

Suggested Time: 15 minutes

1. Have students read the instructions and then the technology column. Elicit from them any other devices or technology they think is missing. Then have them read the headings for the three remaining rows.

2. Have students complete the chart individually. Put students in small groups to compare their charts. Encourage students to give reasons. You might want to put a "master" chart on the board and tally up their answers to see which technologies the class rated as the most and least important.

Link to *NorthStar: Listening and Speaking 4*
Students using the companion text may want to add the additional items listed on page 194 to their charts.

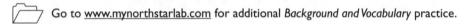

✪✪✪ C BACKGROUND AND VOCABULARY

📁 Go to www.mynorthstarlab.com for *Background and Vocabulary*.

Suggested Time: 20 minutes

1. Have students read about Bill Gates as a businessman, inventor, and philanthropist, and the introductory material on his high-tech home. Then have them read the instructions for the exercise, emphasizing that this is an imaginary interview. Have students read the interview all the way through so that they understand the general meaning before having them reread the text to understand the boldfaced words. You might want to point out to students that it isn't necessary to understand every word to understand the meaning.

2. Have students complete the exercise individually before putting them in pairs to compare their answers. Remind them to scan the text to find the words before choosing the synonym or definition.

3. Go over the answers as a class. You might want to elicit new sentences for the words that cause particular difficulties.

📁 Go to www.mynorthstarlab.com for additional *Background and Vocabulary* practice.

✌2 FOCUS ON READING

◀ SKILLS

Make predictions about the content of the article; differentiate between main ideas and details; make inferences about the main characters' intentions and feelings; express opinions; scan the article for specific information; complete an outline.

✪✪✪ A READING ONE: Inside the House

📁 Go to www.mynorthstarlab.com to read and listen to *Inside the House*.

Suggested Time: 25 minutes

Reading One is an excerpt from the book *The Road Ahead* in which students read about Bill Gates' dream house. The article should make students aware of the potential of technology to enhance our lives, but also to isolate us socially.

1. You might want to discuss the concept of a "dream house" with students before having them read the questions in the book. Ask them to consider what such a house would be like for them and how that might compare with what they already know about Bill Gates's "dream house."

2. Have students read the question and work individually to write answers to the questions. Then have them share their answers with a partner. Have some

volunteers share their answers, possibly writing them on the board or on an overhead transparency to be referred to later.

3. Finally, have students read the text, either in class, for homework, or lab work using MyNorthStarLab. You can also choose to play the recording of the reading and have students listen as they read.

Expansion/Homework

Have students write a paragraph expanding their ideas about their own "dream houses." Ask them to draw a picture to illustrate their "dream houses." They can share their paragraphs and pictures with the class.

READING STRATEGY: Visualization

1. Remind students that they can improve comprehension by visualizing or seeing pictures of descriptions in a text.

2. Have students work with a partner to reread each paragraph and draw rooms in a house with items or symbols to represent the technology that is being described.

✪✪✪ READ FOR MAIN IDEAS   Suggested Time: 10 minutes

Have students work individually to choose the best summaries. Encourage them to refer back to the passage for evidence to support their answers. Go over the summaries together.

REACHING ALL STUDENTS: Read for Main Ideas

- **Less Proficient:** Have students select a main idea from each paragraph.

- **More Proficient:** Have students select the main idea from each paragraph and match it to one of the three ideas listed.

✪✪✪ READ FOR DETAILS   Suggested Time: 20 minutes

1. Review the structure of the outline with students. Point out the lettering and numbering system—the Roman numerals (I, II, III, etc.) identify the main ideas, the capital letters identify the supporting ideas, and that each subsequent level supports the one above it.

2. Read the first main idea as a class and fill in Example 1 (craftsmanship) together. Then have students continue individually. Remind students to scan the text as needed. Move around the room and offer assistance as needed.

3. Put students in pairs to compare their completed outlines with a partner. Encourage students to go back to the text to show their partners where they got the information. Go over students' outlines as a class eliciting all the variations. Discuss any differences.

✪✪✪ MAKE INFERENCES

Suggested Time: 15 minutes

1. Read the instructions with the class. You might want to have students read the first quote and do the first one together as an example.

2. Tell students to read the remaining quotes, checking back in the text for the larger context to help them make their inferences.

3. Go over the inferences as a class, eliciting all the variations. Welcome disagreement, telling students to go back to the text to point out specific details to support their inferences.

Expansion/Homework

Have students work in pairs to write one additional statement they can infer from the reading. Have pairs exchange statements with another pair to find an example from the reading to support the inference.

✪✪✪ EXPRESS OPINIONS

Suggested Time: 15 minutes

Have students read the two discussion questions and then take a few minutes to think about them before getting into small groups to discuss them. You might also suggest that students review the vocabulary in Section C Background and Vocabulary and try to use some of the words in their discussion. If time allows, have selected groups share their responses to one of the two questions with the class.

 Link to *NorthStar: Listening and Speaking 4*

Students who are also using the companion text can extend the discussion to include noise pollution and/or cell phone etiquette.

CRITICAL THINKING

Give students the following questions for discussion in small groups before discussing as a whole class:

1. What are three technologies mentioned in the memoir by Bill Gates?

   Answer: Electronic pin, visual-recognition cameras so that sound and light in the house will move with you; remote controls and consoles to control the entertainment system from every room in the house, still-image database to project pictures onto the walls.

2. How does this house compare to most houses in the U.S.?

   Answers will vary, but will indicate that his house is much more electronically advanced than most houses.

3. Do you think houses like this will make people less social and more isolated?

   Answers will vary, but students can use information from the text and from their own experience to support their opinions.

4. What would you add to the design of this house? Give a reason for your choice.

   Encourage students to have fun and be creative with their answers, as long as they can give reasons for their choices.

✦✦✦ B READING TWO: Thoreau's Home

📁 Go to www.mynorthstarlab.com to read and listen to *Thoreau's Home.*

Suggested Time: 20 minutes

In Reading Two, students read a passage about Thoreau's ideas about simplicity, living in the woods, and building his own house with only a bare minimum of the technology current at the time. The article further challenges students to think about the effects of technology.

1. Read the information about Thoreau to the class. Give students a few minutes to read the question in **Exercise 1** and write their ideas. Have them share their ideas with a partner and invite selected students to share their ideas with the class. Have students work individually to read the passage, either in class or at home. You can also choose to play the recording of the reading and have students listen as they read.

2. Put students in small groups to discuss the four questions in **Exercise 2**. Ask one student from each group to report on their group's ideas. Write the ideas on the board.

✦✦✦ C INTEGRATE READINGS ONE AND TWO

◀ SKILLS

Organize information from the readings in a chart; view the ideas from the perspective of the people in the texts.

STEP 1: Organize   Suggested Time: 15 minutes

1. Look at the chart with students. You may want to elicit examples for the first topic, "year built," together as a class.

2. Have students complete the chart individually, then compare their charts in pairs. You might want to put a "master" chart on the board and use the students' answers to fill in your chart.

STEP 2: Synthesize   Suggested Time: 20 minutes

1. Have students read the instructions and decide whether they want to be Bill Gates or Henry David Thoreau. Have them write their five questions. Move around the room and offer help with the structure and vocabulary of the questions as needed.

2. Have students get into pairs so each pair has one "Bill Gates" and one "Henry David Thoreau." Have them exchange papers and write their answers. Leave time for students to get their papers back and read the answers their partners wrote.

Go to www.mynorthstarlab.com for *Notetaking* and *Academic Skills Practice*.

③ FOCUS ON WRITING

Ⓐ VOCABULARY

◖ SKILLS

Review vocabulary from Readings One and Two; expand understanding of vocabulary through knowledge of word forms and usage; expand vocabulary through study of analogies; use new vocabulary creatively in a cohesive piece of writing.

✪ REVIEW   Suggested Time: 10 minutes

 Go to www.mynorthstarlab.com for *Review*.

1. Review what an antonym is with the class. Have students read the instructions and do the first one together as a class.

2. Have students complete the exercise individually in class or for homework.

✪✪ EXPAND   Suggested Time: 20 minutes

1. Look at the charts in **Exercise 1** with the class. Remind students how sometimes nouns and verbs are spelled the same. Have students work individually to complete the chart. You might want to encourage students to consult each other and their dictionaries before they consult you for the forms they don't know.

2. Check the answers as a class, with students reading their answers aloud to practice pronunciation. Suggest that students try to put the words in sentences to help clarify the meanings for them.

3. Look at the instructions in **Exercise 2** with students. Suggest that they first ascertain which word form is needed in the sentence before deciding which word to choose. Then have students work individually to complete the exercise. Check the words that cause problems as a class, reviewing the function of the word form needed in each blank.

○ CREATE   Suggested Time: 20 minutes

Have students work individually to write responses to the questions as either Bill Gates or Henry David Thoreau. Remind students to use six to ten of the vocabulary words from Exercises 1 and 2 in their responses. Then have students share their responses with a partner.

 Go to www.mynorthstarlab.com for additional *Vocabulary* practice.

✪✪ B GRAMMAR: Future Progressive

 Go to www.mynorthstarlab.com for *Grammar Chart* and *Exercise 2*.

◖ SKILLS

Examine and identify sentences in the readings that are written in the future progressive, and use them in writing with correct use of the auxiliary verb and the correct time phrases, when appropriate.

Suggested Time: 25 minutes

1. For **Exercise 1**, have students work in pairs to read the paragraph and answer the questions that follow.

2. Go over each point in the chart, eliciting more examples and writing them on the board. You may want to draw a timeline on the board to illustrate the time relationship between two actions.

3. Read the instructions for **Exercise 2**. Go over the example. Have students work individually to complete the exercise before reviewing answers with the class.

4. Read the instructions for **Exercise 3** with the class. Check students' comprehension of *tentative*. Have students read the calendar. Then have them read the revised calendar and the remaining instructions. Go over the example with the class.

5. Have students complete the exercise individually. Go over the answers together as a class.

Expansion/Homework
(1) Students can complete the exercises at home and then go over the answers in class. You could also have students expand Exercise 3 and write a paragraph describing Sam's travel plans or trip. (2) For further practice, offer exercises from *Focus on Grammar 4, 3rd Edition* and Azar's *Understanding and Using English Grammar, 3rd Edition*. See the Grammar Book References on page 268 of the student book for specific units and chapters.

 Go to www.mynorthstarlab.com for additional *Grammar* practice.

C WRITING

If you wish to assign a different writing task than the one in this section, see page 258. The Alternative Writing Topics can also be assigned as additional writing topics for homework. The alternative topics relate to the theme of the unit, but may not target the same grammar or rhetorical structures taught in the unit.

◀ SKILLS

Use flowcharts to organize ideas; use signal words; integrate the concepts, vocabulary, grammar, and style focus from the unit to write a cause and effect essay.

✪✪✪ PREPARE TO WRITE: Using a Flowchart

Suggested Time: 10 minutes

1. Read the introductory material on the essay topic with the class. You could put students in groups or pairs to brainstorm their initial thoughts on the effects technology has had on society with each other as a pre-writing technique.

2. Read the background information on flowcharts and the instructions with students. Have them determine individually whether the effects are positive or negative before putting them in pairs to compare and discuss their answers to the questions in **Exercise 1**.

3. For **Exercise 2**, have students create their own flowcharts and mark the effects as positive or negative.

✪✪✪ WRITE: A Cause and Effect Essay

Suggested Time: 30 minutes

1. Have students read the background information on the three possible ways to organize cause and effect essays.

2. Have students read the excerpt and answer the questions in **Exercise 1** in pairs. You might want to point out that in this excerpt, the information highway is causing one main negative effect, which then in turn is causing others.

3. Have students read the boxed information on the different ways to organize cause and effect essays.

4. Go over the instructions in **Exercise 2** with students and then have them answer the questions in pairs.

5. Have students read the outline for Bill Gates's opinion on the Internet in **Exercise 3**. You might want to have students discuss the cause and effect relationships in the information in the outline.

6. Read the instructions for **Exercise 4** and the boxed information with students. Have them complete the outline individually in class or for homework.

7. Read the instructions for **Exercise 5** with the class. You may want to suggest to students that they try making their outlines in different ways to see which works better for what they want to say.

8. Have students make their outlines while you move around the room to offer individual help. Then have them discuss the outlines with a partner. Tell them to ask each other questions about their outlines and the relationships between the information in them.

9. Go over the instructions for **Exercise 6** with students. Have them write their first drafts in class or at home.

✪✪✪ REVISE: Signal Words: Subordinators, Prepositional Phrases, and Transitions

Suggested Time: 25 minutes

1. Go over the background information on using signal words to show cause and effect with the class. Have students read the boxed information individually, or alternatively, go over each section with students, checking comprehension as you go along.

2. Go over the instructions for **Exercise 1** with students. Have them read the paragraph all the way through before attempting to fill in the blanks. You might want to have students label the sentences and clauses as either cause or effect to help them. Then go over their answers as a class.

3. Read the instructions for **Exercise 2** with the class. Explain that many of the sentences can be combined in more than one way with each signal word.

4. Have students complete the exercise individually for homework. Tell them to pay special attention to the punctuation used with each term or phrase. Then go over their answers as a class, eliciting all the various possibilities.

5. For **Exercise 3**, have students review their own drafts for signal words, grammatical problems, and mechanical errors. Move around the room and make comments where appropriate.

⊗⊗⊗ EDIT: Writing the Final Draft

Suggested Time: 25 minutes

Have students write the final draft of their essays. Encourage them to use language and grammar from the unit. Make sure they go through the checklist before submitting their final drafts. Collect the essays and correct them before the next class.

Expansion/Homework
Choose some of the better student essays to illustrate good examples of cause and effect essays, future progressive, and signal words. You can also choose to use student essays to illustrate the topics in the final draft checklist.

 Link to *Northstar: Listening and Speaking 4*
Have the students write an essay on cell phone etiquette and technology today or on noise pollution using information from Unit 10 of the *Listening and Speaking* strand.

 Go to www.mynorthstarlab.com for *Writing the Final Draft*.

✪ ALTERNATIVE WRITING TOPICS

These topics give students an alternative opportunity to explore and write about issues related to the unit theme.

✪ RESEARCH TOPICS

Suggested Time: 20 minutes in class

1. Look at the chart on page 266 and discuss with the class the types of things they can put in each category. Then have them complete the charts, first individually and then in pairs. Have pairs share the results of their discussions.

2. For Step 2, have students think of additional questions and submit them to you for comments and corrections before they conduct their interviews. Students may want to record their interviews and then play the recorded interview in class.

3. Students should take notes during the interview and then write a report summarizing it.

 Go to www.mynorthstarlab.com for *Student Writing Models, Integrated Task, Video Activity, Internet Activity,* and *Unit 10 Achievement Test*.

Student Book Answer Key

UNIT 1

1B SHARE INFORMATION, page 2

1. a
2. b
3. *Suggested answer:* People are only interested in shocking or bad news.
4. *Suggested answer:* The news we receive is controlled by the media.

1C BACKGROUND AND VOCABULARY

2, page 3

1. point of view
2. valid
3. claim
4. assumptions
5. related
6. suffering
7. explain
8. imagine
9. decision
10. examination

READ FOR MAIN IDEAS, page 6

1. a
2. a
3. b
4. b

READ FOR DETAILS, page 6

2. politicians
3. Peter Jennings and the Gennifer Flowers story
4. Oliver Sipple, Rosa Lopez

MAKE INFERENCES, page 7

1. disagrees — paragraph 6
2. disagrees — paragraph 6
3. disagrees — paragraph 6
4. disagrees — paragraph 12
5. agrees — paragraph 5
6. agrees — paragraph 12

1, page 8

Suggested answers:

1. After Jewell discovered the bomb, people were probably grateful and had a lot of respect for him.
2. After Jewell was accused, people were suspicious of him and thought badly of him.
3. The media scrutiny was probably very upsetting. His private life became public.

2, page 9

Suggested answers:

1. He could not work.
2. He could not visit friends.
3. He didn't go out. He could not walk the dog without being followed.
4. Reporters and photographers took all privacy from him.

STEP 1: Organize, page 10

Center box: hounded by media, lost private life, suffered anguish

Richard Jewell: security guard, crime suspect

Oliver Sipple: sexual orientation revealed, ex-marine

Rosa Lopez: maid, retired to native country

Rosa Lopez and Richard Jewell: stopped working

Richard Jewell and Oliver Sipple: hailed as a hero

Oliver Sipple and Rosa Lopez: key witnesses

REVIEW, pages 11–12

2. allegations
3. legitimate
4. suspect
5. besieged
6. scrutiny
7. relevant
8. anguish
9. beg
10. justified
11. judgment
12. Suppose

EXPAND

1, pages 13–14

2. a
3. c
4. a
5. b
6. b
7. c
8. b
9. a
10. b

2, page 14

1. c
2. a
3. e, f
4. d
5. b
6. e

3B GRAMMAR

1, page 15

1. This structure is different from the structure of the active sentences. The grammar structure in the passive sentences is reversed. **Object + *be* + past participle.** Sometimes the person or thing responsible for the action is used, too (***by* + agent**).
2. a hitchhiker, cameras and reporters, people
3. the minister, Rosa Lopez, Richard Jewell
4. The minister, Rosa Lopez, and Richard Jewell are the focus of the passive sentences. The words in the subject position in the passive sentences do not perform the action.

2, page 17

2. was broadcast OR was broadcasted
3. was justified
4. did not return
5. were found
6. decided

7. was read
8. pointed
9. was deflected
10. were questioned

3, pages 17–18

1. was completed
2. was interviewed by the FBI
3. was shot
4. was convicted by the media
5. was married
6. was written by Peter Jennings
7. was found guilty

WRITE

1, page 20

1. News is everywhere.
2. News is everywhere. It serves many different functions.
3. All sentences relate to the ideas in the topic sentence.

2, pages 20–21

1. c   2. b   3. b   4. c

3, page 21

Answers will vary. Suggested answers:

2. The way we receive the news has changed over the years.
3. The media should inform us if a public figure, such as a president, is unfaithful.
4. Reading, like exercise, requires discipline and hard work.

REVISE

1, page 23

Answers will vary. Suggested answers:

1. At first / In the beginning / Initially
2. Later / Then
3. subsequently / then
4. Before
5. After
6. later
7. In the end / Finally / Eventually

UNIT 2

1B SHARE INFORMATION

1, page 26

1. c   2. d   3. a   4. b

2, page 26

Anne Frank had to overcome living in hiding with the fear of being found: physical and emotional obstacles

Lance Armstrong had to overcome cancer: physical obstacle

Walt Disney had to overcome poverty: economic obstacle

Amelia Earhart had to overcome sexism and lack of money: social and economic obstacles

1C BACKGROUND AND VOCABULARY

2, page 27

1. His parents had no money. His father abandoned the family. There was not enough food. They had a small, old house.
2. He enjoyed reading.
3. He was ashamed of his past.

3, page 27

2. meager
3. shame
4. defeated
5. yearned for
6. tormented
7. sordid
8. poverty
9. abandonment
10. hopelessness
11. dilapidated

2A READING ONE, page 28

1. He is in New York.
2. *Suggested answer:* Even though he was the teacher, his students taught him a lot about the world—and himself.
3. *Suggested answer:* He had a successful teaching career.

READ FOR MAIN IDEAS, page 31

1970: Frank McCourt begins teaching at Seward Park High School.

1981: Frank McCourt's mother dies.

1994: Frank McCourt begins to write his book.

1996: *Angela's Ashes* hits the bookstores.

1997: *Angela's Ashes* receives the Pulitzer Prize.

READ FOR DETAILS, page 32

Answers will vary. Suggested answers:

1949 Event: Frank McCourt returned to the United States.	Frank McCourt was 19 years old. He wanted to start a new life.
1970 Event: Frank McCourt began teaching at Seward Park High School.	He began teaching and using his past to connect with his students. His students loved his stories and as he told his stories he realized how his past affected him.
1981 Event: Frank McCourt's mother died.	After his mother died, he realized he had no excuses not to write his memoirs. While his mother was alive, McCourt chose not to write about his childhood out of respect for his mother.
1994 Event: Frank McCourt began to write his book.	He struggled to write his memoirs. It was very difficult at first. He had to dig deep into his past.
1996 Event: *Angela's Ashes* hit the bookstores.	Frank McCourt finally finished his memoirs and named it *Angela's Ashes*. Within weeks, it became a bestseller.
1997 Event: *Angela's Ashes* received the Pulitzer Prize.	Because the book was so good, it won a major award, the Pulitzer Prize. Frank McCourt became famous.

MAKE INFERENCES, pages 32–33

Answers will vary. Suggested answers:

1. People who come from nothing have no value.
2. He recognizes himself and his challenges at their age.
3. He ignored his past prior to teaching.
4. Write about what you know and with your own voice. Don't copy other's ideas.
5. He is suggesting that he has not taken chances with his writing and he should.

2B READING TWO

1, page 34

Answers will vary. Suggested answers:

1. She changed the way we think about people with disabilities.
2. She became an accomplished musician even though she was blind.

2, pages 35–36

Answers will vary. Suggested answers:

1. Schuur and Keller are both blind. They are artistic and enjoy performing in front of people. They were freed from isolation through reading and language. They also needed to be touched by people. Schuur and Keller are different in that Schuur can hear whereas Keller couldn't. In addition, learning to speak was much easier for Schuur because she can hear.

2. • People with handicaps are very capable and should be treated like anyone else.
   • Because blind people can't see, they need some other way to feel connected to people. Being physically touched is one way to feel this connection. In the case of Diane Schuur, she also gets this connection through an audience's appreciation of her music.

STEP 1: Organize, page 36

Answers will vary. Suggested answers:

		Frank McCourt	Diane Schuur
1.	Obstacles they faced	Poverty, abandonment, lack of formal education	Loss of sight
2.	People or person who influenced and inspired them	His students and his mother	Helen Keller
3.	Personal values, traits, or characteristics that helped them face their obstacles	Humor, reading and writing	Reading, playing music
4.	Talent or gift that resulted from the challenges they faced	Writing	Playing music

REVIEW, page 37

Answers will vary. Suggested answers:

Facing an obstacle: confused, darkest, defeated, disenfranchised, hopelessness, isolation, misery, mortified, yearning

Dealing with an obstacle: inquisitiveness, liberate, struggle, transformation

Overcoming an obstacle: achievement, exalted, extraordinary, freedom, master, paradise, utopia

EXPAND, pages 37–38

1. synonym / c
2. antonym / a
3. antonym / b
4. synonym / c
5. antonym / a
6. synonym / c
7. synonym / b
8. synonym / a
9. synonym / c

3B GRAMMAR

1, pages 38–39

1. teaching
2. writing about his childhood
3. reading
4. the base form of the verb + *ing*
5. to deliver
6. New York University, to enroll
7. to write
8. to be
9. *to* + the base form of the verb

2, page 40

b.	6	g.	5
c.	2	h.	1
d.	5	i.	3
e.	4c	j.	4b
f.	4a		

3, pages 40–41

2. As a child, Helen Keller wanted to communicate with people, but she couldn't.
3. McCourt persuaded New York University to allow him to go there.
4. Diane Schuur enjoys performing in front of a crowd.
5. McCourt worried about telling his students that he hadn't gone to high school.
6. Diane Schuur decided to return to the school for the blind.
7. McCourt urged his students to write.
8. It was hard for Helen Keller to learn language.
9. McCourt recalled living in Limerick.
10. Diane Schuur was able to choose which school to go to.

WRITE

1, pages 43–44

1. Overcoming obstacles is the topic of the paragraph. It is in the first and third sentences.
2. The world is full of people who have overcome obstacles and benefited from overcoming them.
3. Underlined sentences: For example, Greg Barton, the 1984, 1988, and 1992 U.S. Olympic medalist in kayaking, was born with a serious disability. He had club feet, his toes pointed inward, and as a result, he could not walk easily. Even after a series of operations, he still had limited mobility. Even so, Greg was never defeated. First, he taught himself to walk, and to even run. Then, he competed on his high school running team. He knew, though, he would never become an Olympic runner, so he looked for other sports that he could play. Happily, he discovered kayaking, a perfect sport for him because it required minimal leg and foot muscles. Using his upper body strength, he was able to master the sport. Finally, after many years of training and perseverance, Greg made the 1984 Olympic team.

These sentences tell how Greg Barton overcame his obstacles and benefited from overcoming them.
4. The concluding sentence is: In short, even though that road was paved with obstacles, he was able to overcome them and achieve the impossible. It summarizes the paragraph.

REVISE

1, pages 44–45

2. Cross out: c
3. Cross out: b
4. Cross out: b

2, page 45

2. Cross out: They are all great writers or musicians. Explanation: The sentence focuses on their talents, not how reading liberated them.
3. Cross out: Furthermore, he lives in England. Explanation: The sentence focuses on where Steven Hawking lives, not on overcoming obstacles.

UNIT 3

1C BACKGROUND AND VOCABULARY

2, pages 49–50

1.	ramifications	7.	effective
2.	debate	8.	acknowledge
3.	treatments	9.	principles
4.	conventional	10.	deny
5.	violate	11.	ailments
6.	entitled		

2A READING ONE, page 50

1. Amy became very sick.
2. Because Amy was very sick and wasn't getting better.
3. *Answers will vary.*

READ FOR MAIN IDEAS, pages 52–53

Answers will vary. Suggested answers:

1. diabetes.
2. she had gone to the doctor.
3. they did not seek conventional medical help.
4. they believe the Hermansons did not hurt their daughter.
5. a. parents' freedom of religion;
   b. a child's right to grow up healthy.

READ FOR DETAILS, page 53

1. T, paragraph 13
2. T, paragraph 10

3. F, paragraphs 2,11, 12. Some of the symptoms of Amy's disease were loss of weight, stomachaches, and dozing off in class.
4. T, paragraph 19
5. T, paragraph 24
6. F, paragraph 21. In Florida, parents can't be judged "abusive or neglectful."

MAKE INFERENCES, pages 53–54

1. b, c   6. a
2. d, e   7. b
3. c, f   8. e
4. f   9. d
5. d, e   10. b

2B READING TWO

1, page 54

Answers will vary. Suggested answers:

1. If you are sick and you think you will get better, you will.
2. Charlie Chaplin is a funny person. He makes people laugh. Laughter helps you feel positive.

2, pages 55–56

Answers will vary. Suggested answers:

1. He was diagnosed with a very serious form of arthritis. He decided to fight the disease.
2. If negative emotions bring negative changes to the body, positive emotions should bring positive changes. Laughter has a positive therapeutic value.
3. Watching funny movies and reading funny books are examples of laugh therapy.
4. He was able to overcome his disease.

STEP 1: Organize, page 56

Answers will vary. Suggested answers:

Both the Hermansons and Norman Cousins:
• Used nonconventional treatments
• Believed conventional medicine is not the only answer

The Hermansons:
• Used prayer
• Saw a practitioner but not a doctor
• Chose alternative therapy for their child, Amy
• Amy died

Norman Cousins:
• Invented his own nonconventional treatment
• Used laugh therapy
• Saw a doctor and used laugh therapy in conjunction with conventional medicine

• Was an adult who made his own choice to use alternative therapy
• Was cured
• Lived 25 more years after using laugh therapy

REVIEW, page 57

2. D	5. S	8. S	11. S
3. S	6. S	9. D	12. D
4. S	7. D	10. D	

EXPAND, pages 57–58

2. a	6. c
3. b	7. b
4. c	8. a
5. b	

3B GRAMMAR

1, pages 58–59

1. T / F
2. T / T
3. T / F

2, page 60

2. F / F	6. F / T
3. T / T	7. T / T
4. F / T	8. F / F
5. T / T	

3, page 61

Answers will vary. Suggested answers:

2. If Peter Deering had used alternative medical treatments, he might have felt better.
3. If Cousins hadn't read extensively about alternative medicine, he might not have tried alternative treatments.
4. Cousins might not have gotten better if he hadn't tried laugh therapy.
5. If William Bullard had been a Christian Scientist, he wouldn't have given his daughter drugs when she was sick.
6. If the teacher hadn't noticed Amy's dozing off in class, she wouldn't have called Amy's parents.
7. If Cousins had liked his doctor's treatment plan, he wouldn't have developed his own laugh therapy treatment.

WRITE

1, pages 63–64

THREE PARTS OF AN ESSAY	NOTES
I. Introduction:	Background information:
Thesis Statement: I believe in the power of spiritual healing and the right of families to choose the treatment they feel is most effective.	• Loving and devoted parent • President of parent-teacher association • Harvard graduate • Lawyer • Christian Scientist
II. Body Paragraph 1 Topic: Personal experience with spiritual healing	**Body Paragraph 1 Support / Evidence:** • Her blood disorder and cure by practitioners' prayers • Experience with her own children
Body Paragraph 2 Topic: Christian Scientists are not breaking the law nor are they irresponsible	**Body Paragraph 2 Support / Evidence:** • Right guaranteed by the Constitution • Scientific studies prove cure of people considered incurable
III. Conclusion: Restate the Thesis I hope that people won't stop looking for alternative treatments because the Hermansons have been found guilty.	
Final Thought / Wrap Up Remember, children die as the result of conventional medical treatment, too, and no one accuses the parents of these unfortunate children of negligence nor brings them to court.	

REVISE

2, page 65

Effective Hooks: 2, 5, 6

UNIT 4

1C BACKGROUND AND VOCABULARY, pages 68–69

1. d 4. j 7. a 10. c
2. k 5. i 8. l 11. h
3. f 6. b 9. e 12. g

READ FOR MAIN IDEAS, pages 73–74

1. 7 4. 10
2. 11 / 12 5. 4
3. 2

READ FOR DETAILS, page 74

Main Ideas	Supporting Ideas
1. Scientists' ideas about exactly what animal intelligence is have changed over time.	• Before the 1960s, scientists believed <u>animals acted without thinking</u>. • Nowadays, scientists think <u>some animals have mental abilities</u>.
2. Trained animals are not exhibiting intelligence because they don't understand what they are doing.	• Many animals appear to be behaving intelligently, but they are simply <u>repeating behaviors they have been trained to do</u>. • For example, the duck that plays the guitar does not <u>understand or appreciate music</u>.
3. Clever Hans wasn't really exhibiting intelligence; he was acting based on cues from people around him.	• Clever Hans was simply observing <u>people's responses</u>. • If no one in the audience knew the answer to the question, Hans <u>could not answer</u>.
4. Scientists' ideas about exactly what human intelligence is are being reevaluated.	• Older, standard IQ tests only measure <u>math</u> and <u>language skills</u>, but not <u>creativity</u>. • However, more than <u>100 factors</u> of intelligence have been written about in <u>scientific literature</u>.
5. Testing animal intelligence is problematic because the idea of intelligence must be seen from the perspective of the animal.	• What is important to an animal is <u>different</u> than what is important to a <u>human</u>. • Therefore tests of animal intelligence must involve situations that <u>have meaning to their lives</u>.

MAKE INFERENCES, pages 75–76

Answers will vary. Suggested answers:

Gracious Gorilla: Perhaps Binki responded to this situation due to animal instinct to protect her young. This is a similar situation to the dog, Villa.

Musical Monkeys: Perhaps these monkeys have simply learned this behavior through training similar to the animals being trained at the IQ Zoo.

Parlez-vous Prairie Dog: This could be an example of animal intelligence because they have developed this form of communication on their own in their own environment.

2B READING TWO

2, page 78

Answers will vary. Suggested answers:

1. Seizure alert dogs are different from seizure response dogs because <u>they were not trained to be seizure alert dogs</u>.
2. Clever Hans and seizure alert dogs are similar because they both <u>aquired their skills without human help. They also applied their skills to new situations.</u>
3. Clever Hans knew when to start or stop tapping his hoof because <u>he "read" / understood people's responses.</u>
4. For Clever Hans to correctly answer a question, two conditions had to be met:
   a. <u>someone in the audience knew the answer</u>
   b. <u>the person was in plain view</u>

STEP 1: Organize, page 79

1. think in a human way / have understood human language / have mastered arithmetic
2. think on his own / "read" the responses of the audience
3. instinct / intelligence
4. very intelligent
5. are just repeating behavior patterns
6. in situations that have meaning to them / just to humans
7. trained to / act / they are intelligent

REVIEW, page 80

Crossed-out words:

1.	signal	5.	gathering	9.	activity
2.	answer	6.	report	10.	attempts
3.	believe	7.	worked	11.	decay
4.	build	8.	characteristics	12.	offered

EXPAND, pages 80–81

Answers in the last two columns will vary. Suggested answers:

Root	Meaning	Reading-Paragraph	Word	Meaning	Other Words with the Same Root
2. cogni-	know/ learn	R2-2 R2-10	cognition recognizing	understanding	cognitive
3. dict-	say/tell	R2-2	predict	to say something will happen	dictation
4. sign-	mark	R1-4	signaling	to send signals	design

Root	Meaning	Reading-Paragraph	Word	Meaning	Other Words with the Same Root
5. cent-	one hundred	R1-5 R2-3	centuries percent	100-year periods; an amount equal to a particular number of parts in every 100 parts	centipede
6. numer-	number	R1-6	numerical	expressed or considered in numbers	innumerable
7. aud-	hear/ listen	R1-7	audience	a group of people who watch and listen to a concert, speech, movie, etc.	audition
8. spect-	see/look	R1-4	spectacular	very impressive and exciting to see or look at	inspect
9. sens-	feeling	R1-7 R2-4	sensitive sense	able to understand other people's feelings; feeling about something	sensible

3B GRAMMAR

1, pages 81–82

1. meaningful situations
2. a person about to have a seizure
3. the afternoon he was able to figure out how Clever Hans was able to answer the questions
4. *that, who, when* / nouns or noun phrases

2, pages 82–83

2.	correct	alternative: in which
3.	incorrect	corrections: which/that
4.	incorrect	correction: whose
5.	correct	alternative: that
6.	correct	alternative: which
7.	incorrect	corrections: who/that
8.	incorrect	corrections: in which/where

3, pages 83–84

Answers will vary. Suggested answers:

3. Binti the gorilla is best known for an amazing incident **which / that** occurred on August 16, 1996.
4. I spoke with a man **who / that** had trained dolphins and killer whales.
5. Psychologists study many animals **which / that** live in zoos.
6. I saw my friend **whose** dog could predict seizures before they started.

7. We saw the dolphin **which / that** performed some spectacular feats.
8. The psychologist **who** developed a new test for animal intelligence had studied at the University of Berlin. OR The psychologist **who** had studied at the University of Berlin developed a new test for animal intelligence.
9. The morning **when** Lulu the pig saved Mrs. Altsman was sunny ands hot.
10. The girl **who / that** was saved by Villa the dog was covered in snow.

WRITE

1, pages 86–87

1. Dorothy Hinshaw is the author of the book *How Smart is Smart.*
2. Scientists in the past fifty years have changed their opinion about what animal intelligence is.
3. Scientists now believe that animals act in ways that show great intelligence, not just instinctual behavior.
4. Hinshaw concludes that when we test animals for intelligence we must test them against measures that have meaning for them, not measures that have meaning for humans. Finding these measures is difficult.

2, pages 87–88

1. a
2. b
3. c
4. a

Answers will vary. Suggested answers:

5. Because of Clever Hans, scientists are careful about attributing intelligence to animals, but perhaps they have become too careful.
6. Scientists have shown that intelligence involves many factors, so it is difficult and complex to measure it.

UNIT 5

1C BACKGROUND AND VOCABULARY, pages 92–93

1. b	4. c	7. c	10. a
2. a	5. c	8. a	11. b
3. b	6. b	9. b	12. c

READ FOR MAIN IDEAS, pages 97–98

Answers will vary. Suggested answers:

Marriage: Marriage is not seen as a lifelong commitment. People assume they will have many marriages to a wide variety of people who will enhance their lives.

Family structure / Relationships: Because people live for hundreds of years there can be 10 or 20 generations of the family living at the same time.

Careers: People will change their careers many times and their careers will be vastly different.

Longevity: No one seems to know how long the human lifespan can be with the Process, but so far, no one has died in the 400 years since the Process was invented.

READ FOR DETAILS, page 98

Answers will vary. Suggested answers:

Topic	Marilisa	Leo
Marriage	First marriage Assumes she'll be married again to a variety of men.	Has been married seven times.
Family Structure/Relationships	Has to deal with multiple stepchildren, much older than her, and ex wives.	Has great relationships with all of his ex-wives and children.
Careers	Has not yet chosen a career, but knows she has lots of time to decide and that she will have the opportunity to have many careers.	Has had at least fifteen or twenty careers, all of them very different. Does this so he always has a challenge—doesn't get bored.
Longevity	Has had her first Prep, but has not yet undergone the Process. Sees an unlimited future	Faithfully does his Process and has been alive for almost four hundred years. Still vigorous and youthful.

MAKE INFERENCES, page 99

1. T
Supporting evidence: One of Leo's previously unknown children turned up unexpectedly.
2. F
Supporting evidence: He is three times (or more) older than Marilisa and yet jokes about being with her after his father tires of her.
3. T
Supporting evidence: He talks humorously about his past.
4. T
Supporting evidence: No one able to afford the Process has died. In other words, some people can't afford it because of the expense.
5. T
Supporting evidence: Leo has done the Process faithfully and it has kept him as dashing and vigorous as a boy.

6. T

Supporting evidence: He jokes about being able to play with her when Leo is done with her.

7. T

Supporting evidence: Marilisa is disturbed by the idea of having the same husband for hundreds of years, but, at the same time, is disturbed by the idea of having many different husbands. She also worries about the "vast amount of time" that is in front of her.

STEP 1: Organize, page 102

Suggested answers:

EFFECT

MARRIAGE Positive Effect	MARRIAGE Negative Effect
R1 you will be able to have many different and interesting spouses **R2** you won't feel you have to stay in a loveless marriage out of inertia	**R1** extremely large age difference between spouses **R2** multiple brief marriages
CAREERS Positive Effect	**CAREERS Negative Effect**
R1 you can "reinvent" yourself by changing careers and finding a fresh challenge **R2** economic productivity will go up; you can try different careers	**R1** no negative effects **R2** fewer job openings; corporations and universities will stagnate without youthful talent and ideas
FAMILY STRUCTURE Positive Effect	**FAMILY STRUCTURE Negative Effect**
R1 No positive effects **R2** more quality time with loved ones; watch future generations grow up	**R1** have to deal with multiple ex-wives / husbands and stepchildren **R2** large age difference in siblings would create different set of social relationships

REVIEW, page 103

Answers may vary. Suggested answers:

Positive	Negative	Neutral
awesome	chilly	disparate
fond	impetuous	immeasurably
punctually	insufferable	simultaneously
vigorous	loveless	tolerable
	presumptuous	ultimately
	worrisome	utterly

EXPAND, pages 104–106

Answers in the last column may vary. Suggested answers:

Death Do Us Part

Suffixes	Example from Text	Definition or Synonym	Example of a New Adjective with the Same Suffix
Paragraphs 1–2			
-ing	shimmering	sparkling	speeding
-ive	impulsive	impetuous	descriptive
Paragraphs 3–5			
-able	insufferable	intolerable	comfortable
-al	ideal	perfect	traditional
Paragraphs 6–15			
-ent	ancient	very old	different
-ous	serious	sincere	curious
Paragraphs 26–33			
-ible	permissible	allowable	invisible
-ic	romantic	passionate	emphatic
Paragraphs 34–38			
-y	misty	foggy	dirty

Toward Immortality

Suffixes	Example from Text	Definition or Synonym	Example of a New Adjective with the Same Suffix
Paragraphs 1–2			
-al	personal	individual	minimal
Paragraphs 3–4			
-ical	practical	sensible	tropical
Paragraphs 5–7			
-less	loveless	without love	homeless
-ing	remaining	still left	smoking
Paragraphs 11–13			
-ed	limited	restricted	skilled
-some	worrisome	troublesome	awesome
-ant	constant	steady	elegant
-ful	youthful	young	hopeful

3B GRAMMAR

1, page 107

1. It happened three years ago.
2. No, he *has been* an architect . . . not he *is*.
3. Yes, they are still searching because the verb is in the continuous form, *searching*, and the sentence states *since the beginning of recorded time*, which is when they started searching.
4. simple past in *a*, present perfect in *b*, and present perfect continuous in *c*.

2, pages 108–109

1. have been searching
2. has been
3. have not been
4. took
5. attended
6. didn't actually start
7. have gone
8. discussed
9. has been doing
10. have had
11. have enjoyed
12. completed
13. has been working

3, pages 109–110

1. has met
2. bought
3. visited
4. has had
5. has been talking
6. met
7. have been studying
8. have figured
9. attended
10. has been doing
11. has written

WRITE

1, page 112

1. The thesis statement is: "My life has been an endless roller coaster ride filled with immeasurable happiness and sadness."

The next paragraphs of the essay will probably be about this happiness and sadness.

Touch: shakes awake

Smell: bitter coffee, burnt toast

Sight: alarm robot, meteor shower

Taste: sour milk, bitter coffee

Sound: loud crack

REVISE

1, page 113

His home is being compared to a lonely cloud because it floats in the sky.

His punctuality is being compared to a Swiss watch because a Swiss watch is precise and dependable.

2, page 113

Paragraph 1: Waterfalls are being compared to cascades of diamonds because they shimmer.

Paragraph 2: Leo is being compared to a boy because he looks so young.

Paragraph 34: Unknown husbands are being compared to swords that fall between Marilisa and Leo because they will destroy her marriage.

3, pages 113–114

The metaphor is: *They are vague chilly phantoms*. She uses this metaphor because they are not real and they are scary like ghosts.

4, page 114

An example of personification is: *The words skewer her*. She uses this personification because hearing the words hurts, as it would hurt if something sharp were pressed into a person.

UNIT 6

1A PREDICT, page 115

Mother Teresa

Bill Gates

Angelina Jolie

Oprah Winfrey

1C BACKGROUND AND VOCABULARY

1, page 116

2. modestly
3. pride
4. amusement
5. uncertain
6. order
7. sell
8. boring
9. appreciate
10. saddened
11. respond
12. scared

2, pages 117–118

1. challenge / manage
   Reason: personal and medical research
2. passion / thrilled / inspired
   Reason: environmental and personal
3. passion / satisfaction / inspired / proudly
   Reason: religious and personal
4. proposal / devote
   Reason: mandatory and personal
5. admiring / determined
   Reason: political and personal

2A READING ONE, page 119

Answers will vary. Suggested answers:

1. The bicycle is in bad condition.
2. Justin wants to fix the bicycle or find another use for it.
3. *Answers will vary.*

READ FOR MAIN IDEAS, page 122

Answers will vary. Suggested answers:

2. Justin needed to find a way to get a lot of used bikes.
3. Justin was able to fix up and donate hundreds of bikes because of the support of his parents and community.
5. Justin is a special boy because he likes to help others.

READ FOR DETAILS, pages 122–123

Answers will vary. Suggested answers:

The Benefits of Community Service	Example of Justin Lebo
Gives a sense of satisfaction and builds self-esteem	After Justin built the first bikes for the Kilbarchin boys, he felt very good knowing that they loved the bikes.
Opens people's eyes to the great variety of people in need	Justin built bikes for all kinds of people in need: women in a women's shelter, people with AIDS, and people in a housing project.
One successful community service experience leads to performing other services	Justin continued to build bikes after the Kilbarchin project.
Helps people to find out who they are, what their interests are, and what they are good at	Justin found out he could take on a big project and complete it. He found out he was good at rebuilding bikes.

MAKE INFERENCES, pages 123–124

1. c   4. a
2. c   5. a
3. b   6. b

2B READING TWO

2, page 127

Answers will vary. Suggested answers:

For Mandatory Volunteering	Against Mandatory Volunteering
1. Constructive way to spend time.	1. Volunteering is a personal choice.
	2. It's an extracurricular activity (personal choice).
2. Gets kids involved in the community.	3. Many students already volunteer.
3. Some people would not know how great an experience volunteering is unless it were required.	4. Students may become resentful and never volunteer again.
	5. Many students don't have time.
	6. The quality of work can suffer.

STEP 1: Organize, page 127

Issues	Reading 1	Reading 2
1. Personal enrichment	Paragraph 24	Paragraphs 5, 10
2. Time commitment	Paragraph 23	Paragraphs 12,13
3. Personal choice	Paragraphs 11, 24	Paragraph 11
4. Dedication to work	Paragraph 22	Paragraphs 4, 14

REVIEW

2, page 130

1. donations
2. inspired
3. passionate
4. challenge
5. proposed
6. resentful
7. opposition

EXPAND, pages 130–131

1. a   3. c   5. c   7. c   9. c
2. b   4. b   6. c   8. b   10. b

3B GRAMMAR

1, page 133

1. Even though Justin was not required by his school to volunteer / he chose to work on bikes and donate them.

   In spite of the fact that many students initially don't want to volunteer / they learn to love it and continue after the school requirements are fulfilled.

   It is a good idea to get students to go out into the community / although it can be frustrating to have to write about it.

2. The concessions introduce a negative opinion.
3. No. If the sentence starts with a concession, there is a comma. If the concession is in the middle of the sentence, there is no comma.
4. The other clauses express the writer's main idea.

WRITE

1, pages 138–140

1. He / She is against cutting school sports.
2. Low team participation, low audience participation, high cost

3.

Arguments to Cut School Sports	Counter Arguments
a. low team participation	a. many teams have high participation numbers so cut back on number of teams
b. low audience participation	b. audience participation numbers are not the only way to measure student support and interest; there is a devoted fan base; sports help spread school spirit
c. high cost	c. cost is worth the long term benefits

REVISE

3, page 143

Introduction 1—Technique a
Introduction 2—Technique c
Introduction 3—Technique b

Conclusion 1—Technique c
Conclusion 2—Technique a b
Conclusion 3—Technique b a

UNIT 7

1B SHARE INFORMATION, page 146

1. 1978 = less than 200,000
    2006 = more than 2,000,000
    2010 = 3,000,000
2. *Answers will vary.*
3. *Answers will vary.*

1C BACKGROUND AND VOCABULARY

2, page 147

1. consultation	5. ambitions	9. avid
2. isolation	6. viable	10. expertise
3. eclectic	7. misconceptions	11. persistence
4. dictated	8. stimulating	

2A READING ONE, page 148

1a. fear of school violence
1b. lack of stimulating courses
2a. parents are solely responsible for instruction
2b. homeschooling inevitably leads to social isolation
2c. homeschooling inevitably leads to decreased participation in music and sports
2d. homeschooling inevitably leads to college rejection letters
3. *Answers will vary.*

READ FOR MAIN IDEAS, page 152

1. T
2. T
3. F / Homeschooling does not prevent students from integrating in their community.
4. F / Parents do not have to be highly educated to homeschool their children.
5. F / All homeschoolers do not follow the same curriculum.

READ FOR DETAILS, pages 152–153

1. a	4. a	7. a	10. b
2. a	5. c	8. c	11. a
3. c	6. c	9. c	

MAKE INFERENCES

1, pages 153–154

Answers will vary. Suggested answers:

1. happily, joy
2. dictated
3. reasonable
4. fear, violence, lack of
5. childish
6. rich, encourage, appeals
7. exemplary
8. abound, remarkable

2, page 154

Answers will vary. Suggested answers:

1. She wants to inform the reader about positive homeschooling experiences.
2. She seems to favor homeschooling over traditional schooling.
3. She chose to report only on successful homeschoolers.

2B READING TWO

2, page 158

1. Tommy discovers a book, which is important because they no longer existed at that time; all reading is done from a computer screen.
2. Margie is excited about the discovery.
3. Margie thinks they had fun in the "old days."
4. *Answer will vary. Possible answer:* He may fear that books would disappear.

STEP 1: Organize, page 158

Answers will vary. Suggested answers:

	Reading One	Reading Two
1. Is there a teacher? If yes, describe the teacher.	Nikki: No, except by correspondence. David: His mother. Andy: Parents, community college instructor, CAP instructor, piano teacher.	The teacher is a computer.
2. Where does the "school" take place?	N: At home, museum. D: At home, natural history museum. A: At home, community college, CAP.	At home
3. Who determines what the students learn and at what pace they learn?	N: American School curriculum; she determines the pace. D: He and his mother; he determines pace. A: He and his parents; his community college; CAP; piano teachers.	The computer and the inspector
4. What happens if students don't understand or can't do something?	N: She phones or writes teachers. D: Not applicable A: He asks community college, CAP, and piano teachers.	Parents, computer, and Inspector
5. When and where do students socialize with friends?	N: At her job, the beach, the museum, and other activities. D: At races and baseball and basketball games. A: At community college, CAP, and volunteering.	With neighbors, after school time, and during breaks.
6. What do the students think about being homeschooled?	They like it a lot.	They don't like it.
7. What do the students think about traditional school?	They don't like it.	They are very interested in the idea and think they would like it a lot.

REVIEW, pages 159–161

dictated	consultation
persistence	nonchalantly
isolation	viable
eclectic	misconceptions
ambition	disputed
avid	stimulating
expertise	

EXPAND, pages 161–162

Noun	Verb	Adjective	Adverb
2. consultation	consult	consulting	X
3. scorn	scorn	scornful	scornfully
4. dictation	dictate	X	X
5. persistence	persist	persistent	persistently
6. misconception	misconceive	misconceived	X
7. dispute	dispute	disputable disputed	disputably
8. expertise	X	expert	expertly
9. isolation	isolate	isolated	X
10. X	X	avid	avidly
11. ambition	X	ambitious	ambitiously
12. eclectic	X	eclectic	eclectically
13. disappointment	disappoint	disappointed	disappointedly
14. adjustment	adjust	adjusted adjustable	X
15. viability	X	viable	viably

3B GRAMMAR

1, page 165

1. Direct speech has commas and quotation marks.
2. The verb tenses used in direct speech will change in indirect speech. For example, simple present in direct speech will change to simple past in indirect speech. In addition, pronouns and possessives change to keep speaker's original meaning. The word *that* may also be added in indirect speech.

2, page 167

2. a		5. b	
3. b		6. a	
4. c		7. c	

3, page 168

2. The inspector told Margie's mother (that) he thought the geography sector had been a little too difficult.
3. He added (that) he'd slowed it up to a ten-year level.
4. Tommy said that was the old kind of school that they had had hundreds and hundreds of years before.
5. Margie told Tommy (that) her mother said a teacher had to be adjusted to fit the mind of each boy and girl it taught.
6. Tommy told Margie (that) she could read the book with him again the next day.

WRITE

1, pages 170–171

1. materials, instructor / teacher, type of student this model is best suited for
2. *Answers will vary. Suggested answers:* grading, time commitment, opportunities for socializing

2, pages 171–172

Answers will vary. Suggested answers:

1. Thesis: When you choose to homeschool, there are many things to consider: the source of your curriculum, whether or not you will have a parent, tutor or other form of guidance, the extra-curricular activities you will do to round out your education, and the type of learner you are.

   The audience is families that are interested in homeschooling.

   The subcategories are introduced in the thesis.

2. The subcategory is traditional homeschooling. The details include:

   • The curriculum is provided by the government or online institution

   • Materials: if government, they are recommended or approved by the government; if an online institution, the institution may provide them

   • Teachers: either parents or tutors; if an online institution, the teachers are online

   • This model of homeschooling is best for students who are independent and like to work at their own pace, but still need guidance and a set curriculum

3. In the next paragraph about unschooling, the details would include how students' interests determine the curriculum, using the home and local environment but no textbooks, that there is little parent/teacher involvement and that learners are self-directed and self-taught.

REVISE

1, page 173

Correct answers: 2, 6, 7
Corrections:

1. tries
3. in the early afternoon
4. stay
5. taking classes

UNIT 8

1C BACKGROUND AND VOCABULARY, pages 176–177

1. a, b
2. b, c
3. a, c
4. b, c
5. a, b
6. b, c
7. a, c
8. a, b
9. a. c
10. b, c
11. b. c
12. a, c

READ FOR MAIN IDEAS

1, page 181

Answers will vary. Suggested answers:

a. Her father was important because he was her first cooking teacher. He told her that we must eat food first with our eyes, then with our minds, then with our noses, and finally with our mouths.

b. Her mother was important because she encouraged Eileen to cook well. Cooking and its ramifications were important to her.

c. Her grandmother was important because she insisted that Eileen be involved in the family table. She made certain that Eileen was in her kitchen whenever Eileen visited her.

2, page 181

Answers will vary. Suggested answers:

• following the classical method, but not as mindless imitators
• superstition
• religion (Buddhism)
• the calendar (astrology)

READ FOR DETAILS

1, page 182

1. T, paragraph 3
2. F, paragraph 5. She knew by instinct how food should be combined. She had never even touched a spatula or wok.
3. F, paragraph 12. They only ate special dumplings during the New Year Festival. OR paragraph 13. She was an observant Buddhist who declined to eat either fish or meat on the first and the fifteenth of each month and for the first fifteen days of the New Year.
4. T, paragraph 12
5. T, paragraph 9
6. T, paragraph 4
7. T, paragraph 2

2, page 182

Answers will vary. Suggested answers:

Cooking process: When we ate raw fish, yue sahng, she taught, one had to prepare the fish in the proper manner.

You hit the fish at the front of its head to stun it, then, when it was still nominally alive, you scaled it, gutted and cleaned it, then sliced it for eating. (Paragraph 6)

Tradition: Aw Pah would consult her Tung Sing, an astrological book, for propitious days on which to begin preparing the special dumplings we made and ate during the New Year festival. (Paragraph 12)

Superstition: She cautioned me to eat every kernel of rice in my bowl, for if I did not, she warned, the man I married would have a pockmarked face, one mark for each uneaten rice kernel. (Paragraph 10)

Religious belief: She was an observant Buddhist who declined to eat either fish or meat on the first and the fifteenth of each month and for the first fifteen days of the New Year. (Paragraph 13)

MAKE INFERENCES, pages 182–183

1. He believes that before you eat any food, you need to appreciate its beauty and how it was cooked.
2. Because he cares so deeply about food.
3. Good cooks are willing and able to change recipes to improve them.
4. Because Aw Paw took her cooking very seriously.
5. Probably not, but she did realize that for Aw Paw food was very important and it should not be wasted.

2B READING TWO, page 186

Answers will vary. Suggested answers:

1. The beliefs of the Slow Food Movement are taking the time to choose, prepare, cook, and enjoy the pleasures of cooking and eating good food and drink.
2. "Local" is important because the food will be fresher.

STEP 1: Organize, pages 186–187

Eating: Her father told her people must first eat their food with their eyes, then with their minds, then with their noses, and finally with their mouths.

Food shopping: Her family shopped at the local vegetable markets frequently. Her grandmother would never eat a vegetable that had been out of the ground for more than two hours.

Family tradition: Her family had many traditions, many of them revolving around New Year's.

REVIEW, pages 187–189

1. specified
2. declined
3. necessitated
4. insisted
5. inextricably linked
6. customary
7. authentic
8. pleasurable
9. proper
10. nominally
11. leisurely
12. literally
13. deference
14. imparting
15. evident

EXPAND, page 189

1. c
2. c
3. a
4. b
5. c
6. c
7. a
8. b

3B GRAMMAR

1, page 190

1. *Throw away, turn off, come up with*
2. *Throw* means to toss, and *throw away* means to discard.
3. *Turn* means to rotate, and *turn off* means to stop.
4. *Come* means to approach, and *come up with* means to invent.

2, pages 192–193

2. invent
3. entered
4. become popular
5. remove from
6. clean
7. discard
8. like
9. exploit
10. eliminate
11. remember
12. examine
13. flip
14. lower
15. start
16. appear

3, page 194

1. come up with
2. take to
3. set foot
4. looked over
5. turned on
6. turned down
7. turn (it) over
8. picked up
9. threw out
10. took off
11. think back on

WRITE

1, page 197–198

1. The topic is a memorable meal. The thesis is that the meal was neither the fanciest nor the most expensive, but it was the most satisfying.
2. **a.** The atmosphere was lovely-white tablecloths, real silverware, and flowers on every table.
   b. They were served all the couscous they could eat in an enormous silver bowl.
   c. They were served delicious French bread, tall glasses of icy cold water with lemon, and the waiter brought them appetizers without even being asked.
3. Beginning: The writer explains the setting, the people, and the event.
   Middle: The writer and friends look for a restaurant.
   End: The writer and friends eat.
4. one day, that night, moments after, when, finally, as soon as, at the very moment, before, after

REVISE

1, page 199

Shortest: It was 1948 in Paris. (5 words)

Longest: Paul and Julia Child, an American couple had come by boat for a stint in the Foreign Service, and their first lunch became the impetus for Mrs. Child's culinary coup of the American diet. (34 words)

2, page 199

Answers will vary. Suggested answers:

My wife and I ate a new restaurant on Center Street with some friends. We ordered a delicious Japanese dish made with tofu. The food wasn't expensive, but unfortunately we all got sick, so we decided we would never go there again.

3, page 199

Answers will vary. Suggested answers:

After an exhausting day of sightseeing, we were looking forward to our meal. However, when the tour bus stopped in front of a pizza parlor instead of a nice restaurant, we all felt very disappointed. We asked the tour leader if we could go to another restaurant with more ambiance and more importantly, authentic food. The tour leader agreed, but said he would have to ask his boss if it was allright. He also said that if we really wanted to go to a restaurant that had food customary for the region, we would have to drive for at least another hour. He added that we would also have to stop for gas because the bus had very little gas left.

UNIT 9

1C BACKGROUND AND VOCABULARY

2, page 203

1.	unhappiness	7.	feelings
2.	imagination	8.	understanding
3.	fear	9.	undervalued
4.	anxious	10.	wish
5.	expected	11.	before
6.	movements	12.	heart

2A READING ONE, page 204

1. *Possible answers:* sadness, disappointment, uncomfortable
2. *Possible answer:* The author will describe her new life. She will discuss how the reality of her new home is different from what she imagined. She will also compare her old home and her new home.

READ FOR MAIN IDEAS, page 206

Answers will vary. Suggested answers:

1. F, paragraph 1. Lucy is uncomfortable in her new country. She wants to go back to where she came from.

2. F, paragraphs 1 and 2. She is disappointed by the reality, ordinariness, and dirtiness of New York. Lucy finds everything different from her home country: the elevator, the food, the climate.
3. T, paragraph 3.
4. F, paragraphs 4 and 5. Lucy was not happy in her home country. She lived in a "not-so-nice" situation and wanted to go somewhere else.
5. T, paragraphs 4 and 5.
6. F, paragraph 5. Lucy's dreams became disappointment in the new country. She suffered from homesickness.

READ FOR DETAILS, page 207

Answers will vary. Suggested answers:

1. Underline *warm and sunny*. The weather was not warm and sunny. Write *cold and gray*.
2. Underline *boat*. She didn't travel by boat. Write *plane*.
3. Underline *beautiful*. She didn't think the sights were beautiful. Write *ordinary, dirty, and worn down*.
4. Underline *just like the one we have at home*. She didn't have a refrigerator in Antigua. Write: *We didn't have a refrigerator at home*.
5. Underline *another bright sunny day*. The sun was not bright. Write *pale, yellow sun*.
6. Underline *just the right thing*. The dress was not right. Write: *It was not warm enough*.
7. Underline *warm*. The weather was not warm. Write *cold*.
8. Underline *enjoyed eating*. She didn't eat pink mullet and green figs. Write *dreamt about*.

MAKE INFERENCES, pages 208–209

1.	b	4.	c
2.	a	5.	b
3.	b	6.	a

2B READING TWO

1, pages 209–210

1. "This country" is the United States.
2. He says that his home country is a "pure flame" and in his new country he is "dying of the cold."

2, page 211

Answers will vary. Possible answers:

chicken and rice, a good cup of coffee, girls, trees, flowers, the river, birds

STEP 1: Organize, page 211

Theme	Reading One	Reading Two
1. weather	Everything is cold and gray. The sun isn't warm.	He's dying of the cold.
2. food	She always ate her grandmother's cooking.	He longs for a dish of chicken and rice and a good cup of coffee.
3. search for a better life	Lucy was unhappy in her home country and thought she could improve her life in America.	He came to establish his store in New York.
4. homesickness	She misses her family.	He misses his country.
5. disappointment with New York	Everything looks ordinary, dirty, and worn down.	What he sees around him is a sad panorama.

Answers will vary. Possible answers:

REVIEW

1, page 212

Answers will vary. Suggested answers:

Home Country: bedazzle, formerly, radiant, took for granted, vigor

New Country: discontent, fright, impatient, nostalgia, realization, to long

Both Countries: established, fantasy, predictable, sensation, soul

EXPAND

2, pages 212–213

2. c	5. c	8. a	11. c
3. b	6. c	9. b	12. b
4. a	7. a	10. a	

3B GRAMMAR

1, pages 213–214

1. She imagined what New York looked like first.
2. No. She put on her summer dress first.
3. Her longing to go there happened first.
4. The verb tenses and the time words *(by the time, when, before).*

2, pages 215–216

2. 2 / 1	5. 1 / 2
3. 1 / 2	6. 1 / 2
4. 2 / 1	7. 1 / 2

3, pages 216–217

Answers will vary. Suggested answers:

2. By the time she published *Autobiography of My Mother,* she had already published *Lucy.*
3. Jamaica Kincaid had moved to Bennington, Vermont, before she published *A Small Place.*
4. As soon as she had moved to New York, she found a domestic job.
5. By 1977, she had worked as a staff writer at *The New Yorker* magazine.
6. She had already worked as a staff writer at *The New Yorker* magazine when she married Allen Shawn, son of *The New Yorker* publisher.
7. After she had published a story in *The Village Voice* newspaper, she worked as a staff writer at *The New Yorker* magazine.

WRITE

2, page 221

a. point by point
b. block
c. point by point

REVISE

1, page 222

1. *In the same way* introduces ideas that are similar. *While, in contrast,* and *whereas* introduce ideas that are different.
2. The four topics are climate, living conditions, food, and problems.

2, pages 223–224

2. Dávila dislikes harsh winter with its bare trees; in the same way, Lucy dislikes the pale winter sun. *similarly*
3. Lucy misses her grandmother's home cooking; ~~in the same way,~~ Dávila misses his country's native food.
4. Dávila opened his store in New York; on the other hand, Lucy worked for a family as a nanny.
5. Lucy is a young woman; in contrast, Dávila is an older man.
6. While "Poor Visitor" was written in the last half of the twentieth century, "Nostalgia" was written in the first half of the twentieth century.

UNIT 10

1C BACKGROUND AND VOCABULARY, pages 229–230

1. b	5. b	9. b
2. a	6. c	10. c
3. c	7. c	11. a
4. b	8. c	

READ FOR MAIN IDEAS, pages 233–234

1. a   2. b   3. b

READ FOR DETAILS, pages 234–236

I. **Thinking about home in the late 1980s**
   A. Style preferences
      1. craftsmanship
      2. not ostentatious
   B. Must accommodate sophisticated and changing technology
      1. not obtrusive
      2. functions as servant, not master

II. **Selecting the perfect property**
   A. Location
      1. shore of Lake Washington
      2. easy commuting distance
   B. Living space—average size
      1. living room
         a. size = 14 x 28 feet
         b. area for watching television or listening to music
      2. other cozy spaces for one or two people
      3. large reception hall
         a. accommodates one hundred

III. **Controlling the home environment with an electronic pin**
   A. Tells the home who and where you are
   B. House uses pin information to meet your needs
      1. light follows you
      2. music follows you
      3. movie or news follows you
      4. a phone call follows you

IV. **Other readily and easily available technology**
   A. Hand-held remotes and consoles in each room
      1. controls tell monitors
         a. to become visible
         b. what to display
   B. Visual displays
      1. large choice
         a. thousands of pictures
         b. recordings
         c. movies
         d. television programs
         e. many options for selecting information
      2. house can control visual displays
         a. materialize when you enter and vanish when you leave rooms
         b. house can change programming depending on who is in the room

V. **State-of-the-art database**
   A. First homeowner to have it
   B. Database has more than 1 million still images
      1. includes photographs
      2. includes art reproductions
   C. Guests can call up anything they like
      1. portraits of presidents
      2. pictures of sunsets
      3. skiing in the Andes, etc.

VI. **Future availability of quality images**
   A. On the information highway
   B. In homes in the future

VII. **Fears about the information highway**
   A. Reduces the time people spend socializing
      1. homes will become too cozy and self-contained
      2. people will become isolated
   B. Not in agreement
      1. people are social animals
      2. highway only provides more entertainment and communication options
         a. personal
         b. professional
         c. employment
      3. people will decide to spend as much time out of their homes

VIII. **Benefits of the information highway**
   A. Makes it easier to
      1. maintain distant relationships
      2. find new companions
   B. Makes life more interesting
      1. people will meet in person
      2. meet people with common interests

IX. **Conclusion: Experimenting and the future**
   A. Bill Gates enjoys experimenting and may decide to
      1. conceal monitors
      2. throw away electronic pins
   B. Hopes
      1. may like everything
      2. wonders how he got along without it

MAKE INFERENCES, page 237

Answers will vary. Suggested answers:

1. You'll be presented with an electronic pin to clip on your clothes. This pin will tell the home who and where you are, and the house will use this information to try to meet and even anticipate your needs (Paragraph 3). . . . You'll be able to choose from among thousands of pictures, recordings, movies, and television programs and you'll have all sorts of options available for selecting information (Paragraph 4). . . . If you're planning to visit Hong Kong soon, you might ask the screen in your room to show you pictures of the city. . . . If you and I are enjoying different things and one of us walks into a room where the other is sitting, the house might continue the audio and video imagery for the person who was in the room first, or it might change to programming both of us like (Paragraph 5). . . . If you are a guest, you'll be able to call up portraits of . . . on screens throughout the house (Paragraph 6).

2. Unoccupied rooms will be unlit . . . the lights ahead of you gradually coming up to full brightness and the lights behind you fading. (Paragraph 3)

3. The product is a database of more than a million still images, including photographs and reproductions of paintings. (Paragraph 6)
4. The family living room is about 14 by 28 feet. (Paragraph 2)
5. I enjoy experimenting, and I know some of my concepts for the house will work out better than others. (Paragraph 11)
6. I found some property on the shore of Lake Washington. (Paragraph 2; photograph on page 231)
7. You won't be confronted by the technology, but it will be readily and easily available. (Paragraph 4)
8. Some worry that . . . we'll become isolated. I don't think that's going to happen. As behaviorists keep reminding us, we're social animals. (Paragraph 9)

2B READING TWO

2, page 240

Answers will vary. Suggested answers:

1. Answers will vary. It may mean that we cannot understand all the complex things in the world, so it's the simple things—like the beauty of nature (the wind)—that we should appreciate.
2. The solitude and being in a natural setting.
3. He kept the price low by using second-hand materials, doing the work himself, and also by transporting the materials himself.
4. He probably felt proud.

STEP 1: Organize, page 240

	Reading One	Reading Two
1. Year built	Late 1980s	1845
2. Size of house	Average for a large house	10 feet by 15 feet
3. Cost of house	Estimated as between $53 and $97 million	$28.12 1/2
4. Location	Shore of Lake Washington	By Walden Pond outside of Concord, Massachusetts
5. Accomodations for friends	Reception hall for 100, large selection of movies, music, and artwork to choose from …	Thoreau noted that he had three chairs in his cabin: "One for solitude, two for friendship, three for society."
6. Luxuries/technology in the house	Electronic pin and hand-held remotes which control automatic lighting, music, movies, art.	Books, hinges, screws, hoe, axe
7. Philosophy of luxuries/technology	Technology should be the servant, not the master. It should be unobtrusive but easily available.	Live life in the simplest of ways. He did not believe luxuries or comforts were necessary. He felt they actually stopped human progress.

REVIEW, page 241

1. a   3. s   5. s   7. a   9. a
2. s   4. a   6. s   8. s   10. a

EXPAND

1, page 242

Noun	Verb	Adjective	Adverb
anticipation	anticipate	anticipated	X
access accessibility	access	accessible	X
craftsmanship	craft	X	X
opposition	oppose	opposite opposing	X
accommodation	accommodate	accommodated accommodating	accommodatingly
ostentation	X	ostentatious	ostentatiously
X	X	cozy	cozily
option	opt	optional	X
X	X	unobtrusive	unobtrusively
concealment	conceal	concealed concealing	X
confrontation	confront	confrontational	confrontationally
occupation	occupy	occupied unoccupied	X
intention	intend	intentional intended	intentionally
communication	communicate	communicable	X
variety	vary	various	X

2, pages 243–244

2. intention
3. intentionally
4. unobtrusively
5. intentional
6. opposite/opposing
7. communication
8. options
9. communicate
10. opposes
11. optional
12. anticipate
13. accessible
14. variety
15. accessability
16. access

3B GRAMMAR

1, page 245

1. future events
2. the fact that events are ongoing

2, page 246

2. will be meeting
3. will be trying
4. will be checking
5. talks
6. will be eating
7. will be testing
8. will be spending
9. will be
10. eats
11. will be talking
12. will have
13. will be sleeping
14. won't be waiting

3, pages 247–248

2. In February, Sam won't be visiting Walt Whitman's home in New York. He'll be going on a winter camping trip.

3. In March, Sam will be building a model of the cabin at Walden Pond.

4. In April, Sam won't be walking the beaches of Cape Cod. He'll be building the cabin.

5. In May, Sam won't be building the cabin. He'll be living in it.

6. In June, Sam won't be living in the model of Walden Pond cabin. He'll be walking the beaches of Cape Cod and writing about his experiences.

7. In July, Sam will be traveling by boat on the Concord River.

8. In August, Sam won't be studying transcendentalist philosophy. He'll be taking the railroad from Concord to Bangor.

9. In September, Sam won't be taking the railroad from Concord. He'll be living in the backwoods of Maine.

10. In October, Sam won't be living in the backwoods of Maine. He'll be traveling by boat on the Merrimack River.

11. In November, Sam won't be traveling by boat on the Merrimack River. He'll be studying transcendentalist philosophy.

12. In December, Sam will be writing about his experiences following Thoreau's footsteps.

WRITE

1, page 250

1. The Internet will reduce the time people spend socializing and people will become isolated. Reducing the time people spend socializing will lead to isolation.

2. The Internet will provide more entertainment and communication options and it will make it easier to keep up with friends and make new friends and this will make life more interesting. Life will be more interesting as a result of the Internet and the options it provides.

3. Gates is more interested in discussing the effects and is more interested in their positive aspects.

2, page 251

1. It will provide a way to keep up with old friends.
   It will create many new options for people.
   Homes will become cozy entertainment providers.
   It will provide a way to make new friends with similar interests.

2. The Internet / will provide a way to make new friends with similar interests / people may choose to meet new friends in person / will make life more interesting.

4, page 253

I. Henry David Thoreau wanted to live a simple life, free from dependence on the modern technology of his time, relying on nature and himself.

  A. Henry David Thoreau wanted solitude
    1. decided to <u>leave his family home</u>
    2. decided to build a home in the woods
  B. <u>Thoreau didn't have a lot of money for the house</u>
    1. built home with his own labor
    2. <u>used cheap second-hand materials</u>
  C. Thoreau needed to live cheaply
    1. <u>he fished and hunted for food</u>
    2. he planted vegetables to eat and took good care of them
      a. the vegetables thrived
        1) <u>he had lots to vegetables to eat</u>
        2) he made money by selling excess vegetables
          a) <u>he used the money to buy oil for lamps</u>
            (1) <u>he was able to read at night</u>

REVISE

1, page 256

Answers will vary. Suggested answers:

As a result
consequently
due to
For this reason
because

Because of
As a result
due to the fact
For this reason

2, pages 256–258

2. E / C
   Since many people have cell phones, it is easy to stay in contact with people even when they are not at home.
   Many people have cell phones; therefore, it is easy to stay in contact with them . . .

3. E / C
   E-mail allows us to have daily contact with people around the world; consequently, many families are in closer contact than in the past.
   Due to the fact that e-mail allows us to have closer contact with people around the world, many families are in closer contact than in the past.

4. E / C
   Technology has given us many new advances in medicine; as a result, there is a higher frequency of early detection of many types of cancer.
   Technology has given us many new advances in medicine; thus, there is a higher frequency of early detection of many types of cancer.

5. C / E

   Because smart home technology turns off electricity when it is not being used, homeowners save money and help cut down on the use of fossil fuels.

   Smart home technology turns off electricity when it is not being used, so homeowners save money and help cut down on the use of fossil fuels.

6. E / C

   Many students use the Internet for research; for this reason, the use of libraries for traditional research has declined.

   Because of the fact that many students use the Internet for research, the use of libraries for traditional research has declined.

7. C / E

   Since playing video games has become a very popular hobby with young people, they are becoming more socially isolated and less physically active.

   Playing video games has become a very popular hobby with young people; as a consequence, they are becoming more socially isolated and less physically active.

Unit Word List

The **Unit Word List** is a summary of key vocabulary from the student book. The words are presented by unit, in alphabetical order.

UNIT 1

allegation
allege
anguish
around the clock
beg
besieged
clear one's name
convicted in the court of public opinion
fair game
have an endless hunger for
hounded by
judgment
justified

justify
keep to oneself
legitimate
on one's deathbed
perspective
play ostrich
relevant
scrutiny
speculation
spread the word
suppose
suspect
the price one pays

UNIT 2

abandonment
achievement
confused
confusion
darkest
defeated
dilapidated
disenfranchised
embarrassment
enlivened
exalted
exceptional
extraordinary
failure
falling apart
freedom
hopeful
hopelessness
immoral
inquisitiveness
isolated
isolation
leaving behind

liberate
liberated
liberation
longing
master
meager
misery
mortified
noble
overcome
paradise
plentiful
poverty
shame
sordid
struggle
tormented
transformation
understanding
utopia
wealth
yearn for
yearning

UNIT 3

accuse
acknowledge
acknowledgement
admit
agreement
ailment
alternative
ask advice of
belief
benefit
consult
conventional
debate
defend
deny

diagnosis
disobey
doubtful
effect
effective
elicit
entitled
principle
produce
ramification
skeptical
symptom
treatment
unconventional
violate

UNIT 4

attribute
audience
candidate
capacity
centuries
cognition
concept
conditioned
controversy
evaluate
evolve
factor
feat
numerical

perceive
predict
prevail
psychiatrist
psychologist
psychology
recognize
resemble
sense
sensitive
signaling
spectacular
standard
zoo

UNIT 5

ancient	personal
awesome	practical
chilly	presumptuous
constant	prolonged
disparate	punctually
fond of	remaining
ideal	romantic
immeasurably	serious
immortality	shimmering
impetuous	simultaneously
impulsive	tolerable
insufferable	ultimately
limited	utterly
loveless	vigorous
misty	worrisome
permissible	youthful

UNIT 6

admiration	indignation
admiring	inspiration
call up	inspire
challenge	inspired
clear out	keep on
determination	manage
determined	management
devote	oppose
devotion	opposition
donate	passion
donation	pick up
dry up	proposal
end up	proudly
figure out	resentful
find out	resentment
fix up	ridiculous
fulfill	satisfaction
fulfillment	sit around
hope	thrilled

UNIT 7

adjust	expertise
adjustment	isolation
ambition	misconception
avid	nonchalantly
consultation	persistence
dictate	scorn
dictation	scornful
disappoint	stimulating
disappointed	stimulation
disappointment	viability
dispute	viable
eclectic	

UNIT 8

authentic	necessitate
come to	nominally
customary	pleasurable
decline	prepare
deference	proper
evident	set foot in
grow up	specify
impart	take advantage of
inextricably linked	take back
insist	take to
leisurely	throw away
literally	turn off

UNIT 9

anxious	misunderstanding
arbitrary	movements
bedazzle	nostalgia
concept	overvalued
desire	patient
discomfort	predictable
discontent	radiant
emotion	random
energetic	reality
established	realization
fantasy	saddens
formerly	sensation
fright	signal
frightens	soul
garment	surprising
gesture	take for granted
homesick	unexpected
impatient	vigor
long (for)	vigorous

UNIT 10

access	different
accessibility	intend
accommodate	intention
accommodation	modest
anticipate	occupation
anticipation	occupied
avoid	opposing
choice	opposite
communicable	opposition
communication	option
conceal	ostentation
concealment	ostentatious
confront	provided
confrontation	reveal
confrontational	unobtrusive
conspicuous	unoccupied
cozy	variety
craftsmanship	various

Achievement Tests
Unit 1

Name: _____

Date: _____

PART 1: READING

1.1 *Read the beginning of an article from a photography magazine. Check (✔) the best prediction of what the reading is about. There is only one right answer.*

Most journalists are well aware of the dangers of reporting false information. Of course, they want to satisfy the endless hunger of the public for more and more juicy bits of gossip. At the same time, they must work to present news fairly.

By comparison, photographers may feel that they are safe from the possible allegations faced by reporters. But are they?

_____ **A.** journalists' responsibility for accuracy

_____ **B.** the fairness of gossip magazines

_____ **C.** the relative safety of photographers from allegations

_____ **D.** professional concerns of photographers

1.2 *Now read the entire article. Use the information to choose the correct answers.*

Photographers Beware

Most journalists are well aware of the dangers of reporting false information. Of course, they want to satisfy the endless hunger of the public for more and more juicy bits of gossip. At the same time, they must work to present news fairly.

By comparison, photographers may feel that they are safe from the possible allegations faced by reporters. But are they?

Consider the recent photo of a restaurant taken from a public street. In the restaurant, a man and woman can be seen holding hands across a table. The photo was used on the front page of a community magazine.

Now, the photographer is being sued by both people, who say that there was an invasion of their privacy. In other words, the couple believes that they had a reasonable expectation of privacy in the restaurant, which is actually owned by the pictured woman.

Furthermore, both parties claim that they've suffered anguish as a result of the photo. The man and woman were married. However, they were not married to each other. Each person's spouse saw the photograph and recognized their partner. Since then, each person's spouse has filed for a divorce.

Now, the courts must scrutinize a scramble of tricky concepts in determining the photographer's liability. In determining a judgment, several relevant factors will be considered:

1. Was the photograph taken from a public place?
2. Is the restaurant itself a private place?
3. Does the photo directly relate to the content of the article?

Just like reporters, photographers must use their best judgment in taking and printing images. Otherwise, they may pay the price.

Check (✔) the best answer to complete each sentence.

1. The writer of the article warns photographers about _____

   when taking and printing images.

   _____ **A.** using good judgment

   _____ **B.** picturing couples

   _____ **C.** the judgments of courts

   _____ **D.** scrutiny of the public

2. The writer of the article thinks that both photographers and journalists

   _____ .

   _____ **A.** are eager to gather juicy information

   _____ **B.** have some of the same professional concerns

   _____ **C.** focus too often on people's private information

   _____ **D.** fail to consider complex factors

3. The photograph shows _____ .

   _____ **A.** a married couple

   _____ **B.** a community meeting

   _____ **C.** an unmarried couple

   _____ **D.** restaurant employees

4. The people in the photograph suffered anguish because _____ .

   _____ **A.** their spouses filed for divorce

   _____ **B.** they have lost money

   _____ **C.** they have lost their jobs

   _____ **D.** they will probably be sued

1.3 *Read the passage from "Peeping Tom Journalism" by Nancy Day in* NorthStar: Reading *and* Writing 4, *Unit 1. Use the information from this reading and "Photographers Beware" to complete the activity. The first one has been done for you.*

Peeping Tom Journalism

When Sara Jane Moore pointed a gun at President Ford, a man in the crowd knocked her hand, deflecting the shot. The man, Oliver W. Sipple, became an instant hero. He was thirty-three years old and a Marine veteran. What else did the public want or need to know about him? Initial reports did not mention Sipple's sexual orientation. But when a San Francisco news columnist said that local gay leaders were proud of Sipple's actions, other papers began to report it. Sipple sued the columnist and several newspapers for invading his privacy. He said that he suffered "great mental anguish, embarrassment, and humiliation." Lawyers argued that by becoming involved in an event of worldwide importance, Sipple had given up his right to privacy because the public has a legitimate interest in his activity.

	Oliver Sipple	Photographed Couple	Both
Felt there was an invasion of privacy			✓
1. Publication of information caused anguish			
2. Lawyers thought that the public had a legitimate interest in the information			
3. Others learned of possible sexual interests			
4. Was a hero			
5. Participated in a private act that could be seen from a public location			

PART 2: VOCABULARY

2.1 *Read the quotations from "Peeping Tom Journalism." Then check (✔) the word that is closest in meaning to the boldfaced word and best completes each sentence.*

1. "Journalists must rely on their own **judgment**."

   Journalists must weigh the facts in order to make good _____ .

   _____ **A.** suggestions   _____ **C.** images

   _____ **B.** decisions   _____ **D.** impressions

2. "The reporter who actually faced these decisions decided to mention the gun, the sandwich, the fishing tackle, and the condition of the car, but not the magazine or any **speculation**."

   The reporter avoided making _____ .

   _____ **A.** guesses   _____ **C.** evidence

   _____ **B.** jokes   _____ **D.** statements of fact

3. "Some of the interest can be **justified** on the basis that character affects how people perform their jobs."

   The connection between character and job-performance _____ the interest.

   _____ **A.** explains   _____ **C.** contradicts

   _____ **B.** weakens   _____ **D.** creates

4. "When Gennifer Flowers **alleged** a twelve-year affair with President Bill Clinton, she first told the story to the tabloid *Star*."

   Gennifer Flowers _____ she had an affair with Bill Clinton.

   _____ **A.** denied   _____ **C.** implied

   _____ **B.** proved   _____ **D.** claimed

5. "He said that he suffered 'great mental **anguish**, embarrassment, and humiliation.'"

   He said that he had experienced _____ .

   _____ **A.** scars   _____ **C.** suffering

   _____ **B.** weakness   _____ **D.** instability

2.2 *Complete the idioms with the correct verb from the box. Be sure to use the correct form of the verb. Not all of the verbs will be used.*

be	clear	convict	keep	lose	pay	play	spread

When Isabella Sotin was on her deathbed, she stunned her family by confessing to

manslaughter. She had killed her husband 47 years prior. But she had never

_____ the price for her crime. Instead, her husband's brother had been
    1.

found guilty. In fact, he had been _____ in the court of public opinion
                              2.

before he ever went to trial, as he had a long history of violence. As for Isabella, her

name had been _____. After the murder trials, the Sotin family
                     3.

_____ mostly to themselves. When Isabella finally confessed, the Sotin
      4.

family _____ the word of their eldest son's innocence.
         5.

PART 3: SKILLS FOR WRITING

3.1 *Complete the sentences. Put the verb in parentheses in the passive voice.*

1. Sometimes, information may accidentally _____ .
                                         (misrepresent)

2. For example, recently, a picture of a crowded street in New York

    _____ on the front of a major magazine.
          (feature)

3. In the middle of the picture, a popular athlete could _____
                                                       (see)

    quite clearly.

4. The article itself _____ on sports figures involved in drug
                                    (focus)

    scandals.

5. The magazine _____ by the pictured man for misrepresenting
                          (sued)

    him as someone who uses drugs.

3.2 *Read the paragraph and the possible topic sentences. Check (✓) the sentence that would work best as the topic sentence for this paragraph.*

_____ . For example, in the recent Hollywood movie, *Bruce Almighty*, the actor Jim Carrey gets God's private phone number. For a moment on the screen, the number is visible. What movie-makers didn't anticipate was the fact that the number was real. It was the mobile phone number of at least two people: Andy Green, a sandwich shop manager, and Dawn Jenkins, a glassmaker. Both received many calls from people who wanted to speak to God. For a while, Green was getting up to seventy calls a day. He claimed he was losing sleep. He even considered taking legal action against the movie-maker, whose presentation of his number caused him such anguish.

_____ **A.** Andy Green's phone number was shown in a Hollywood movie.

_____ **B.** Journalists, reporters, and movie-makers all need to beware.

_____ **C.** Revealing private contact information, such as a phone number or address, may be grounds for a lawsuit.

_____ **D.** Movie-makers rarely make mistakes.

3.3 *Complete the sentences with the correct transition words from the box.*

in the beginning	some time later
in the end	then

_____, Andy Green's phone number was mostly private, used by
      1.

friends and family. _____ *Bruce Almighty* was released.
      2.

_____ calls began coming from strangers who wanted to make
      3.

requests to be forgiven and to talk to God. _____ , the number of
      4.

callers dropped, but Green considered suing the movie-makers.

PART 4: WRITING

A Summary Paragraph (20 minutes)

Write a summary paragraph about a time when you (or somebody you know) felt that your (his/her) privacy was violated.

- Make sure your paragraph has a topic sentence and a controlling idea.
- Make the content of the rest of the paragraph relate to the topic sentence.
- Use time transitions correctly.
- Use the vocabulary and grammar from Unit 1.

Unit 1 Vocabulary Words				
allegation	beg	justify	perspective	speculation
anguish	besieged	legitimate	relevant	suppose
be hounded by	judgment	pay the price	scrutiny	
Unit 1 Grammar: Passive Voice				
• It *was made clear* to the photographer that she needed a model release.				

Achievement Tests
Unit 2

Name: _____

Date: _____

PART 1: READING

1.1 *Read the beginning of an interview from a company newsletter about a new employee, Denny Clayton. Check (✔) the best prediction of what the reading is about. There is only one right answer.*

INTERVIEWER: Welcome to Teen Counseling, Denny.

DENNY: Thank you. For a long time, I yearned for a job where I would feel that I was part of a family, and that's how I feel here at the Counseling Center.

INTERVIEWER: You've had an interesting career path. Can you tell us about how you got interested in counseling?

_____ **A.** Denny Clayton's career in counseling

_____ **B.** the Teen Counseling Center

_____ **C.** the importance of family

_____ **D.** Denny Clayton's interest in teenagers

1.2 *Now read the entire interview. Use the information to choose the correct answers.*

A Dream Job

INTERVIEWER: Welcome to Teen Counseling, Denny.

DENNY: Thank you. For a long time, I yearned for a job where I would feel that I was part of a family, and that's how I feel here at the Counseling Center.

INTERVIEWER: You've had an interesting career path. Can you tell us about how you got interested in counseling?

DENNY: Well, I originally studied business in college. I was raised to think that I'd end up in a business-related career, like my parents. In fact, I did work at a small import-export firm for a few years, crunching numbers, working on contracts. In that job, though, I always felt so isolated.

INTERVIEWER: It sounds like you really struggled to find meaning in your desk job.

DENNY: I did. It was confusing for me. Over time, I started feeling real hopelessness in my job. Finally, I quit the import-export company and started working in my parents' restaurant. That was a dead end[1] too.

INTERVIEWER: How did you get from your restaurant job into counseling?

DENNY: Well, one day, an extraordinary thing happened. I was in a restaurant and I overheard a couple of the waitresses chatting about various things—school, their parents, their friends, their jobs. I immediately

_____

[1] **dead end:** a path that ends, or an uninteresting path

related to their issues, and I wanted to help them. That night, I went home and got online and started researching careers in counseling. Immediately, I felt this sense of freedom. I knew that I needed to go back to school and become a counselor.

INTERVIEWER: Then you enrolled in the Clover Hill Community College?

DENNY: I did, and as soon as I started school, my world was transformed. I loved my instructors and my classes. I was eager to do my homework and learn more. I could hardly wait to start actually counseling kids.

INTERVIEWER: That's when you ended up here at Teen Counseling?

DENNY: Right. Teen Counseling had an opening for an intern. For me, the position was a dream-come-true. Now, every day, I get the chance to talk with young people about their lives . . . and I get paid for it! I feel that I am making a real connection with them, literally touching their lives, and it is like paradise for me. Plus, at the same time that I was counseling them about finding themselves, I myself was just starting to understand that I could be myself, too. I didn't have to fit into the career path that my parents had set up for me. I feel that I've really "found my calling."[2]

_____

[2] **find one's calling:** to identify the activity that brings a person the most satisfaction

Check (✔) the best answer to complete each sentence.

1. Denny talks a lot about his _____ .

   _____ **A.** parents' careers

   _____ **B.** need for a family

   _____ **C.** job in the import-export firm

   _____ **D.** path to a counseling career

2. In his job at the import-export firm, Denny probably _____ .

   _____ **A.** traveled a lot

   _____ **B.** sat in an office

   _____ **C.** worked on ships and planes

   _____ **D.** coordinated his work with a college

(continued on next page)

3. Denny started looking for another career for all of the following reasons *except*

_____ .

_____ **A.** he felt isolated

_____ **B.** he wanted to earn more money

_____ **C.** he wasn't interested in working in his parents' business

_____ **D.** the waitress's conversation drew him in

4. When he started to study counseling, Denny felt _____ .

_____ **A.** enthusiastic

_____ **B.** nervous

_____ **C.** isolated

_____ **D.** stuck

1.3 *Read the passage from "The Miracle" by Diane Schuur in* NorthStar: Reading and Writing 4, *Unit 2. Use the information from this reading and "A Dream Job" to complete the activity. The first one has been done for you.*

The Miracle

I can say the word *see*, I can speak the language of the sighted. That's part of the first great achievement of Helen Keller. She proved how language could liberate the blind and the deaf. She wrote, "Literature is my utopia. Here I am not disenfranchised." But how she struggled to master language. In her book, *Midstream*, she wrote about how she was frustrated by the alphabet, by the language of the deaf, even with the speed with which her teacher spelled things out for her on her palm. She was impatient and hungry for words, and her teachers' scribbling on her hand would never be as fast, she thought, as the people who could read the words with their eyes. I remember how books got me going after I finally grasped Braille. Being in that school was like being in an orphanage. But words—and in my case, music—changed that isolation. With language, Keller, who could not hear and could not see, proved she could communicate in the world of sight and sound— and was able to speak to it and live in it. I am a beneficiary of her work. Because of her example, the world has given way a little. In my case, I was able to go from the state school for the blind to regular public school from the age of 11 until my senior year in high school. And then I decided on my own to go back into the school for the blind. Now I sing jazz.

I hate the word *handicapped*. Keller would too. We are people with inconveniences. We're not charity cases. Her main message was and is, "We're like everybody else. We're here to be able to live a life as full as any sighted person's. And it's okay to be ourselves."

That means we have the freedom to be as extraordinary as the sighted. Keller loved an audience and wrote that she adored "the warm tide of human life pulsing round and round me." That's why the stage appealed to her, why she learned to speak and to deliver speeches. And to feel the vibrations of music, of the radio, of the movement of lips. You must understand that even more than sighted people, we need to be touched. When you look at a person, eye to eye, I imagine it's like touching them. We don't have the convenience. But when I perform, I get that experience from a crowd. Helen Keller must have as well. She was our first star. And I am very grateful to her.

Experiences of Finding a Way to Connect with Others	Helen Keller	Diane Schuur	Denny Clayton
Felt free	✓	✓	✓
1. Struggled to find his/her calling			
2. Felt eager to pursue his/her new activities			
3. Ended a feeling of isolation			
4. Hated the word *handicapped*			
5. Realized it was okay to be himself/herself			

PART 2: VOCABULARY

2.1 *Choose either a synonym or an antonym for the word given. Circle the word.*

1. confused _____ (*synonym*)
   A. mixed up   **B.** foolish   **C.** clear

2. extraordinary _____ (*antonym*)
   A. rare   **B.** unusual   **C.** ordinary

3. freedom _____ (*synonym*)
   A. flexibility   **B.** liberation   **C.** feeling

4. hopeless _____ (*antonym*)
   A. hopeful   **B.** energetic   **C.** ambitious

5. paradise _____ (*antonym*)
   A. beautiful place   **B.** fantasy   **C.** unhappy place

2.2 *Check (✔) the word that best completes each sentence.*

1. Teachers tend to appreciate _____ students because their curiosity can make the class more interesting.

   _____ **A.** inquisitive

   _____ **B.** mortified

   _____ **C.** confused

   _____ **D.** hopeless

2. As a result of being able to understand books, Schuur's world was

   _____ .

   _____ **A.** exalted

   _____ **B.** hopeless

   _____ **C.** transformed

   _____ **D.** disenfranchised

3. People who love a particular sport, such as skiing or biking, describe the experience of doing that sport as a kind of _____ .

   _____ **A.** utopia

   _____ **B.** struggle

   _____ **C.** misery

   _____ **D.** yearning

4. A person who spends years to _____ a musical instrument can appreciate its value all the more.

   _____ **A.** exalt

   _____ **B.** master

   _____ **C.** struggle

   _____ **D.** defeat

5. Because the town was small and the community was close-knit, the scandal in the mayor's office _____ residents.

   _____ **A.** yearned for

   _____ **B.** defeated

   _____ **C.** disenfranchised

   _____ **D.** mortified

PART 3: SKILLS FOR WRITING

3.1　*Combine the sentences using both underlined words. Use either a gerund or an infinitive of the boldfaced verb.*

Alvin Ailey loved **to dance**. It <u>was</u> important to him.

　　<u>Dancing was important to Alvin Ailey.</u>

1. Alvin Ailey **danced** as a child. He <u>was</u> interested in it.

　　_____

2. Alvin Ailey **danced** with Lester Horton. He <u>studied</u> it in his studio.

　　_____

3. He <u>wanted</u> to show his memories. He **danced** in order to do this.

　　_____

4. He **pulled** from his experience with gospel and the blues. He <u>felt free</u> in doing this.

　　_____

5. Alvin <u>thought about</u> how to teach young people to dance in a school. He **founded** the Ailey School.

　　_____

3.2　*Read the paragraph. Then write the letters of the correct sentences.*

(**A**) In a self-assessment questionnaire, music lovers repeatedly rank their emotional response to music as one of the greatest pleasures of their life. (**B**) The questionnaire, distributed to twenty-seven music listeners, asked respondents to rank their experience of music on a scale of one to six. (**C**) Additionally, the questionnaire asked them to rank their enjoyment of other common pleasures: eating, activities with friends, pursuing a favorite hobby, and relaxing. (**D**) I like all of these things, too. (**E**) Respondents typically ranked their love of certain hobbies, eating, and friends with the high rank of four or five. (**F**) But among the most avid of music listeners, their exaltation at listening to a specific piece of music regularly ranked a six. (**G**) In short, by their own assessment, their appreciation of music was one of the most extraordinary experiences of their life.

1. The topic sentence is sentence _____ .

2. One sentence that does not belong in this paragraph is _____ .

(continued on next page)

3. The following sentence of support would fit best between sentences _____ and
   _____: "One was *low in exaltation* and six was *high in exaltation*."

4. The following sentence of support would fit best between sentences _____ and
   _____: "For many, certain physical pleasures ranked even higher, at a five or six."

5. The concluding sentence is sentence _____ .

PART 4: WRITING

A Biographical Paragraph (20 minutes)

*Write a biographical paragraph about a person you know who feels strongly about a
personal or career interest in his or her life.*

- Include a topic sentence, supporting ideas, and a concluding sentence.
- Include your opinion about the main idea.
- Use the vocabulary and grammar from Unit 2.

Unit 2 Vocabulary Words				
achievement	extraordinary	inquisitive	paradise	utopia
confused	freedom	isolation	struggle	yearn for
darkest	hopelessness	master	transformation	
Unit 2 Grammar: Gerunds and Infinitives				

[gerund]
- Frank McCourt enjoys **writing**.
[infinitive]
- He wanted **to write** about his experiences.

Achievement Tests
Unit 3

Name: _____

Date: _____

PART 1: READING

1.1 *Read the beginning of a brochure from a holistic medicine clinic. Check (✔) the best prediction of what the reading is about. There is only one right answer.*

Many people visit our office because they are concerned about their physical bodies. They are frequently looking for the quick treatment of a physical symptom. However, we believe that effective medical consultation involves more than looking at symptoms. It involves addressing the underlying emotional and psychological connection between our physical selves and our mental selves: the mind-body connection. Using alternative forms of therapy based on the principles of the mind-body connection, practitioners at the Psysoma Clinic aim to involve clients emotionally in their own well-being. So, what can you do to elicit change in your own body? Here are some first steps.

_____ **A.** medical treatment

_____ **B.** ways to improve your physical health with your mind

_____ **C.** Psysoma Clinic's beliefs and practices

_____ **D.** psychological illnesses

1.2 *Now read the entire brochure. Use the information to choose the correct answers.*

The Mind-Body Connection

Many people visit our office because they are concerned about their physical bodies. They are frequently looking for the quick treatment of a physical symptom. However, we believe that effective medical consultation involves more than looking at symptoms. It involves addressing the underlying emotional and psychological connection between our physical selves and our mental selves: the mind-body connection. Using alternative forms of therapy based on the principles of the mind-body connection, practitioners at the Psysoma Clinic aim to involve clients emotionally in their own well-being. So, what can you do to elicit change in your own body? Here are some first steps:

1. Focus your mind.

   Studies show that people who take time to focus their thoughts are less likely to get stressed and scattered by daily events. This focus could involve a formal activity, such as meditation, or it could be an informal focus on your thoughts and intentions.

(continued on next page)

2. Envision the outcome you want.

   Envisioning is a powerful tool. Studies show that patients who envision overcoming their pain actually feel less pain. Likewise, you may envision feeling happy, focusing your mind, or letting go of symptoms.

3. Allow yourself to relax.

   Many people think that if they're relaxed, they're not being productive. This is not true! Commit yourself to relaxing, even while you work. Your body will thank you.

4. Set time aside to do something that you like to do.

   In busy, modern-day society, many people schedule virtually every minute with work, family, or other obligations. Remember, you are entitled to pursue activities for the purpose of pleasure. Choose one and set aside time to do it for a half-hour every day.

5. Set one achievable goal for each day.

   If you don't know your goal, you won't know when you've reached it. This can lead to dissatisfaction. Set an achievable goal each day, and when you achieve it, congratulate yourself on your success.

6. Concentrate on positive thoughts and feelings.

   Hans Selye's book (1956) established the connection between negative feelings and health. Since then, practitioners have repeatedly shown the same connection between positive feelings and health. Concentrate on positive thinking. It's the beginning of all treatment.

Check (✔) the best answer to complete each sentence.

1. The brochure gives suggestions on how to benefit from _____ .

   _____ **A.** positive thinking

   _____ **B.** treatment of symptoms

   _____ **C.** herbal treatments

   _____ **D.** Hans Selye's book

2. According to the brochure, patients can involve their _____ in improving their health.

   _____ **A.** learning

   _____ **B.** experiences

   _____ **C.** emotions

   _____ **D.** physical selves

3. One benefit of focusing the mind is that it _____ .

_____ **A.** helps to minimize stress

_____ **B.** encourages meditation

_____ **C.** requires only an informal effort

_____ **D.** takes little time

4. Based on the brochure, a person who envisioned failing would

_____ .

_____ **A.** get stressed

_____ **B.** feel powerful

_____ **C.** be more likely to fail

_____ **D.** know an outcome in advance

5. The reading advises people to spend time on activities with the purpose of

_____ .

_____ **A.** enjoyment

_____ **B.** being productive

_____ **C.** congratulating themselves

_____ **D.** knowing their own feelings

6. All of the following are benefits of setting an achievable goal *except*

_____ .

_____ **A.** you'll know when you've reached it

_____ **B.** achieving it can give you satisfaction

_____ **C.** it will help you to define success

_____ **D.** it will inspire you to work harder

1.3 *Read the passage from Norman Cousins's "Laugh Therapy" in* NorthStar: Reading and Writing 4, *Unit 3. Write the number of the health step prescribed in "The Mind-Body Connection" next to the steps that Norman Cousins took. The first one has been done for you.*

Laugh Therapy

Despite the diagnosis, Cousins was determined to overcome the disease and survive. He had always been interested in medicine and had read *The Stress of Life* (1956), the work of organic chemist Hans Selye. This book discussed the idea of how body

(continued on next page)

chemistry and health can be damaged by emotional stress and negative attitudes. Selye's book made Cousins think about the possible benefits of positive attitudes and emotions. He thought, "If negative emotions produce (negative) changes in the body, wouldn't positive emotions produce positive chemical changes? Is it possible that love, hope, faith, laughter, confidence, and the will to live have positive therapeutic value?"

He decided to concentrate on positive emotions as a remedy to heal some of the symptoms of his ailment. In addition to his conventional medical treatment, he tried to put himself in situations that would elicit positive emotions. "Laugh therapy" became part of his treatment. He scheduled time each day for watching comedy films, reading humorous books, and doing other activities that would bring about laughter and positive emotions. Within eight days of starting his "laugh therapy" program, his pain began to decrease and he was able to sleep more easily. His body chemistry even improved. Doctors were able to see an improvement in his condition! He was able to return to work in a few months' time and actually reached complete recovery after a few years.

_____3_____ He let himself relax.

_____ **1.** He made time to watch funny movies and read funny books.

_____ **2.** He focused his mind on positive feelings.

_____ **3.** He saw in his mind the benefits of laughing and relaxation on the body.

PART 2: VOCABULARY

2.1 *Circle the word that best completes the analogy.*

1. alternative: other = conventional: _____

    A. traditional   **B.** meeting   **C.** effective

2. beliefs: ideas = draw out: _____

    A. dismiss   **B.** describe   **C.** elicit

3. practitioner: doctor = educator: _____

    A. teacher   **B.** diagnosis   **C.** comedian

4. inspire: encourage = consult: _____

    A. confirm   **B.** ask   **C.** include

5. cause: effect = disease: _____

    A. host   **B.** treatment   **C.** symptom

2.2 *Complete the sentences using the words from the box. Not all of the words will be used.*

alternative	effective	entitle	produces
consult	effects	principles	symptoms

1. The _____ of some drugs cannot be identified until they are traced in the offspring of the user.

2. Laughter actually _____ a chemical in the brain that leads to a feeling of happiness.

3. Fatigue is often one of the first _____ of depression.

4. The decision to prescribe a drug may or may not be based on the prescriber's _____ .

5. In the USA, _____ forms of medicine have gained a lot of popularity in the last couple of decades.

PART 3: SKILLS FOR WRITING

3.1 *Write a sentence about each situation. Use the past unreal conditional.*

1. Mary sunbathed for hours every day as a teenager. Then she got skin cancer.

   _____

2. Bob drank lots of soda when he was young. He developed a lot of cavities.

   _____

3. The student read a lot of books in school. He graduated from college at 19.

   _____

4. The artist brought her portfolio to the interview. The company offered her the job.

   _____

5. The teacher graded students too easily. The students didn't try very hard.

   _____

3.2 *Read the introductory paragraph and answer the questions that follow. Write the letters of the correct sentences. Some may be used more than once. Not all of the sentences will be used.*

(**A**) My brother is deaf and he is a happy member of Deaf culture. (**B**) While many hearing people at first feel sorry for him when they meet him, they only feel sorry for him because they don't know him. (**C**) If they knew him like I do, they would know that he accepts his deafness, and he is proud to be a member of the Deaf community. (**D**) The broader society often sees deafness as a disability. (**E**) However, many deaf people, including my brother, do not see it this way. (**F**) Instead, they see themselves as part of a minority group, and they like the group. (**G**) Members of the dominant, hearing culture would be wise to follow the lead of deaf people in defining their own groups, their own limitations, and their own acceptance of themselves.

Sentence __A__ states who the writer is and why her opinion matters.

1. Sentence _____ hooks the reader with something surprising.

2. Sentences _____, _____, and _____ provide background information about the topic.

3. Sentence _____ is the thesis statement.

PART 4: WRITING

An Opinion Essay (20 minutes)

Reread "The Mind-Body Connection" in Part 1.2. Then write an opinion essay about one of the six suggestions in the reading.

- Include an introduction with a thesis statement, a body paragraph, and a conclusion.
- Make sure your introduction has a hook.
- Provide evidence and reasons for your ideas.
- Use the vocabulary and grammar from Unit 3.

Unit 3 Vocabulary Words				
alternative	conventional	elicit	principles	symptom
beliefs	effect	entitled	produce	treatment
consult	effective			

Unit 3 Grammar: Past Unreal Conditionals
• If my aunt **hadn't gotten** sick, I **wouldn't have spent** so much time with her.

Achievement Tests
Unit 4

Name: _____

Date: _____

PART 1: READING

1.1 *Read the first diary entry from an imaginary employee who worked with an actual chimpanzee who studied American Sign Language. Check (✔) the best prediction of what the reading is about. There is only one right answer.*

June 14, 1966: The new baby chimpanzee has arrived at the laboratory. Her name is Washoe. The doctors think that she is a prime candidate for learning American Sign Language. Washoe seems very happy in her new environment. The doctors have worked hard to set up the conditions necessary for learning a language. They've arranged a very stimulating environment, including games, books, magazines, and tools. The doctors predict that Washoe has the capacity to learn ASL.

_____ **A.** a chimpanzee's progress in learning ASL

_____ **B.** American Sign Language

_____ **C.** second language learning

_____ **D.** a laboratory environment

1.2 *Now read all of the diary entries. Use the information to choose the correct answers.*

Washoe's ASL Development

June 14, 1966: The new baby chimpanzee has arrived at the laboratory. Her name is Washoe. The doctors think that she is a prime candidate for learning American Sign Language. Washoe seems very happy in her new environment. The doctors have worked hard to set up the conditions necessary for learning a language. They've arranged a very stimulating environment, including games, books, magazines, and tools. The doctors predict that Washoe has the capacity to learn ASL.

July 26: Washoe's caretakers speak to her constantly using sign language, and slowly, she seems to understand some of their communication. Having a model of speakers using a language is a primary factor for learners of the language, so researchers are using this concept to teach the chimpanzee.

October 9: Today, Washoe used the sign for "toothbrush." I saw it myself. She pointed to her toothbrush and made the sign clearly. It is her 19th sign. The researchers recorded it in the book as a reliable sign. In order to be evaluated as reliable, the sign needs to be observed by three different observers in three different uses. Then, it needs to be used again 15 days in a row.

(continued on next page)

December 6:   Washoe is making up some of her own signs now. It's quite a feat! We cannot understand them all. However, today she used "water" and "bird" when she saw a swan. As for her list of reliable signs, she has learned over 200 signs and uses them all regularly.

February 5:   Newspaper reporters have been here all week, watching Washoe and the other chimps. Some linguists are skeptical of Washoe's success. For example, the famous linguist Noam Chomsky thinks that the ability to produce language did not evolve in chimpanzees. Rather, he argues that they simply do acts that will earn them rewards.

March 7:   Washoe signs regularly to her other chimp-friends, Tutu, Loulis, and Dar. They are learning signs without any intervention from the researchers, but they don't know nearly as many as Washoe does.

Check (✔) the best answer to complete each sentence.

1. Doctors worked with the chimpanzee to _____ .

    _____ **A.** teach her American Sign Language

    _____ **B.** compare her learning to humans' learning

    _____ **C.** understand environments for language learning

    _____ **D.** dispute Noam Chomsky's theory

2. According to the reading, all of the following are necessary for learning a second language *except* _____ .

    _____ **A.** an interesting environment

    _____ **B.** learning materials

    _____ **C.** models of the language

    _____ **D.** a primary caretaker

3. Researchers counted a sign as reliable when Washoe used it _____ , and then used it again for weeks.

    _____ **A.** while holding a toothbrush

    _____ **B.** three separate times, each observed by a different viewer

    _____ **C.** 19 times

    _____ **D.** with other chimpanzees

4. The sentence that offers the best summary of the December 6 diary

   entry is _____ .

   _____ **A.** Washoe uses hundreds of signs and is creating some of her own.

   _____ **B.** Washoe has created two hundred signs.

   _____ **C.** While she uses many signs, it is hard to know which are reliable.

   _____ **D.** Researchers can only guess at the meaning of "swan," for example.

5. Noam Chomsky believed that researchers were just giving Washoe

   _____ .

   _____ **A.** credit for signs she didn't use

   _____ **B.** rewards for using signs

   _____ **C.** the ability to learn language

   _____ **D.** an evolutionary advantage

6. Washoe's teaching her chimpanzee friends sign language was interesting

   because _____ .

   _____ **A.** researchers were not involved

   _____ **B.** her friends signed to her and to each other

   _____ **C.** they couldn't learn all that Washoe knew

   _____ **D.** she did it regularly

1.3 *Read the passage from "How Smart Is Smart?" in NorthStar: Reading and Writing 4, Unit 4. Use the information from this reading and "Washoe's ASL Development" to complete the activity. Write the letter of the factor of intelligence next to the sentence that describes it. The first one has been done for you.*

How Smart Is Smart?

We humans recognize a "smart" person when we meet one; we know who is a "brain" and who is not. In school, we take IQ tests, which are supposed to give a numerical measure of our "intelligence." But these days, the whole concept of intelligence is being reevaluated. The older, standard IQ tests measure only a limited range of mental abilities, concentrating on mathematics and language skills. Creativity, which most people would agree is a critical element in the meaningful application of intelligence, has not traditionally been evaluated by such tests, and other important mental skills have also been ignored. But things are changing. Many scientists believe that dozens of different talents are a part of intelligence. In fact, more than a hundred factors of intelligence have been written about in scientific literature. Psychologists are now developing tests that measure intelligence

(continued on next page)

more accurately and more broadly. The SOI (Structure of Intellect) test, for example, evaluates five main factors of intelligence: cognition (comprehension), memory, evaluation (judgment, planning, reasoning, and critical decision making), convergent production (solving problems where answers are known), and divergent production (solving problems creatively). Each of these is broken down further into many subcategories.

But what about animals? We can't hand them a pencil and paper and give them a test, and we can't ask them what they're thinking. We must find other ways of measuring their "smarts." And that's not the only problem. Since the lives of animals are so different from ours, we can't apply human standards to them. We must develop different ideas of what animal intelligence might be.

   A. cognition

   B. memory

   C. evaluation

   D. divergent production

   __D__   Washoe taught other chimps to sign.

   _____ **1.** Washoe understood the meaning of many signs.

   _____ **2.** Washoe remembered more than 250 signs.

   _____ **3.** Washoe figured out new signs for words by deciding which signs paired together to make new meanings.

PART 2: VOCABULARY

2.1 *Cross out the vocabulary item in each group that does not relate to the others.*

1. candidate	participant	prisoner	entrant
2. evaluate	judge	assess	reject
3. prevail	weaken	dominate	lead
4. capacity	capability	ability	hope
5. subject	observer	scientist	researcher
6. resemble	look like	review	appear as

2.2 *Complete the sentences using the words from the box. Not all of the words will be used.*

attributed	conditioned	evolution	prevail
concepts	evaluation	predicted	resemble

1. Scientists _____ that the rats would continue to push the button even after the scientists had stopped giving them rewards.

2. The _____ of learning, performing, imitating, and seeking reward are similar but different in important ways.

3. Some researchers _____ the horse's performance to boredom.

4. When researchers pose a research question, it may actually affect their _____ of the results.

5. Because of its short lifespan and relatively quick _____, the common housefly is an excellent subject of study.

PART 3: SKILLS FOR WRITING

3.1 *Read the article about a boy's experiment in training a goldfish. Write five more adjective clauses from the article.*

Guillermo bought two goldfish and kept them in separate bowls. He planned to teach one goldfish to anticipate its feeding time, and he planned to use the other goldfish as his "control."

Every day before feeding the goldfish ~~that he was trying to train~~, Guillermo placed a music box next to the fish's bowl. Then he played a loud song that the fish could hear for one minute. After the minute, Guillermo fed the fish.

Guillermo put the control fish in a place where it couldn't hear the music. "I fed the control fish directly, without playing any music," explained Guillermo.

To Guillermo's surprise, the fish that got the music before his feedings almost immediately learned that food would follow the music. Guillermo reported that within a few days, "as soon as the music started, the fish swam quickly to the surface" to eat. In fact, he swam to the surface just as fast as the fish who didn't hear the music.

(continued on next page)

Later, Guillermo stopped feeding the fish after playing the music. Still, Guillermo wrote in his diary, "Even if I played the music when it wasn't feeding time, the fish would rush to the surface." Guillermo realized that he had conditioned the fish to swim up whenever it heard the music.

that he was trying to train _____

1. _____

2. _____

3. _____

4. _____

5. _____

3.2 *Check (✔) the better paraphrase for each quotation.*

Guillermo said, "I want to set up a casual experiment to study the fishes' intelligence."

✔ **A.** Guillermo explained that he wanted to do an informal experiment to test fish intelligence.

____ **B.** Guillermo said that he wanted to set up a casual experiment to study the fishes' intelligence.

1. Guillermo thought that "one minute should be long enough for the fish to recognize the sound of music."

____ **A.** Guillermo anticipated that the fish would be able to recognize the music within one minute.

____ **B.** Guillermo thought that one period of 60 seconds should be long enough for the fish to recognize the sound of music.

2. "I fed the control fish directly, without playing any music," explained Guillermo.

____ **A.** Guillermo said that he did not play music before feeding the control fish.

____ **B.** Guillermo explained that playing music for the control fish would have confused his study.

3. Guillermo reported that within a few days, "as soon as the music started, the fish swam quickly to the surface" to eat.

_____ **A.** Guillermo reported that within a few days of the start of his experiment, the fish who heard the music swam quickly to the surface of the water after the music had begun to play.

_____ **B.** Guillermo reported that the fish who heard the music swam rapidly to the surface.

4. Guillermo wrote in his diary, "Even if I played the music when it wasn't feeding time, the fish would rush to the surface."

_____ **A.** Guillermo wrote all of his findings and observations in his diary, including the fish's behavior when music was played.

_____ **B.** Guillermo wrote that the fish ultimately would swim to the surface any time the music was played.

PART 4: WRITING

A Summary Paragraph (20 minutes)

Reread "Washoe's ASL Development." Then write a summary of Washoe's experience learning ASL.

- Include the thesis.
- Include only the important details.
- Use your own words.
- Use the vocabulary and grammar from Unit 4.

Unit 4 Vocabulary Words				
attribute	concept	evolve	perceive	resemble
candidate	conditioned	factor	predict	standard
capacity	evaluate	feat	prevail	
Unit 4 Grammar: Adjective Clauses				
• The student **who studied the fish** learned that fish were smarter than he had originally thought.				

Achievement Tests
Unit 5

Name: _____

Date: _____

PART I: READING

1.1 *Read the passage from an autobiographical story. Check (✔) the best prediction of what the reading is about. There is only one right answer.*

In industrialized nations today, the average life expectancy hovers around 70 to 75 years. While this may sound young, compare modern life expectancies to those from previous generations. For example, in ancient Egypt, most people died between 30 and 40. Dying at such a young age may seem insufferable to us, yet the Egyptians expected it. The life of King Tutankhamun illustrates how this earlier age of death accelerated the ancient Egyptians' life cycle.

_____ **A.** modern life expectancies around the world

_____ **B.** the life cycle of ancient Egyptians

_____ **C.** the causes or premature death in ancient Egypt

_____ **D.** health care in industrialized nations

1.2 *Now read the entire story. Use the information to choose the correct answers.*

Life Expectancy in Ancient Egypt

In industrialized nations today, the average life expectancy hovers around 70 to 75 years. While this may sound young, compare modern life expectancies to those from previous generations. For example, in ancient Egypt, most people died between 30 and 40. Dying at this young age may seem unacceptable to us, yet the Egyptians expected it. The life of King Tutankhamun illustrates how this earlier age of death accelerated the ancient Egyptians' life cycle.

King Tut became king at age 9 and led his empire from 1333 to 1322 BC. Considering this, the young king had little time to train or plan for his leadership. Instead, he moved directly from childhood to adult responsibilities.

Like other ancient Egyptians, King Tut married at a young age. Whereas the modern day search for a marriage partner may take decades, the ancient Egyptians had no such leisure to make prolonged marriage decisions.

King Tut and his wife had two children who died as babies. While such deaths would lead to shock and immeasurable grief today, they were common then. So, parents could not count on watching their children grow up. Unlike modern humans, few Egyptians would have ever dreamed of holding their grandchildren in their arms, though some city-dwellers may have achieved this goal, as they had a lower mortality rate compared to village residents.

Other causes of a shorter life expectancy included tuberculosis, polio, and malnutrition. Diseases occasionally broke out, causing utter devastation. Many of these diseases were fatal, and unlike today, few could be cured or even treated. Still, today's scholars dispute why King Tut died at an age that was considered young even then: 19. King Tut possibly died from an infection that, even if it had been vigorously treated, would have required antibiotics not yet in existence. Ultimately, his doctors' techniques were limited because they lived before modern medicine.

   Since the time of the ancient Egyptians, humankind has made great strides in prolonging life expectancy. In fact, by ancient Egyptian standards, modern longevity is truly awesome. The Egyptians would be shocked to know that these days, some people even discuss immortality as a future possibility. While it may be presumptuous to think that we could ever achieve that, might it be possible to double life expectancy again over the next three thousand years?

Check (✔) the best answer to complete each sentence.

1. _____ illustrates the life cycle of ancient Egyptians.

   _____ **A.** King Tutankhamun's life

   _____ **B.** The search for a marriage partner

   _____ **C.** The life expectancy of modern humans

   _____ **D.** King Tutankhamun's children

2. According to the reading, in ancient Egypt, a long period of dating in order to find a mate was _____ .

   _____ **A.** important for a king

   _____ **B.** a luxury

   _____ **C.** a wasted effort

   _____ **D.** childish

3. Ancient Egyptians took their life expectancy to be _____ .

   _____ **A.** insufferable

   _____ **B.** normal

   _____ **C.** devastating

   _____ **D.** improvable with medical technology

4. The cause of King Tut's death is _____ .

   _____ **A.** hard to find

   _____ **B.** presumptuous

   _____ **C.** awesome

   _____ **D.** debated

1.3 *Read the passage from "Toward Immortality: The Social Burden of Longer Lives" in*
NorthStar: Reading and Writing 4, *Unit 5. Use the information from this reading and*
"Life Expectancy in Ancient Egypt" to complete the activity. Check (✔) the story in which
each idea is mentioned. The first one has been done for you.

Toward Immortality: The Social Burden of Longer Lives

<u>A Doubled Lifespan</u>

If scientists could create a pill that let you live twice as long while remaining free of
infirmities, would you take it?

If one considers only the personal benefits that longer life would bring, the
answer might seem like a no-brainer[1]: People could spend more quality time with
loved ones; watch future generations grow up; learn new languages; master new
musical instruments; try different careers; or travel the world.

But what about society as a whole? Would it be better off if lifespans were
doubled? The question is one of growing relevance, and serious debate about it goes
back at least a few years to the Kronos Conference on Longevity Health Sciences in
Arizona. Gregory Stock, director of the program on Medicine, Technology, and
Society at UCLA's School of Public Health, answered the question with an emphatic
"Yes." A doubled lifespan, Stock said, would "give us a chance to recover from our
mistakes, lead us towards longer-term thinking, and reduce healthcare costs by
delaying the onset of expensive diseases of aging. It would also raise productivity by
adding to our prime years."

Bioethicist Daniel Callahan, a cofounder of the Hastings Center in New York,
didn't share Stock's enthusiasm. Callahan's objections were practical ones. For one
thing, he said, doubling lifespans won't solve any of our current social problems.
"We have war, poverty, all sorts of issues around, and I don't think any of them
would be at all helped by having people live longer," Callahan said in a recent
telephone interview. "The question is, 'What will we get as a society?' I suspect it
won't be a better society."

Others point out that a doubling of the human lifespan will affect society at
every level. Notions[2] about marriage, family, and work will change in fundamental
ways, they say, as will attitudes toward the young and the old.

<u>Marriage and Family</u>

Richard Kalish, a psychologist who considered the social effects of life extension
technologies, thinks a longer lifespan will radically change how we view marriage.

---

[1] **no-brainer:** something that you do not have to think about because it is easy to
understand

[2] **notions:** ideas, beliefs, or opinions

Ideas	"Toward Immortality: The Social Burden of Longer Lives"	"Life Expectancy in Ancient Egypt"
Limited techniques for doctors		✓
1. Not necessarily a better society		
2. Less shock and grief at the death of an infant		
3. Humans and immortality		
4. Change in ideas about marriage and family		
5. Life cycle accelerated		

PART 2: VOCABULARY

2.1 *Complete the sentences using the correct adjective or adverb form of a word from the box.*

awe	immeasurable	presume	vigor
chill	love	tolerate	worry

1. All ancient Egyptians struggled with their climate's hot days and _____ nights.

2. In many cultures, people think it is _____ and arrogant for young people to believe that they can choose a marital partner well.

3. Strong bonds among the living family members made their many losses more _____ .

4. The development of antibiotics _____ advanced modern medicine.

5. The ancient Egyptians farmed _____ and saved as much food as they could in case of famine.

2.2 *Fill in the chart with words from the box that describe feelings and time. Not all of the words will be used.*

chilly	insufferable	prolonged	simultaneously
disparate	productive	punctually	utterly

Feelings		Time	
1.		**3.**	
2.		**4.**	
		5.	

PART 3: SKILLS FOR WRITING

3.1 *Read the article about the Fountain of Youth. Complete each sentence with the verb in the correct tense: simple past, present perfect, or present perfect continuous.*

In 1513, Juan Ponce de Leon, the governor of Puerto Rico, started to look for the Fountain of Youth. He continued his search for years, ultimately coming very close to Warm Mineral Spring. Still popular today, this spring _____ for
1. (use)
thousands of years. It is possible that Leon never _____ whether the
2. (learn)
spring was the fountain he was seeking, because he _____ his life in
3. (lose)
battle there.

   People from many cultures and many religious backgrounds

_____ the Fountain for thousands of years. Most recently, the well-
4. (seek)
known American magician, David Copperfield, claimed that he had discovered the true Fountain of Youth amid islands in the Bahamas. Copperfield

_____ that when dying bugs are put in contact with the water, they
5. (report)
will fly again. Copperfield purchased the island group, and since then, scientists

_____ experiments of the waters to determine their restorative
6. (conduct)
powers. The island group _____ to visitors for the past several years.
7. (close)

3.2 *Complete the sentences that use figurative language with a word from the box. Not all of the words will be used.*

as	blew	glow	like	~~saucer~~	hummed

The moon was a golden _____*saucer*_____ hanging in the sky.

1. The sound of the ocean was _____ the brass section of a band.

2. The wind _____ a tune of mystery and horror.

3. The setting sun was as red _____ fire.

PART 4: WRITING

A Descriptive Essay (20 minutes)

Write a description of your current life, imagining that your life expectancy is only 30.

- Write an interesting introduction.
- Describe your imaginary life using sensory details of smell, sight, sound, taste, and touch.
- Include figures of speech in your descriptions.
- Include a clear conclusion.
- Use the vocabulary and grammar from Unit 5.

Unit 5 Vocabulary Words				
awesome	immeasurably	presumptuous	ultimately	worrisome
chilly	immortality	prolonged	utterly	
disparate	insufferable	tolerable	vigorously	

Unit 5 Grammar: Contrasting Simple Past, Present Perfect, and Present Perfect Continuous

- [simple past] [present perfect continuous]
  Leo **rented** this movie on Thursday, and he **has been trying** to finish it all week.
  [present perfect]
- Now he **has returned** the movie to the store.

Achievement Tests
Unit 6

PART 1: READING

1.1 *Read the passage from an inspirational article. Check (✔) the best prediction of what the reading is about. There is only one right answer.*

People often say that they want to make the world a better place. However, they may feel that in order to make a difference, in order to impact society in a major way, they need to give a lot of time or a lot of money. Actually, they don't need to do either. Anne Herbert's words, now a well-known bumper sticker, have inspired many to a different level of donation, "Practice random acts of kindness and senseless acts of beauty." Let us propose some simple ways that you can devote yourself to making the world a better place, starting today.

_____ **A.** people who have impacted society in a major way

_____ **B.** a woman named Anne Herbert

_____ **C.** the randomness of kindness

_____ **D.** little steps that people can take to improve their community

1.2 *Now read the entire article. Use the information to choose the correct answers.*

Random Acts of Kindness

People often say that they want to make the world a better place. However, they may feel that in order to make a difference, in order to impact society in a major way, they need to give a lot of time or a lot of money. Actually, they don't need to do either. Anne Herbert's words, now a well known bumper sticker, have inspired many to a different level of donation, "Practice random acts of kindness and senseless acts of beauty." Let us propose some simple ways that you can devote yourself to making the world a better place, starting today.

1. Greet another person by saying "good afternoon" or by smiling.
   The simple act of extending greetings connects us to our fellow beings in a brief but fulfilling way. Say "good morning" to the next person you meet. You'll both end up with a smile.

2. Help a stranger.
   Get a shopping cart at the grocery store for somebody whose hands are full. Donate old furniture to a homeless shelter. When you are determined to help the next guy, it'll make you happy, too.

3. Treat the environment with respect.
   Plant a flower. Pick up a piece of trash. Turn off a running faucet. If you treat public places proudly, you challenge others to behave to a higher standard, too!

4. Compliment someone with conviction.
In our busy commercial culture, compliments often come and go in an empty way. The next time you praise somebody, put some passion into your praise. Tell them specifically what you admire, and why. Make it personal.

5. Relax when there's a problem.
Big or small, problems are a part of life. Relax! If somebody spills soda in your path, say, "No problem." You'll enjoy the satisfaction of staying cool when others might end up angry.

Have a nice day!

Check (✔) the best answer to complete each sentence.

1. According to the article, when you do kind things to others, you may feel that

the act is _____ .

_____ **A.** short

_____ **B.** satisfying

_____ **C.** premature

_____ **D.** simple

2. The article recommends getting a shopping cart _____ .

_____ **A.** when your hands are full

_____ **B.** at a homeless shelter

_____ **C.** when you smile

_____ **D.** for somebody else

3. The article says that treating the environment well can _____ .

_____ **A.** increase natural beauty at parks

_____ **B.** encourage others to do the same

_____ **C.** save taxpayers' money

_____ **D.** make you feel more respect for your surroundings

4. According to the article, you can show praise that is _____ .

_____ **A.** admirable

_____ **B.** focused on commercial goods

_____ **C.** specific and personalized

_____ **D.** part of a busy day

(continued on next page)

5. The author probably thinks that people mostly like to feel _____ .

_____ **A.** happy

_____ **B.** important

_____ **C.** challenged

_____ **D.** useful

1.3 *Read the passage from "Justin Lebo" in* Northstar: Reading and Writing 4, *Unit 6. Use the information from this reading and "Random Acts of Kindness" to complete the activity. Not all of the statements will be used. The first one has been done for you.*

Justin Lebo

Reporters and interviewers have asked Justin Lebo the same question over and over: "Why do you do it?" The question seems to make him uncomfortable. It's as if they want him to say what a great person he is. Their stories always make him seem like a saint, which he knows he isn't. "Sure it's nice of me to make the bikes," he says, "because I don't have to. But I want to. In part, I do it for myself. I don't think you can ever really do anything to help anybody else if it doesn't make you happy."

"Once I overheard a kid who got one of my bikes say, 'A bike is like a book: it opens up a whole new world.' That's how I feel, too. It made me happy to know that kid felt that way. That's why I do it."

A. ~~One act of devotion may inspire others.~~

B. Doing good things should be voluntary.

C. Giving a gift can open up a new world.

D. Good acts make the doer feel happy.

E. Donating shows that the doer is a good person.

F. Acts of kindness make the world a better place.

G. Every kid should have a bike.

"Justin Lebo"   Both   "Random Acts of Kindness"

1. _____

2. ___ A ___

3. ___

4. _____

PART 2: VOCABULARY

2.1 *Read the letter from a boy in the Kilbarchan home to Justin. Use the words from the box to fill in the blanks. Not all of the words will be used.*

determine	keep on	passion	proud
fulfilling	managed	propose	sit around

Dear Justin,

Thank you so much for my bicycle! I don't know how you _____ to
             1.

make a used bike look so new. I _____ thinking about your hard work
             2.

on the bike. It must have taken you a long time to fix it up so well. I bet you feel

really _____ of your work. Your success makes me want to find a useful
      3.

hobby, too. I don't have mechanical skills like you do, but I have a lot of

_____ for painting. For me, it's a very _____ hobby. So, I am
    4.   **5.**

starting to make some paintings that I can give to other boys here to hang in

their rooms. I hope they will enjoy them as much as I am enjoying the bicycle.

                         Thanks again!

                         Tommy

2.2 *Complete the sentences using the correct word from the chart.*

Noun	Verb	Adjective	Adverb
admiration	admire	admiring	admiringly
challenge	challenge	challenging	X
determination	determine	determined	X
inspiration	inspire	inspired inspirational	inspirationally
pride	X	proud	proudly
proposal	propose	proposed	X

1. Jacob was _____ to build a bicycle for every boy in the home.

2. Those who know about Mother Teresa's acts of devotion look at her with great

   _____ .

3. The generosity of Oprah Winfrey may _____ many donors to
   give money.

4. Some schools _____ that community service should be a
   requirement.

5. Jacob rebuilt the bikes _____ knowing they would go to good
   use.

PART 3: SKILLS FOR WRITING

3.1 *Read a notice about Linus, one of the dogs at the Prince George County Animal Shelter. Write four more sentences that have concessions.*

Adopt a Pet

Meet Linus. ~~Even though she just arrived at the shelter one week ago, we are already searching for her home, because we are sure that the right, loving family will feel lucky to find Linus~~.

Linus is about three years old, a mixed breed, mostly terrier. This breed is usually very devoted, and terriers can end up by your side all day long. Despite the fact that she likes a lot of attention, Linus seems to have a reasonable sense of independence and can spend up to four hours alone.

Linus is a friendly dog who likes to be held and petted. Although she likes to be petted, she is quite uncomfortable around young children. So, Linus is looking for a home with adult caretakers.

She is fully house-trained and usually follows simple commands such as "sit" and "come." Even though she clearly has had good training, she still needs work in learning to walk with a leash.

Linus was found in a rural area with no tags, and the people who found her say that she was very stressed by her ride in their car. In spite of this, she may be able to travel comfortably in a dog carrier, depending how she was trained as a puppy.

If Linus sounds like a good fit for your home, call the Prince George County Animal Shelter today: 555-3322.

Even though she just arrived at the shelter one week ago, we are already

searching for her home, because we are sure thet the right, loving family will

feel lucky to find Linus.

1. _____

_____

2. _____

_____

3. _____

_____

4. _____

_____

3.2 *Combine each pair of sentences using the concessions in parentheses. Imagine that you support animal shelters, pet adoption, and mandatory animal obedience classes.*

1. Supporters of pet adoption argue that it saves animals' lives. Critics of pet adoption counter that many adopted pets are mistreated and end up back in a shelter. (although)

   _____

   _____

2. Supporters of pet adoption claim that it usually benefits both the animal and the adoptee. Critics of pet adoption argue that it is risky to bring an unknown animal into a home. (in spite of)

   _____

   _____

3. Supporters of mandatory animal obedience classes say that well trained animals make better pets. Opponents of mandatory animal obedience classes say that each person should be able to decide how to train a pet. (even though)

   _____

   _____

3.3 *Read three other possible introductions for the article "Adopt a Pet." Label them A, B, or C from the box.*

> A. Tells why the topic is important.
> B. Asks a provocative question.
> C. Tells a relevant story.

_____ 1. Have you ever considered adopting a pet? If so, you'll never find a dog nicer than Linus. Even though she just arrived at the shelter one week ago, we are already searching for her home, because we are sure that the right, loving family will feel lucky to find Linus.

_____ 2. Every day, three new dogs are brought to the Prince George Animal Shelter, and in order to survive, they need to find a caring home. Even though she just arrived at the shelter one week ago, we are already searching for her home, because we are sure that the right, loving family will feel lucky to find Linus.

_____ 3. Our shelter has a new dog. Her name is Linus. Even though she just arrived at the shelter one week ago, we are already searching for her home, because we are sure that the right, loving family will feel lucky to find Linus.

PART 4: WRITING

A Persuasive Essay (20 minutes)

Write a five-paragraph persuasive essay to convince somebody to commit to perform one act of kindness every day.

- Include a thesis statement in your introduction.
- Support your position with details and reasons.
- Include a possible counter argument and refute it.
- Write a conclusion that makes a prediction, asks a question, or tells a story.
- Use the vocabulary and grammar from Unit 6.

Unit 6 Vocabulary Words				
admiring	donate	inspired	passion	satisfaction
challenge	end up	keep on	proposal	sit around
determined	fulfilling	manage	proudly	thrilled
devote				

Unit 6 Grammar: Concessions
• ***Even though*** Justin wasn't required to volunteer, he chose to repair and donate bikes.

Achievement Tests
Unit 7

Name: _____

Date: _____

PART 1: READING

1.1 *Read the passage about online courses. Check (✔) the best prediction of what the reading is about. There is only one right answer.*

Do you consider online classes to be a viable alternative to traditional face-to-face classrooms? If so, you're not alone. The enrollment rate for online classes is soaring. While some students never fully adjust to the new medium, others swear by[1] it.

_____ **A.** the popularity of alternative learning situations

_____ **B.** the benefits and some drawbacks of online classes

_____ **C.** how to adjust to online classes

_____ **D.** how to enroll in both traditional and online courses

1.2 *Now read the entire article. Use the information to choose the correct answers.*

Learners Weigh Online Option

Do you consider online classes to be a viable alternative to traditional face-to-face classrooms? If so, you're not alone. The enrollment rate for online classes is soaring. While some students never fully adjust to the new medium, others swear by it.

Many students who like online classes enjoy the convenience. Diana Morgan's story is quite typical. Ms. Morgan explains, "A specific situation dictated my participation in online courses. I was working as a medical assistant and caring for my children. My ambition was to become a nurse, but I was overwhelmed. Learning online let me take stimulating nursing classes from home. The class saved me time and money."

Others approach online learning with more doubt, but even among those, many are soon converted. After completing an online marketing class, Julia Jackson said, "I felt that studying online would be a more limited experience than in a traditional classroom. However, this was a misconception. My class was enriched by the eclectic professional backgrounds of my classmates. They were also from many different geographic locations. Several students even had expertise in running their own businesses."

Some aspects of online learning turn out to be positive for some students and negative for others. Raymond Zamora says he doesn't like to be with other people. He is also an avid fan of science fiction—the subject of his first online course. "Being physically isolated let me communicate my ideas without interruption. What a great experience!" By comparison, Alicia Branson could never get used to the isolation. "Without face-to-face interaction with my instructor, I felt less motivated. My persistence declined as the class continued."

_____

[1] **swear by:** promise something to be true

T-42

© 2009 by Pearson Education, Inc. Permission granted to reproduce for classroom use.

One indisputable[2] drawback of online study is that fewer students who enroll complete their courses compared to those in traditional classroom courses. Educational researchers dispute the reasons behind the pattern. Registration for courses is so easy that it may attract learners who are less serious.

Knowing if online learning would suit you may ultimately depend on your learning style. However, until you try it, you can't be sure!

_____

[2] **indisputable:** something that can't be argued because it's a fact

Check (✔) the best answer to complete each sentence.

1. The article focuses on _____ experiences with online classes.

   _____ **A.** working professionals'

   _____ **B.** instructors'

   _____ **C.** typical students'

   _____ **D.** medical patients'

2. Diana Morgan took an online class primarily because _____ .

   _____ **A.** she wanted to save money

   _____ **B.** she was busy at work and at home

   _____ **C.** there were no traditional nursing schools available

   _____ **D.** her employer dictated it

3. Based on Julia Jackson's experience, she would probably be most likely to

   _____ .

   _____ **A.** limit the time she studies

   _____ **B.** think her misconceptions were true

   _____ **C.** start her own business

   _____ **D.** take another online course

4. Raymond Zamora and Alicia Branson were both _____ .

   _____ **A.** science fiction fans

   _____ **B.** friendly

   _____ **C.** convinced that online classes were great

   _____ **D.** students in online classes

(continued on next page)

5. Compared to the dropout rate in traditional classrooms, the rate in online

   courses is _____ .

   _____ **A.** higher

   _____ **B.** the same

   _____ **C.** lower

   _____ **D.** hard to track

1.3 *Read the passage from "The Satisfied Learner: How Families Homeschool Their Teens" in NorthStar: Reading and Writing 4, Unit 7. Use the information from this reading and "Learners Weigh Online Option" to complete the activity. The first one has been done for you.*

The Satisfied Learner: How Families Homeschool Their Teens

Maybe it's the fear of school violence or the lack of stimulating courses, but the number of homeschooling teenagers is on the rise. Some parents balk at the very thought of homeschooling their teen. After all, it's one thing to teach your daughter how to read. It's quite another to teach her trigonometry. But the idea that parents are solely responsible for instruction is just one of the many misconceptions about home education. Some other incorrect notions include that homeschooling inevitably leads to social isolation, decreased participation in music and sports, and college rejection letters. The following families' stories speak the truth: Socially and intellectually satisfying, homeschooling is an extremely viable option—for both parent and child.

Statements	Homeschooling	Online Courses	Both
People have misconceptions about this type of schooling.			✓
1. People think that the classes will not be as stimulating as traditional classes.			
2. People think that parents do all the teaching.			
3. Many people consider this educational alternative a reasonable possibility.			
4. Fewer students complete the work.			

PART 2: VOCABULARY

2.1 *Fill in the chart with the noun form of the words.*

Noun	Verb	Adjective	Adverb
1.	consult	consulting	X
2.	isolate	isolated	X
3.	misconceive	misconceived	X
4.	stimulate	stimulating	X

2.2 *Complete the sentences using the words from the box. Not all of the words will be used.*

adjust	dispute	isolation	persistence	viable
dictate	eclectic	misconception	stimulate	

1. Some learners can never _____ to studying alone behind a computer screen.

2. While online courses may be _____ for some learners, they require self-motivation and discipline.

3. While _____ is a good trait for any student, it cannot guarantee your success.

4. Some students _____ their grades, regardless of their performance.

5. They may have a _____ that their grades should be high whether their work is excellent or not.

6. A talented professor can _____ even the brightest of students.

PART 3: SKILLS FOR WRITING

3.1 *Write the direct speech statements in indirect speech.*

1. Professor Endendel said, "Few students followed the actual assignment."

   _____

2. One student raised her hand and said, "I want to do the assignment again."

   _____

3. The professor said, "I'll think about offering an alternative assignment tomorrow."

   _____

4. My girlfriend tells me, "I always do the extra credit work so that I get the extra points."

   _____

5. After class, I said, "I might do extra credit from now on, too."

   _____

3.2 *Complete each sentence with the correct form of the word in parentheses. Make sure that your sentence has parallel structure.*

Most learners rely primarily on reading the course book, listening to lectures, or ____*watching*____ the tapes.
           (watch)

1. Jason gets frustrated, distracted, and _____ when there is noise in the
                                              (irritation)
   library.

2. The counselor always tries to stimulate students, to explain their options, and
   _____ them to do their best.
        (motivate)

3. The hikers went up the mountain with perseverance, energy, and high
   _____.
        (ambition)

4. The designer has both experience and _____ in working on web
                                              (expert)
   pages.

5. The crew members discuss their work shifts, _____ with the shift
                                                    (consultation)
   manager, and post their conclusions.

PART 4: WRITING

A Classification Essay (20 minutes)

Write a four-paragraph essay about different ways of learning outside of a school setting, such as being tutored, being self-taught, observing others, or traveling.

- In the introduction paragraph, interest your reader and include a thesis statement.
- Discuss one category in each body paragraph.
- Include the parallel points in each body paragraph.
- Restate the thesis in your conclusion paragraph.
- Use the vocabulary and grammar from Unit 7.

<table>
<tr><td colspan="5" align="center">Unit 7 Vocabulary Words</td></tr>
<tr><td>adjust
ambition
avid</td><td>consultation
dictate
dispute</td><td>eclectic
expertise
isolation</td><td>misconception
persistence
stimulate</td><td>viable</td></tr>
<tr><td colspan="5" align="center">Unit 7 Grammar: Direct and Indirect Speech</td></tr>
<tr><td colspan="5">• DIRECT: Mary said, "I am going to the store this afternoon."
• INDIRECT: She said that she was going to the store this afternoon.</td></tr>
</table>

Achievement Tests
Unit 8

PART 1: READING

1.1 *Read the book recommendation from a bookstore employee. Check (✔) the best prediction of what the reading is about. There is only one right answer.*

Our staff readers recommend *Corfu Banquet: A Memoir with Seasonal Recipes*, by Emma Tennant. The memoir takes place on the Greek island of Corfu. The author's parents built a house there in the 1960s. *Corfu Banquet* is more than a story of a house. It brings alive the tastes, smells, and colors that are inextricably linked to the island.

_____ **A.** a Greek island named Corfu

_____ **B.** the author, Emma Tennant

_____ **C.** how the house was built on Corfu

_____ **D.** what impressed the staff readers in the memoir

1.2 *Now read the entire recommendation. Use the information to choose the correct answers.*

Corfu Banquet: An Excellent Book

Our staff readers recommend *Corfu Banquet: A Memoir with Seasonal Recipes*, by Emma Tennant. The memoir takes place on the Greek island of Corfu. The author's parents built a house there in the 1960s. *Corfu Banquet* is more than a story of a house. It brings alive the tastes, smells, and colors that are inextricably linked to the island.

On Corfu, residents enter the rhythms of the earth. They cook local, seasonal foods and celebrate the rich bounty of the land. *Corfu Banquet* brings alive the sumptuous sights and smells of the Mediterranean so that you can literally taste its flavors. This is a pleasurable experience. Readers imagine picking the basil that imparts its sweet fragrance from great pots on the porch. You can almost taste the light pink homemade ice cream.

Beyond the flavors, the author's description of authentic details adds texture to the reader's understanding of the land. For example, we can see *mourga* clouding the autumn waters. This is the mush of olive skins that are customarily thrown away from the village press. Readers can also enjoy the leisurely experience of joining Tennant's family meals, where they enjoy food and drink for hours.

Corfu Banquet leaves out nothing. It even gives deference to Maria, the "spirit of the house." Tennant includes several family recipes, and a few original paintings. Her book is an eye-opening celebration of the art of one family in the Greek isles.

Check (✔) the best answer to complete each sentence.

1. According to the reviewer, the rhythms of the earth can be seen in

   _____ .

   _____ **A.** the tides of the Mediterranean

   _____ **B.** the building of a house

   _____ **C.** the local foods

   _____ **D.** the land of the island

2. Reading this book offers the reader _____ .

   _____ **A.** a good education about Corfu

   _____ **B.** lots of excitement

   _____ **C.** a sense of the island's simple pleasures

   _____ **D.** a brief history of Greece

3. *Mourga* can best be described as _____ .

   _____ **A.** the meat of the olives

   _____ **B.** leftover olive skins that are thrown away

   _____ **C.** cloudy waters

   _____ **D.** a tasty spread made of mashed olives

4. Who is Maria? _____ .

   _____ **A.** A ghost

   _____ **B.** The family cook

   _____ **C.** The author's maternal grandmother

   _____ **D.** One of the author's parents

1.3 *Read the passage from "'Slow Food' Movement Aims at Restoring the Joy of Eating" in NorthStar: Reading and Writing 4, Unit 8. Use the information from this reading and "Corfu Banquet: An Excellent Book" to complete the activity. The first one has been done for you.*

"Slow Food" Movement Aims at Restoring the Joy of Eating

"It was just a game at first," says founder Carlo Petrini, "a chance to remind people that food is a perishable art, as pleasurable in its way as a sculpture by Michelangelo."

Today, Slow Food is 20,000 strong in Italy, where the joy of the table is a matter of national pride. And there are Slow Food organizations in more than 15 countries, from Switzerland to Singapore.

Although the movement is new to these shores, adherents say they believe Americans will take to it like pigs to truffles. "Every year Americans are going to more restaurants, asking and learning more about food," says Paul Bartolotta, Slow Foodist and owner of Chicago's Spiaggia restaurant.

He says the USA is ripe for Slow Food. "Ten years ago, there were hardly any (farmers) markets, we were fast-food-driven, and there was less interest in food and wine. It has dramatically changed. Now there are organic supermarkets."

Slow Food could even tame America's obsession with dieting, White says. "If you only feed the body, you get fat. It's important not to deny the spiritual aspects of eating, to milk the most joy out of the bodily function of eating."

"And time at the table is time well spent," says Bartolotta. "The Slow Food movement's message is, 'Let's eat well and enjoy it.' No matter how crazy and hectic our lives are, the pleasure of the table is a fundamental right."

Statements	"'Slow Food' Movement"	*Corfu Banquet*	Both
Food is a form of art.			✓
1. Dining should be done at a leisurely pace.			
2. The people eat at fast food restaurants too often.			
3. Food is tied to the land where it is grown.			
4. Mealtime is a family activity.			
5. Enjoying food means more than simply eating and swallowing.			

PART 2: VOCABULARY

2.1 *Read the quotations. Then check (✔) the word that is closest in meaning to the boldfaced word and best completes each sentence.*

1. "He would show me the correct way to prepare rice, telling me that if our rice was old then perhaps more water than **customary** might be needed to give our congee its fine and silky finish."

    Cooking old rice may require more water than _____ .

    _____ **A.** rice   _____ **B.** usual   _____ **C.** the recipe

2. "When we ate raw fish, uye sahng, she taught, one had to prepare the fish in the proper manner."

    The fish needed to be prepared _____ .

    _____ **A.** in advance   _____ **B.** religious   _____ **C.** correctly

3. "When it was still **nominally** alive, you scaled it, gutted and cleaned it, then sliced it for eating."

    The fish could be prepared when it was still _____ alive.

    _____ **A.** officially   _____ **B.** completely   _____ **C.** not

4. "She would eat no vegetables that were older than two hours out of the ground, which **necessitated** repeated trips to the markets by her servants."

    Her desire for fresh vegetables _____ several trips to the market.

    _____ **A.** disrupted   _____ **B.** prevented   _____ **C.** required

5. "'Do not shout in the kitchen,' Ah Paw would **insist**."

    Ah Paw _____ that people not shout in the kitchen.

    _____ **A.** demanded   _____ **B.** preferred   _____ **C.** thought

2.2 *Complete the sentences with the words from the box. Not all of the words will be used.*

authentic	imparts	pleasurable	specify
decline	leisurely	properly	throw it away

1. The _____ Greek dish called *spanokopeta* is made from a flaky

   pastry in layers with various fillings.

2. To prepare it _____, you need to use butter.

3. The butter _____ a rich flavor and smell.

4. If the thin dough tears, there is no need to _____ .

5. Some recipes _____ the filling, but more experienced cooks

   may use meats, cheese, or even fried leeks in their filling.

PART 3: SKILLS FOR WRITING

3.1 *Rewrite the sentences. Replace the boldfaced verb with a phrasal verb from the box. You may need to change the form of the verb. Not all of the phrasal verbs will be used.*

catch on	do away with	look over	take advantage of	turn up
come up with	grow up	pick up	turn on	

1. Turkish cooks have **invented** a version of spanokopeta that has fewer

   calories and less fat.

   _____

   _____

2. Using yogurt instead of butter, Turkish cooks **remove** about 50% of the calories

   in their spanokopeta.

   _____

   _____

3. In fact, yogurt is the standard ingredient in this pastry, and you'll see it if you **examine** any Turkish cookbook.

_____

_____

4. Turkish chefs have also **exploited** the idea that the pastry top does not need to be flaky and brown.

_____

_____

5. Instead, they **increase** the heat while cooking, and when they remove it from the oven, they cover it with a towel, making the pastry soft.

_____

_____

6. Turkish-style spanokopeta, however, has not **become popular** in the USA.

_____

_____

3.2 *Read the paragraph. Then read the chart and match the parts of the sentences to form complete sentences. Write the correct letter on the line.*

The melon pickers stood in a long chain. They passed melons all day. They passed from one person to the next. Their backs got tired. Finally, they couldn't catch any more. The field looked like dance. It was elegant. The pickers' arms danced. Their melons flew. The melons were fragile.

____1. The melon pickers stood in a long chain,	**A.** like an elegant dance.
____2. They passed from one person to the next	**B.** and fragile melons flying through the air.
____3. The field looked	**C.** and they passed melons all day long.
____4. It was the dance of pickers' arms	**D.** until their backs got so tired that they couldn't catch any more.

PART 4: WRITING

A Narrative Essay (20 minutes)

Write a four-paragraph essay about an experience that focused on food: cooking, planting, harvesting, preparing, canning, etc. Your essay should include the components of narrative: an interesting thesis, examples and details that support your thesis, a clear chronology that uses transition words to show the order of events in time.

- Introduce your topic and write a clear thesis.
- Use examples and details to support your thesis.
- Use transition words to show how events are related in time.
- Vary the length of your sentences.
- Use the vocabulary and grammar from Unit 8.

Unit 8 Vocabulary Words				
authentic	evident	insist	necessitate	proper
customary	impart	leisurely	nominally	specify
decline	inextricably linked	literally	pleasurable	throw away
deference				

Unit 8 Grammar: Phrasal Verbs
• She **turned off** the lights in the restaurant kitchen.

Achievement Tests
Unit 9

Name: _____

Date: _____

PART 1: READING

1.1 *Read the passage from a pamphlet about naturalization. Check (✔) the best prediction of what the reading is about. There is only one right answer.*

Nearly eight million permanent residents of the United States are able to become U.S. citizens through a process called naturalization. Many of these residents will choose to apply for naturalization. They will spend significant amounts of time and money. Often, they even hire lawyers to help them through confusing paperwork, governmental requirements, restrictions, and fine print. They take tests and pay fees and struggle, with impatience, toward their goal. These details can become so complicated that some applicants may actually forget or overlook the emotional element of their decision.

_____ **A.** the emotional challenge of choosing to naturalize

_____ **B.** how to choose a good immigration lawyer

_____ **C.** restrictions on naturalization

_____ **D.** the time and financial cost of the naturalization process

1.2 *Now read the entire pamphlet. Use the information to choose the correct answers.*

Is Naturalization Right for You?

Nearly eight million permanent residents of the United States are able to become U.S. citizens through a process called naturalization. Many of these residents will choose to apply for naturalization. They will spend significant amounts of time and money. Often, they even hire lawyers to help them through confusing paperwork, governmental requirements, restrictions, and fine print. They take tests and pay fees and struggle, with impatience, toward their goal. These details can become so complicated that some applicants may actually forget or overlook the emotional element of their decision.

In order to become a citizen, a person must take an oath.[1] In the oath, this person must state support of the U.S. Constitution. He or she must agree to obey the laws of the United States and take back any foreign allegiance.[2] This means that naturalized citizens must actually give up their loyalty to their former country. They must establish a new allegiance to the United States.

Changing one's native, patriotic commitment may be easy for some. It could be especially easy for those who have suffered mistreatment, poverty, or terrible discontent in their native country.

(continued on next page)

---

[1] **oath:** a promise
[2] **allegiance:** loyalty to something

However, for many others, the realization of giving up native loyalties can be difficult in one's soul. Many new residents to the United States, or to any new country, may long for their native land. They may miss the people, the geography, the food, the music, and the traditions. They may think back with nostalgia to the land of their birth. Some may even realize that they took for granted certain comforts of home. For these residents, is it really so easy to let go of their commitment to their home country?

Some applicants for naturalization approach the process with vigor. They may not even think about the emotional impact of their choice. However, sooner or later, it is predictable that they will come face to face with the reality of this decision. Then they must ask: Is naturalization right for me?

Check (✔) the best answer to complete each sentence.

1. Becoming a citizen may be especially difficult for a person's _____ .

   _____ **A.** body   _____ **C.** home country

   _____ **B.** soul   _____ **D.** lawyer

2. A person who takes the oath of allegiance is supposed to _____

   his loyalty to the United States.

   _____ **A.** take back   _____ **C.** switch

   _____ **B.** learn   _____ **D.** make equal

3. Even if people don't think about the emotional impact of naturalization at first,

   later they will _____ .

   _____ **A.** need a lawyer   _____ **C.** feel like a foreigner

   _____ **B.** be more comfortable   _____ **D.** wonder if they made the
                                                    right choice

4. "Patriotic commitment may be easy for some" probably means that these

   people _____ .

   _____ **A.** are glad to leave their country   _____ **C.** have money for lawyers

   _____ **B.** are more patriotic   _____ **D.** are more patient

5. After adopting a new country, many people may feel _____ their

   native country.

   _____ **A.** increased passion for   _____ **C.** confusion about

   _____ **B.** decreased love for   _____ **D.** strange in

1.3 *Read the poem "Nostalgia" from* NorthStar: Reading and Writing 4, Unit 9. *Use the information from this reading and "Is Naturalization Right for You?" to complete the activity. The first one has been done for you.*

Nostalgia
By Virgilio Dávila (1869–1943)

1   "Mamma, Borinquen[1] calls me,
     this country is not mine,
     Borinquen is pure flame
     and here I am dying of the cold."

2   In search of a better future
     I left the native home,
     and established my store
     in the middle of New York.
     What I see around me
     is a sad panorama,[2]
     and my spirit calls out,
     wounded by much nostalgia,
     for the return to the home nest,
     Mamma, Borinquen calls me!

3   Where will I find here
     like in my criollo[3] land
     a dish of chicken and rice,
     a cup of good coffee?
     Where, oh where will I see
     radiant in their attire
     the girls, rich in vigor,
     whose glances bedazzle?[4]
     Here eyes do not bedazzle,
     this country is not mine!

4   If I listen to a song here
     of those I learned at home,
     or a danza[5] by Tavarez,
     Campos, or Dueño Colon,
     my sensitive heart
     is more enflamed with patriotic love,
     and a herald[6] that faithful proclaims
     this holy feeling
     the wail "Borinquen is pure flame!"
     comes to my ears.

5   In my land, what beauty!
     In the hardest winter
     not a tree is seen bare,
     not a vale[7] without green.
     The flower rules the garden,
     the river meanders talkative,
     the bird in the shadowy wood
     sings his arbitrary[8] song,
     and here . . . The snow is a shroud,[9]
     here I am dying of the cold.

---

[1] **Borinquen:** the name the people of Puerto Rico use when referring to their homeland; the Borinquen Indians, or Boriqueños, were the original inhabitants of Puerto Rico

[2] **panorama:** a view over a wide area of land

[3] **criollo:** Spanish-American

[4] **bedazzle:** to impress, surprise

[5] **danza:** a type of dance music from the nineteenth century

[6] **herald:** messenger

[7] **vale:** a wide, low valley

[8] **arbitrary:** decided or arranged without a reason or plan; random

[9] **shroud:** a cloth that is wrapped around a dead person's body before it is buried

Statements	"Nostalgia"	"Is Naturalization Right for You?"	Both
Passion toward one's native country may always remain strong.			✓
1. People may feel impatient about the process of becoming a citizen.			
2. In a new country, a person may long for the food, the people, and the culture of "home."			
3. The old country is warm and the earth is green, whereas the new country is cold.			
4. Leaving one's homeland can be very hard for the soul, or spirit.			

PART 2: VOCABULARY

2.1   *Circle the word that best completes each analogy.*

1. establish: create = begin: _____

   A. end   **B.** consider   **C.** start

2. formerly: time = north: _____

   A. direction   **B.** foods   **C.** signal

3. sensation: feeling = ache: _____

   A. love   **B.** pain   **C.** celebration

4. discontent: unhappiness = hurry: _____

   A. rush   **B.** slow down   **C.** maintain speed

5. predictable: expected = unknown: _____

   A. frightening   **B.** known   **C.** learned

2.2 *Complete the sentences with the words from the box. You may need to change the word form. Not all of the words will be used.*

fright	impatient	radiant	take for granted
gesture	long for	realization	vigor

1. Dávila opened his business with passion and _____ .

2. Applicants for citizenship usually have to wait only six months, so they get less _____ than people who used to wait years.

3. Dávila writes of the _____ beauty of Puerto Rican women.

4. She thanked them for their business and waved good-bye in one

   _____ .

5. After his wife moved away, Charlie realized that he had _____ her delicious home-cooked meals.

PART 3: SKILLS FOR WRITING

3.1 *Each of the sentences talks about two events that happened in the past. The individual events are below each sentence. In what order did the events happen? Write 1 for the first (earlier) event and 2 for the second (later) event.*

1. The door had snapped off by the time Mary realized how hard the wind was blowing.
   ____ The door snapped off.
   ____ Mary realized how hard the wind was blowing.

2. As soon as the door had flown into the neighbor's yard, the neighbor stepped outside.
   ____ The door flew into the neighbor's yard.
   ____ The neighbor stepped outside.

3. The door had just hit the neighbor in the head when the neighbor fell down.
   ____ The neighbor fell down.
   ____ The door just hit the neighbor in the head.

4. By the time the ambulance arrived, the neighbor had regained consciousness.
   ____ The neighbor regained consciousness.
   ____ An ambulance arrived.

5. Mary had fixed her door by the time the wind stopped blowing.
   ____ The wind stopped blowing.
   ____ Mary fixed her door.

3.2 *Read the story about Peter and Barbara's hike. Write the correct subordinator or transition in parentheses to complete each sentence.*

Peter and Barbara had a difficult hiking trip. They forgot to pack water!

_____While_____ they didn't have any water, they did have some juice.
  (While / In contrast)

_____, they really wanted to complete their hike. By the time
  1. (As / However)

they reached the top of the mountain, they had drunk all of their juice, and they

were really thirsty. _____, they were getting hungry. So, they
              2. (Similary / On the other hand)

hiked down as fast as they could. When they got to their car, they found a new

surprise. _____ that they had left their food in the car, they had
        3. (In the same way / However)

left their keys on the top of the mountain! _____ neither wanted
                             4. (In contrast / Whereas)

to hike back up, they had to. _____ they were hungry and thirsty
              5. (Just as / Likewise)

on their first round-trip, this time they would be even hungrier and thirstier!

PART 4: WRITING

A Comparison and Contrast Essay (20 minutes)

Write a four-paragraph essay comparing and contrasting a major change in your lifestyle, such as your current and past school, a current and past hobby, or a current and past job.

• Include background information and a thesis statement about the two topics in your introduction.
• Support your thesis with examples and details.
• Use point-by-point or block organization.
• Summarize the main idea in your conclusion.
• Use the vocabulary and grammar from Unit 9.

Unit 9 Vocabulary Words				
discontent	fright	nostalgia	realization	take for granted
establish	gesture	predictable	sensation	to long for
fantasy	impatient	radiant	soul	vigor
formerly				

Unit 9 Grammar: Past Perfect
• By the time they reached the top of the mountain, they **had eaten** all of their snacks.

Achievement Tests
Unit 10

Name: _____

Date: _____

PART 1: READING

1.1 *Read the passage from an autobiographical story. Check (✔) the best prediction of what the reading is about. There is only one right answer.*

Many people have seen the Amish portrayed in Hollywood movies. Many more associate the Amish with their fine craftsmanship in creating wood products or in quilt making. These are classic images of this small Christian group. But few non-Amish people really know much about the Amish. With about 200,000 followers living in the United States and Canada, the Amish present an interesting picture in today's society.

_____ **A.** the Amish as depicted in Hollywood movies

_____ **B.** stereotypes about Amish people

_____ **C.** the modern-day lifestyle of Amish people in North America

_____ **D.** Amish arts and crafts

1.2 *Now read the entire story. Use the information to choose the correct answers.*

Today's Amish

Many people have seen the Amish portrayed in Hollywood movies. Many more associate the Amish with their fine craftsmanship in creating wood products or in quilt making. These are classic images of this small Christian group. But few non-Amish people really know much about the Amish. With about 200,000 followers living in the United States and Canada, the Amish present an interesting picture in today's society.

One very influential Amish belief in modern-day society is their special regard for living modestly. This belief influences how the Amish confront technology. The Amish often opt to avoid trends of modern society. So, the Amish do not watch TV or surf the Internet. They do not drive cars for local travel. A horse and buggy moving along the roadside has become a classic and conspicuous sign of a nearby Amish community.

As technology advances, this difference in lifestyles between the Amish and the non-Amish becomes even stronger. The Amish approach to technology has a major impact on how the Amish spend their free time. When work and chores are done and they are unoccupied, the Amish often enjoy recreation time outdoors. Their entire community may meet for a game of volleyball or sledding. Afterward, they may talk and relax in front of a cozy fire. Their community is the center of their lives. They tend to make community traditions and social relationships a priority.

Some Amish groups, however, do allow limited new technology. For example, a visit to an Amish barn may reveal a chainsaw sitting in the corner. An unobtrusive glance at a buggy may show that it has electric turn signals. Whether such new technology should be accommodated is decided by the local church.

(continued on next page)

While nobody can anticipate where the Amish will stand on technology 100 years from now, one thing is certain. They have shown steady resistance to the ostentatious lifestyles that seem to have taken over much of North America.

Check (✔) the best answer to complete each sentence.

1. The reading discusses the choice of Amish people to _____ technology in their lives.

   _____ **A.** learn more about

   _____ **B.** consider using

   _____ **C.** limit

   _____ **D.** destroy

2. Amish people tend to prefer to live _____ .

   _____ **A.** ostentatiously

   _____ **B.** comfortably

   _____ **C.** modestly

   _____ **D.** elaborately

3. Amish people would be unlikely to do all of the following *except* _____ .

   _____ **A.** ride a horse

   _____ **B.** drive a car

   _____ **C.** buy something on the Internet

   _____ **D.** own an electric drill

4. Which outdoor activity would the Amish most likely not do? _____ .

   _____ **A.** baseball

   _____ **B.** snowmobiling

   _____ **C.** swimming

   _____ **D.** tag

5. _____ decides which technology will be allowed.

   _____ **A.** Each family

   _____ **B.** The local church

   _____ **C.** Buggy owners

   _____ **D.** Amish farmers

1.3 *Read the passage from "Inside the House" by Bill Gates in* NorthStar: Reading and Writing 4, *Unit 10. Use the information from this reading and "Today's Amish" to complete the activity. The first one has been done for you.*

Inside the House

I began thinking about building a new house in the late 1980s. I wanted craftsmanship but nothing ostentatious. I wanted a house that would accommodate sophisticated, changing technology, but in an unobtrusive way that made it clear that technology was the servant, not the master.

I found some property on the shore of Lake Washington within an easy commuting distance of Microsoft. Living space will be about average for a large house. The family living room will be about fourteen by twenty-eight feet, including an area for watching television or listening to music. And there will be cozy spaces for one or two people, although there will also be a reception hall to entertain one hundred comfortably for dinner.

First thing, as you come in, you'll be presented with an electronic pin to clip on your clothes. This pin will tell the home who and where you are, and the house will use this information to try to meet and even anticipate your needs—all as unobtrusively as possible. Someday, instead of needing the pin, it might be possible to have a camera system with visual-recognition capabilities, but that's beyond current technology. When it's dark outside, the pin will cause a moving zone of light to accompany you through the house. Unoccupied rooms will be unlit. As you walk down a hallway, you might not notice the lights ahead of you gradually coming up to full brightness and the lights behind you fading. Music will move with you, too. It will seem to be everywhere, although, in fact, other people in the house will be hearing entirely different music or nothing at all. A movie or the news or a phone call will be able to follow you around the house, too. If you get a phone call, only the handset nearest you will ring. . . .

One of the many fears expressed about the information highway is that it will reduce the time people spend socializing. Some worry that homes will become such cozy entertainment providers that we'll never leave them, and that, safe in our private sanctuaries, we'll become isolated. I don't think that's going to happen. As behaviorists keep reminding us, we're social animals. We will have the option of staying home more because the highway will create so many new options for home-based entertainment, for communication—both personal and professional—and for employment. Although the mix of activities will change, I think people will decide to spend almost as much time out of their homes.

(continued on next page)

Statements	Bill Gates	The Amish	Both
Fine craftsmanship is valuable.			✓
1. It's not desirable to be ostentatious.			
2. Unobtrusive technology works well in a home.			
3. Combining a little new technology with old ways is possible.			
4. Social relationships are important.			

PART 2: VOCABULARY

2.1 *Circle the antonym for each word in the first column.*

1. **anticipated**	**A.** planned	**B.** unexpected	**C.** rejected
2. **confront**	**A.** avoid	**B.** consider	**C.** fight
3. **conspicuous**	**A.** obvious	**B.** rude	**C.** hidden
4. **cozy**	**A.** spacious	**B.** small	**C.** crowded
5. **unobtrusive**	**A.** loud	**B.** ostentatious	**C.** cheerful

2.2 *Complete the sentences with the adjective form of the words from the box.*

access	conceal	occupy	option
accommodate	modesty	opposite	reveal

1. The backyard of the house is _____ both from inside the house and from either side.

2. _____ trees and bushes make it impossible to see Gates's driveway from the road.

3. In front of the _____ window on the other side of the room is a large table.

4. Even though Gates's home is huge, it looks quite _____ from the exterior.

5. I wonder if wearing an electronic pin is _____ in Gates's house, or if it's required to get the lights on and off.

PART 3: SKILLS FOR WRITING

3.1 *Read a note from a woman to her next-door neighbor. Complete the sentences using the future progressive of the verbs in parentheses.*

Dear May,

As you know, we _will be leaving_ for Hawaii tomorrow morning. You may see
                     (leave)

various people at our house while we're gone, so we just don't want you to worry

about it.

1. Jacob, the Dells' son, _____ our flowers in the late afternoon.
                            1. (water)

2. On Thursday, Fresh Paint painters _____ the fence.
                                        2. (paint)

3. Mary _____ our mail and newspaper for the whole week.
          3. (pick up)

You have probably noticed the boxes on our porch. Those are donations. They

_____ there for another week, because the pick-up truck didn't come
    4. (sit)

last week.

If you need to contact us, our number is (555) 333-3333. We _____
                                                              5. (stay)

at the Radiant Sands Hotel on Oahu.

By the way, _____ you _____ to Oklahoma in August? You
                                    6. (go)

mentioned that you might go visit your daughter.

Have a good week!

Beatrice

T-65

3.2 *Complete the causal chain about somebody's cell phone. Write the letter of each cause / effect. Not all of the causes / effects will be used.*

    A. I get lots of calls.

    B. I feel like I never have time alone.

    C. Lets anybody call me any time.

    D. I feel like I have to answer all of the calls.

    E. Cell phones are expensive.

    F. I think I'll get rid of my cell phone.

    G. My cell phone has more features than I use.

Cause	Effect (becomes Cause)	Effect (becomes Cause)	Effect (becomes Cause)	Effect (becomes Cause)	Effect
My cell phone	C	1.	2.	3.	4.

PART 4: WRITING

A Cause-and-Effect Essay (20 minutes)

Write a four-paragraph cause-and-effect essay about a technological device that you use often in your life and how that technology affects your personal relationships.

- Write an introduction with a thesis statement.
- In the body paragraphs, include the steps in the causal chain. Focus more on the effects than the causes.
- Use signal words to show causes and effects.
- Write a conclusion that is a prediction, a solution, or a summary of your main points.
- Use the vocabulary and grammar from Unit 10.

Unit 10 Vocabulary Words				
access	conceal	cozy	option	unobtrusive
accommodate	confronted by	craftsmanship	ostentatious	unoccupied
anticipate	conspicuous	modest	reveal	

Unit 10 Grammar: Future Progressive
• The neighbor **will be picking up** our mail while we're gone.

Achievement Tests Answer Key

UNIT 1

1.1
C

1.2
1. A   2. B   3. C   4. A

1.3
1. Both
2. Sipple
3. Both
4. Sipple
5. Photographed Couple

2.1
1. B   2. A   3. A   4. D   5. C

2.2
1. paid
2. convicted
3. cleared
4. kept
5. spread

3.1
1. be misrepresented
2. was featured
3. be seen
4. was focused
5. was sued

3.2
C

3.3
1. In the beginning
2. Then OR Some time later
3. Then OR Some time later
4. In the end

PART 4
Answers will vary. See the scoring rubric on page T-71.

UNIT 2

1.1
A

1.2
1. D   2. B   3. B   4. A

1.3
1. Keller, Schuur, Clayton
2. Keller, Schuur, Clayton
3. Keller, Schuur, Clayton
4. Keller, Schuur
5. Keller, Schuur, Clayton

2.1
1. A
2. C
3. B
4. A
5. C

2.2
1. A   2. C   3. A   4. B   5. D

3.1
1. Alvin Ailey was interested in dancing as a child.
2. Alvin Ailey studied dancing with Lester Horton in his studio.
3. He wanted to dance to show his memories.
4. He felt free to pull from his experience with gospel and the blues.
5. Alvin thought about founding the Ailey School to teach young people how to dance.

3.2
1. A
2. D
3. B and C
4. E and F
5. G

PART 4
Answers will vary. See the scoring rubric on page T-71.

UNIT 3

1.1
B

1.2
1. A   2. C   3. A   4. C   5. A   6. D

1.3
1. 4   2. 6   3. 2

2.1
1. A   2. C   3. A   4. B   5. C

2.2
1. effects
2. produces
3. symptoms
4. principles
5. alternative

3.1
1. If Mary hadn't sunbathed for hours every day as a teenager, she wouldn't have gotten skin cancer.
2. If Bob hadn't drunk lots of soda when he was young, he wouldn't have developed so many cavities.
3. If the student hadn't read a lot of books in school, he wouldn't have graduated from college at 19.
4. If the artist hadn't brought her portfolio to the interview, the company wouldn't have offered her the job.
5. If the teacher hadn't graded the students so easily, the student would have tried harder.

3.2
1. A 2. D, E, F 3. G

PART 4

Answers will vary. See the scoring rubric on page T-71.

UNIT 4

1.1
A

1.2
1. A 2. D 3. B 4. A 5. B 6. A

1.3
1. A 2. B 3. C

2.1
1. prisoner 3. weaken 5. subject
2. reject 4. hope 6. review

2.2
1. predicted 4. evaluation
2. concepts 5. evolution
3. attributed

3.1
1. that the fish could hear
2. where it couldn't hear the music
3. that got the music before his feedings
4. who didn't hear the music
5. when it wasn't feeding time

3.2
1. A 2. A 3. B 4. B

PART 4

Answers will vary. See the scoring rubric on page T-71.

UNIT 5

1.1
B

1.2
1. A 2. B 3. B 4. D

1.3
1. "Toward Immortality" 4. "Toward Immortality"
2. "Life Expectancy" 5. "Life Expectancy"
3. "Life Expectancy"

2.1
1. chilly 4. immeasurably
2. presumptuous 5. vigorously
3. tolerable

2.2
1. chilly 4. punctually
2. insufferable 5. simultaneously
3. prolonged

3.1
1. has been used 5. reported
2. learned 6. have conducted
3. lost 7. has been closed
4. have been seeking

3.2
1. like 2. hummed 3. as

PART 4

Answers will vary. See the scoring rubric on page T-71.

UNIT 6

1.1
D

1.2
1. B 2. D 3. B 4. C 5. A

1.3
1. C 2. B 3. D 4. F

2.1
1. managed 4. passion
2. keep on 5. fulfilling
3. proud

2.2
1. determined 4. propose
2. admiration 5. proudly
3. inspire

3.1
1. Despite the fact that she likes a lot of attention, Linus seems to have a reasonable sense of independence and can spend up to four hours alone.
2. Although she likes to be petted, she is quite uncomfortable around young children.
3. Even though she clearly has had good training, she still needs work in learning to walk with a leash.
4. In spite of this, she may be able to travel comfortably in a dog carrier, depending how she was trained as a puppy.

3.2
Answers may vary slightly. Suggested answers:
1. Although many adopted pets are mistreated and end up back in a shelter, pet adoption saves animals' lives.
2. In spite of the fact that it is sometimes risky to bring an unknown animal into a home, in most cases, pet adoption benefits both the animal and the adoptee.

3. Even though pet owners should have some freedom in training their animals, mandatory animal obedience classes would make better pets.

3.3
1. B   2. A   3. C

PART 4
Answers will vary. See the scoring rubric on page T-71.

UNIT 7

1.1
B

1.2
1. C   2. B   3. D   4. D   5. A

1.3
1. Both   3. Both
2. Homeschooling 4. Online courses

2.1
1. consultation   3. misconception
2. isolation   4. stimulation

2.2
1. adjust   4. dispute
2. viable   5. misconception
3. persistence   6. stimulate

3.1
1. Professor Endendel said that few students followed the actual assignment.
2. One student raised her hand and said that she wanted to do the assignment again.
3. The professor said that she/he would think about offering an alternative assignment tomorrow.
4. My girlfriend tells me that she always does the extra credit work so that she gets the extra points.
5. After class, I said that I might do extra credit from now on, too.

3.2
1. irritated   4. expertise
2. to motivate   5. consult
3. ambition

PART 4
Answers will vary. See the scoring rubric on page T-71.

UNIT 8

1.1
D

1.2
1. C   2. C   3. B   4. B

1.3
1. Both   4. Corfu Banquet
2. Slow Food   5. Both
3. Both

2.1
1. B   2. C   3. A   4. C   5. A

2.2
1. authentic   4. throw it away
2. properly   5. specify
3. imparts

3.1
1. Turkish cooks have <u>come up with</u> a version of spanokopeta that has fewer calories and less fat.
2. Using yogurt instead of butter, Turkish cooks <u>do away with</u> about 50% of the calories in their spanokopeta.
3. In fact, yogurt is the standard ingredient in this pastry, and you'll see it if you <u>look over</u> any Turkish cookbook.
4. Turkish chefs have also <u>taken advantage of</u> the idea that the pastry top does not need to be flaky and brown.
5. Instead, they <u>turn up</u> the heat while cooking, and when they remove it from the oven, they cover it with a towel, making the pastry soft.
6. Turkish-style spanokopeta, however, has not <u>caught on</u> in the USA.

3.2
1. C   2. D   3. A   4. B

PART 4
Answers will vary. See the scoring rubric on page T-71.

UNIT 9

1.1
A

1.2
1. B   2. C   3. D   4. A   5. A

1.3
1. "Naturalization" 3. "Nostalgia"
2. Both   4. Both

2.1
1. C   2. A   3. B   4. A   5. A

2.2
1. vigor   4. gesture
2. impatient   5. taken for granted
3. radiant

3.1

1. 1 The door snapped off.
   2 Mary realized how hard the wind was blowing.
2. 1 The door flew into the neighbor's yard.
   2 The neighbor stepped outside.
3. 2 The neighbor fell down.
   1 The door just hit the neighbor in the head.
4. 1 The neighbor regained consciousness.
   2 An ambulance arrived.
5. 2 The wind stopped blowing.
   1 Mary fixed her door.

3.2

1. However	4. Whereas
2. Similarly	5. Just as
3. In the same way	

PART 4

Answers will vary. See the scoring rubric on page T-71.

UNIT 10

1.1

C

1.2

1. C   2. C   3. A   4. B   5. B

1.3

1. Both	3. The Amish
2. Bill Gates	4. Both

2.1

1. B   2. A   3. C   4. A   5. B

2.2

1. accessible	4. modest
2. concealing	5. optional
3. opposite	

3.1

1. will be watering	4. will be sitting
2. will be painting	5. will be staying
3. will be picking up	6. will . . . be going

3.2

1. A   2. D   3. B   4. F

PART 4

Answers will vary. See the scoring rubric on page T-71.

NorthStar 4 Achievement Test Scoring Rubric: Writing

Score	Description
5	A response at this level contains relevant information from the test reading passage; the information is generally coherent and connected and is marked by several of the following: • adequate organization; effective use of transition words and phrases to display unity and progression of information • a clearly identifiable introduction, body, and conclusion although the introduction or conclusion might need more development. There is a main idea and multiple supporting sentences per paragraph. • consistent, generally correct use of word order, pronouns, relative clauses, modals, and auxiliary + main verbs; sentences often include multiple clauses or subordination • appropriate use of a variety of vocabulary items from the unit • several language errors throughout
4	A response at this level contains relevant information from the test reading passage; the information is somewhat coherent and connected and is marked by several of the following: • somewhat adequate organization; there is generally effective use of transition words and phrases to sequence and organize information • a clearly identifiable introduction and body, but a conclusion may not be clearly identifiable; there is a main idea and multiple supporting sentences per paragraph • consistent, generally correct use of subject-verb agreement, pronouns, relative clauses, infinitives, modals, and simple verb tenses • appropriate use of a variety of vocabulary items from the unit • several language errors throughout
3	A response at this level contains relevant information from the test reading passage; the information is not coherent or connected and is marked by several of the following: • somewhat adequate organization; there is a somewhat effective attempt to use transition words and phrases to sequence and organize information • more than one paragraph; there is a main idea and multiple supporting sentences per paragraph • consistent, correct use of subject-verb agreement, pronouns, relative clauses, infinitives, modals, and simple verb tenses • appropriate use of a variety of vocabulary items from the unit • several language errors throughout
2	A response at this level contains some information from the test reading passage and is marked by several of the following: • some organization; the writer is just beginning to use transition words to sequence information, but more practice is needed • only one paragraph; there is a simple main idea and several supporting sentences • generally consistent, correct use of subject-verb agreement, pronouns, relative clauses, infinitives, modals, and simple verb tenses • appropriate use of several vocabulary items from the unit • several language errors in paragraph
1	A response at this level contains little information from the test reading passage and is marked by several of the following: • a lack of organization of information • several complete sentences; there is a simple main idea and few supporting sentences • generally consistent, correct use of subject-verb agreement, personal pronouns, WH- relative clauses, and simple verb tenses • appropriate use of 1–2 vocabulary items from the unit • numerous language errors per sentence
0	A response at this level contains very little information from the test reading passages, and is marked by several of the following: • very little organization of information • few complete sentences to form a short paragraph; an inadequate attempt to provide a main idea and supporting sentences • somewhat consistent, correct use of subject-verb agreement and simple verb tenses • inappropriate use of vocabulary from the unit • numerous language errors per clause A response at this level might also be blank.